T0224205

Communications
in Computer and Information Science   **994**

Commenced Publication in 2007
Founding and Former Series Editors:
Phoebe Chen, Alfredo Cuzzocrea, Xiaoyong Du, Orhun Kara, Ting Liu,
Dominik Ślęzak, and Xiaokang Yang

Weixia Xu · Liquan Xiao
Jinwen Li · Zhenzhen Zhu (Eds.)

Computer Engineering and Technology

22nd CCF Conference, NCCET 2018
Yinchuan, China, August 15–17, 2018
Revised Selected Papers

 Springer

Editors
Weixia Xu
National University of Defense Technology
Changsha, China

Jinwen Li
National University of Defense Technology
Changsha, China

Liquan Xiao
National University of Defense Technology
Changsha, China

Zhenzhen Zhu
National University of Defense Technology
Changsha, China

ISSN 1865-0929   ISSN 1865-0937 (electronic)
Communications in Computer and Information Science
ISBN 978-981-13-5918-7   ISBN 978-981-13-5919-4 (eBook)
https://doi.org/10.1007/978-981-13-5919-4

Library of Congress Control Number: 2018966321

This Springer imprint is published by the registered company Springer Nature Singapore Pte Ltd.
The registered company address is: 152 Beach Road, #21-01/04 Gateway East, Singapore 189721, Singapore

Preface

We are pleased to present the proceedings of the 22nd Annual Conference on Computer Engineering and Technology (NCCET 2018). Over its short 22-year history, NCCET has established itself as one of the major national conferences dedicated to the important and emerging challenges in the field of computer engineering and technology. Following the previous successful events, NCCET 2018 provided a forum to bring together researchers and practitioners from academia and industry to discuss cutting-edge research on computer engineering and technology.

We are delighted that the conference continues to attract high-quality submissions from a diverse and national group of researchers. This year, we received 120 submissions, among which 17 papers were accepted. Each paper received three or four peer reviews from our Technical Program Committee (TPC) comprising a total of 42 TPC members from academia and industry.

The pages of this volume represent only the end result of an enormous endeavor involving hundreds of people. Almost all this work is voluntary, with some individuals contributing hundreds of hours of their time to the effort. Together, the 42 members of the TPC, the ten members of the External Review Committee (ERC), and the 12 other individual reviewers consulted for their expertise wrote over 300 reviews.

Every paper received at least two reviews and many had three or more. With the exception of submissions by the TPC, each paper had at least two reviews from the TPC and at least one review from an outside expert. For the fifth year running, most of the outside reviews were done by the ERC, which was selected in advance, and additional outside reviews beyond the ERC were requested whenever appropriate or necessary. Reviewing was "first read double-blind," meaning that author identities were withheld from reviewers until they submitted a review. Revealing author names after initial reviews were written allowed reviewers to find related and previous material by the same authors, which helped greatly in many cases in understanding the context of the work, and also ensured that the author feedback and discussions at the PC meeting could be frank and direct. We allowed PC members to submit papers to the conference. Submissions co-authored by a TPC member were reviewed exclusively by the ERC and other outside reviewers, and these same reviewers decided whether to accept the PC papers; no PC member reviewed a TPC paper, and no TPC papers were discussed at the TPC meeting.

After the reviewing was complete, the PC met in Changsha on July 7 and 8 to select the papers. Separately, the ERC decided on the PC papers in email and phone discussions. In the end, 17 of the 120 submissions (14%) were accepted for the conference.

First of all, we would like to thank all researchers who submitted manuscripts. Without these submissions, it would be impossible to provide such an interesting technical program. We thank all PC members for helping to organize the conference program. We thank all TPC members for their tremendous time and efforts during the paper review and selection process. The efforts of these individuals were crucial in constructing our successful technical program. Last but not least, we would like to thank the organizations and sponsors that supported NCCET 2018. Finally, we thank all the participants of the conference and hope that you have a truly memorable NCCET 2018 in Yinchuan, China. See you in Enshi next year.

August 2018   Weixia Xu
                                                          Zhang Minxuan
                                                            Liquan Xiao

Organization

Organizing Committee

General Co-chairs

Xu Weixia	National University of Defense Technology, China
Gao Yuzhuo	Ningxia University, China
Zhang Minxuan	National University of Defense Technology, China

Program Chairs

Xiao Liquan	National University of Defense Technology, China
Wu Linbo	Ningxia University, China

Publicity Co-chairs

Zhang Chengyi	National University of Defense Technology, China
Li Jinwen	National University of Defense Technology, China

Local Arrangements Co-chairs

Sun Xuehong	Ningxia University, China
Li Jinwen	National University of Defense Technology, China

Registration and Finance Co-chair

Zhang Junying	National University of Defense Technology, China

Program Committee

Han Wei	Xi'an Aviation Institute of Computing Technology, China
Jin Lifeng	Jiangnan Institute of Computing Technology, China
Xiong Tinggang	709 Institute of China Shipbuilding Industry, China
Zhao Xiaofang	Institute of Computing Technology Chinese Academy of Sciences, China
Yang Yintang	Xi Dian University, China
Feng Feng	Ningxia University, China

Technical Program Committee

Dou Qiang	National University of Defense Technology, China
Du Huimin	Xi'an University of Posts and Telecommunications, China
Fan Dongrui	Institute of Computing Technology Chinese Academy of Sciences, China
Fan Xiaoya	Northwestern Polytechnical University, China

Fu Yuzhuo	Shanghai Jiao Tong University, China
Guo Donghui	Xiamen University, China
Guo Wei	Tianjin University, China
Xu Jiangtao	Tianjin University, China
Wei Jizeng	Tianjin University, China
Huang Jin	Xidian University, China
Li Ping	University of Electronic Science and Technology of China, China
Li Yun	Yangzhou University, China
Lin Kaizhi	Inspur, China
Lin Zhenghao	Tongji University, China
Sun Yongjie	National University of Defense Technology, China
Tian Ze	Aviation Industry Corporation of China, China
Wang Yaonan	Hunan University, China
Wang Yiwen	University of Electronic Science and Technology of China, China
Wang Yongwen	National University of Defense Technology, China
Xue Chengqi	Southeast University, China
Yang Xiaojun	Institute of Computing Technology Chinese Academy of Sciences, China
Yu Zongguang	CECT, China
Zeng Yun	Hunan University, China
Zhang Lixin	Institute of Computing Technology Chinese Academy of Sciences, China
Zhang Minxuan	National University of Defense Technology, China
Zhang Shengbin	Northwestern Polytechnical University, China
Zhang Shujie	Huawei, China
Zhao Yuelong	South China University of Technology, China
Zhou Ya	Guilin University of Electronic Technology, China
Jiang Xu	Hong Kong University of Science and Technology, China
Jiang Jiang	Shanghai Jiao Tong University, China
He Weifeng	Shanghai Jiao Tong University, China
Han Jun	Fudan University, China
Meng Jianyi	Fudan University, China
Tang Hongwei	Institute of Computing Technology Chinese Academy of Sciences, China
Zhang Ke	Institute of Computing Technology Chinese Academy of Sciences, China
Liang Huaguo	HeFei University of Technology, China
Wang Wei	HeFei University of Technology, China
Zhang Duoli	HeFei University of Technology, China
Liu Yongpan	Tsinghua University, China
Sun Guangyu	Peking University, China
Pei Songwen	University of Shanghai for Science and Technology, China

Contents

Design and Application for Sealing of Strengthening Computer for Anti-hard Environment

Qianqian Yang[✉]

The Computer Department, Jiangsu Automation Research Institute,
Lianyungang, China
yqq1203@126.com

Abstract. Reasonable sealing is an effective protective measure for the reinforced computer from corrosion and electromagnetic interference in harsh environment. In this paper, we analysed the sealing problem of the reinforced computer from the aspects of sealing material selection and sealing structure design. As a result, it is proposed that a solution to the problem of computer sealing against harsh environment. Taking a certain type of reinforced computer as an example, the sealing design was completed and relative tests were perfectively accomplished, in accordance with the requirements of the national military standard. The test results show that the problems, such as the leakage and electromagnetic interference did not take place in this type of reinforced computer. Fortunately, this solution improves the reliability of the reinforced computer.

Keywords: Reinforced computer · Anti-hard environment · Sealing material · Sealing structure

1 Introduction

The anti-hard environment computer is a kind of computer that can reliably work under certain harsh conditions. As a military electronic device, it cannot be eroded by water and cannot be contaminated by salt mist, sand, dust, industrial atmosphere, and other harmful substances. At the same time, it cannot be affected from the electromagnetic interference. The reinforced crate is an important part of computers that are resistant to harsh environment. It requires the installation of cover plates, panels, connectors, and many other components. Therefore, the seams will be inevitably filled with the reinforcement crate. In order to eliminate the adverse effects of the joints on the internal components of the crate and themselves, it is necessary to seal and reinforce the crate by the way of selecting the suitable sealing material and designing the properly sealing structure. In this paper, combining engineering practice experience, it is analyzed that the types of sealing materials and their respective applicable scopes. The commonly used sealing structures are used to optimize and perfect the sealing structure of the reinforcement computer, and the sealing measures for a certain type of reinforcement computer are given.

© Springer Nature Singapore Pte Ltd. 2019
W. Xu et al. (Eds.): NCCET 2018, CCIS 994, pp. 1–15, 2019.
https://doi.org/10.1007/978-981-13-5919-4_1

2 Selection of Sealing Materials

Sealing materials include liquid sealing materials and solid sealing materials, and the sealing mechanisms of liquid and solid sealing materials vary from each other. The sealing mechanism of liquid sealing materials mainly includes mechanical theory, diffusion theory, electrostatic theory and adsorption theory, etc. The sealing mechanisms of solid sealing materials mainly include blocking theory, self-sealing theory and interference theory [1]. In order to meet the requirements of the reinforced enclosure's sealing and electromagnetic shielding, the selected sealing material must not only have waterproof function, but also should have electromagnetic shielding capability. Electromagnetic shielding materials with sealing effect can also be referred to as conductive sealing materials. At present, the conductive seal materials developed and applied are mainly divided into solid conductive sealing materials and liquid conductive sealing materials.

2.1 Solid Conductive Sealing Materials

The solid conductive sealing material is a kind of polymer composite material prepared by filling conductive filler into the matrix material. According to different conductive filler and matrix materials, solid conductive sealing materials are divided into three categories: metal filler conductive rubber materials, non-metallic filler conductive rubber materials and wire mesh composite conductive rubber materials [2]. The conductive filler includes metal, graphite, conductive copolymer, conductive polymer, and the like. The base material includes rubber, plastic, and the like. Common solid conductive seal materials include conductive rubber, closed-cell conductive foam, wire mesh gaskets, and flexible graphite.

2.1.1 Conductive Rubber

Conductive rubber is made by adding conductive filler to the rubber matrix, which not only retains the elasticity and seal ability of the matrix rubber, but also has the conductivity of the conductive filler. Conductive rubber has many advantages such as light weight, easy processing and forming, low cost, mature technology, good water and air tightness, and excellent electromagnetic shielding performance. It is widely used in aviation, spaceflight, navigation and other weapons and equipment systems, which is the most commonly used conductive seal material [3].

According to different conductive fillers, conductive rubber is divided into sterling silver conductive rubber, carbon black conductive rubber, silver-plated silver conductive rubber, nickel-plated silver conductive rubber, aluminum silver-plated conductive rubber and nickel-plated graphite conductive rubber. According to different molding processes, conductive rubber is divided into extruded conductive rubber and molded conductive rubber. Users can customize various shapes of conductive rubber products, such as conductive rubber strips and conductive rubber mats, as needed. Conductive rubber strip has the advantages of simple structure, small footprint, which can adapt to various structural routes, good sealing performance and excellent conductive effect. It is currently widely used for reinforce chassis frames and covers, frames and panels, doors and panels and other components. Conductive rubber pads are mainly used for the sealing of connectors and reinforced chassis.

2.1.2 Closed-Cell Conductive Foam

Closed-cell conductive foam is prepared by using polyurethane as a sponge core and externally wrapping a material containing a nickel-copper metal plating layer. Closed-cell foam cores have excellent elasticity, higher flame retardancy, and better tightness. Nickel-copper metal plating has good electrical conductivity. Therefore, closed-cell foam has excellent shielding performance and good sealing performance. Closed-cell conductive foam is mainly used to seal components such as chassis and screen doors, chassis and covers.

2.1.3 Wire Mesh Gaskets

The wire mesh gasket is a combination of a braided wire mesh and rubber, which not only provides electromagnetic shielding but also seals. The commonly used metals include tin-plated phosphor bronze, tin-coated copper-clad steel, aluminum alloy, Monel, etc. Rubber can be solid or sponged with neoprene, silicon rubber, fluorosilicone rubber, and butyl rubber. Wire mesh gaskets can be effectively fixed to the chassis with pressure sensitive adhesive. Users can choose different shapes and different sizes of gaskets according to their needs. They are mainly used for the shielding of chassis shields, fan guards, and cable connectors.

2.1.4 Flexible Graphite

Flexible graphite is a new type of engineering material obtained after special treatment of graphite. In addition to the characteristics of natural graphite, it also has special flexibility and elasticity, which is an ideal sealing material. In 1968, the United States successfully developed a flexible graphite sealing material that solved the problem of leakage of atomic energy valves. Subsequently, some developed countries began to develop and produce, such as Germany, Japan, and France At present, flexible graphite and its composite materials have been widely used in petrochemical, machinery, metallurgy, electric power, and atomic energy, Aviation and other departments, whose benefits are very significant [4]. At present, flexible graphite has not yet been applied to the reinforced chassis.

2.2 Liquid Conductive Sealing Material

The liquid conductive seal material mainly guides the electric adhesive. The conductive adhesive is generally not used alone, but is used together with the solid conductive seal material.

At present, there are many brands of conductive adhesives. According to their different substrates, they can be divided into the following categories: (1) Epoxy. The base material is epoxy resin, filled with conductive metal particles mainly Ag, Ni, Cu (Ag plating); (2) silicones. The base material is silicone, whose filled conductive metal particles are mainly Ag, Cu (Ag plating); (3) polymers. The matrix material is a polymer, and the filled conductive metal particles are mainly Ag [5]. Conductive adhesives generally cure at room temperature and can be used to connect or install conductive rubber pads, conductive rubber strips, and wire mesh gaskets.

2.3   Basic Principles for Sealing Materials Selection

The sealing materials used by computers for harsh environment must meet the following requirements:

(1) Must have both conductivity and moisture barrier properties.
(2) With suitable mechanical strength and hardness, excellent compression performance.
(3) No softening at high temperatures, no hardening at low temperatures, excellent anti-corrosion properties, and excellent wear resistance.

In addition, when selecting the sealing material, the characteristics of the sealed part and the sealing material should be comprehensively considered, and a mature and reasonable sealing process method should be used as far as possible.

3   Design of Sealing Structure

3.1   Selection of Sealing Structure

Through the analysis of the sealing structure, the sealing effect of the reinforcement of the computer is influenced by the factors including the structural form and the processing precision of the sealing parts. According to the principle whether the seal structure is detachable, the sealing structure can be divided into non-detachable seal structure and detachable seal structure. Non-detachable sealing structure, usually welded to achieve the permanent seal, which can prevent air or moisture into the internal reinforcement. As a result, it can effectively protect the internal electronic components of the crate. However, the non-detachable sealing structure has a fatal disadvantage that it is not conducive to reinforcing the subsequent maintenance of the crate. The detachable sealing structure facilitates the maintenance and debugging of the reinforced crate, although the sealing effect is slightly inferior to the non-detachable sealing structure. The detachable sealing structure has various forms. The common sealing structure is shown in a-e of Fig. 1, and the extended sealing structure is shown in f-l of Fig. 2. According to the different sealing parts and the need of commissioning and maintenance, the reinforced crate can choose any one or two types of sealing structures.

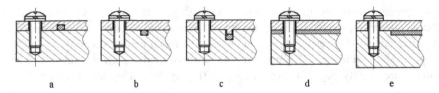

a   b   c   d   e

Fig. 1. The sealing structures are shown above.

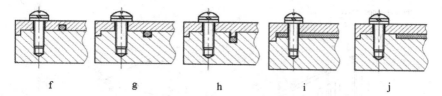

Fig. 2. The extended seal structures are shown above.

The seal structure a, b and c shown in Fig. 1 usually selects sealing strip as the sealing material, and these three structures are suitable for casting, die-casting or machined crate. The conductive seals can be prepared in advance, and then press the conductive seals into the grooves, or use conductive sealant to achieve stick. Although these seals take possion of simple structures, they can achieve the purpose of water vapor seal and electromagnetic shielding. The characteristic of a and b in Fig. 1 is that the sealing area is large, and it is only necessary to process the mounting groove of the conductive seal on one of the parts. Compared to a and b in Fig. 1, the characteristic of c in Fig. 1 is that the sealing area is small. The sealing force is small, the required installation screw diameter is small, and so the structure size of the sealed part is also small. In the three sealing structures a, b and c in Fig. 1, the sealing performance of c is the best. However, c in Fig. 1 needs to be in the mounting groove of the conductive seal is machined on the part and the boss is machined on the other part. Therefore, the processing of c in Fig. 1 is the most difficult.

The sealing structure d and e shown in Fig. 1 usually selects the gland as the sealing material. The advantage is that the structure is simple. The disadvantage is that the sealing shape is more complicated. The difference between d and e in Fig. 1 is that the former needs to process the mounting holes of the screws on the gasket, and the latter does not need to process the mounting holes. In order to avoid the screws, the shape of the gasket used in Fig. 1 e is more complicated than that of d.

Based on the seal structure shown in Fig. 1, the design concept in Fig. 2 is to provide a boss and a groove at the edges of the sealed member, respectively, in order to increase the length of invasion path such as water vapor and increase the sealing effect. The structure f in Fig. 2 has been applied on a certain type of reinforced crate, and the sealing effect is good.

In addition, regardless of the type of construction chosen, the amount of compression of the chosen sealing material must be considered.

3.2 Design of Sealing Structure

Taking a certain type of reinforcement computer as an example, a sealing structure design was performed. A certain type of reinforcement computer is shown in Fig. 3, and its structure mainly includes a crate frame, a crate panel, a crate upper cover, a crate lower cover, and various connectors. The crate frame is vacuum brazed and permanently sealed, which is non-removable. The seal between the crate panel, the upper cover of the crate, the lower cover plate of the crate and the crate frame, and the seal between the connector and the crate panel are detachable seals. This article focuses on the design of the seal between the crate cover and the crate frame, between the connector and the crate panel.

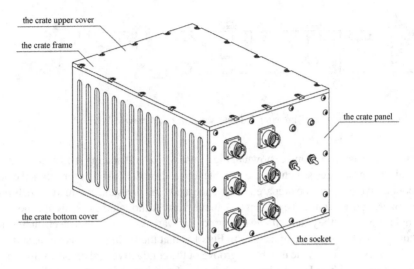

Fig. 3. Some type of reinforced crate is shown above.

3.2.1 Sealing Design Between Crate Cover and Crate Frame

By analyzing the size of the sealing groove and the diameter of the fixing screw, a sealing scheme between the crate cover and the crate frame of a certain type of reinforced computer is determined.

The crate frame and the panel are all made by CNC machine tools. The material is aluminum alloy. A silver-plated conductive rubber strip with a circular cross-section is used as the conductive sealing material. The sealing structure adopts f in Fig. 2, and its cross-sectional structure and dimensions are shown in Fig. 4. Crate frame and crate cover are connected by the screw. The screw material is low carbon steel and its yield limit $[\sigma s] = 100$ MPa. The physical parameters and dimensional parameters of the material of the aluminum silver-plated conductive rubber strip are shown in Tables 1 and 2, respectively, and the cross-sectional shape thereof is shown in Fig. 5.

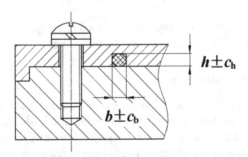

Fig. 4. The structure and size of cross-section for some reinforced crate is shown above.

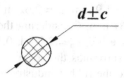

$$d \pm c$$

Fig. 5. The cross-sectional shape of conductive rubber strip is shown above.

Table 1. The physical parameters and dimensional parameters of conductive rubber strips are shown below.

Physical parameters	Hardness	Shear Modulus	Poisson's ratio	Metal and rubber friction coefficient	Diameter	Diameter tolerance
Value	70	$G = 6.7$ MPa	$\mu = 0.47$	$f = 0.6$	$d = 2.62$ mm	$c = 0.15$ mm

1. Solve Out the Size of Sealing Groove

$$[(d+c) - (h - c_h)]/(d+c) \leq \varepsilon_{max}. \tag{1}$$

$$[(d-c) - (h + c_h)]/(d-c) \geq \varepsilon_{min}. \tag{2}$$

Among them,

ε_{max}: the maximum compression of aluminum-plated silver conductive rubber strips;

ε_{min}: the minimum compression of aluminum-plated silver conductive rubber strips;

h: the depth of sealing groove;

c_h: the depth tolerance of sealing groove.

Through input parameters d = 2.62 mm, c = 0.15 mm, εmax = 0.35, εmin = 0.15, combining formula (1) and formula (2), we can find ch ≤ 0.1495 mm, h ≤ 1.95 mm. Considering the machined error, we can calculate the depth of the seal groove h ± ch = 1.9 ± 0.15 (mm).

Assuming that the conductive rubber strips are filled with the entire seal groove after compression, the cross-sectional areas of the conductive rubber strip before and after deformation are equal.

$$S_{before} = \pi \times d^2/4. \tag{3}$$

$$S_{after} = h \times b. \tag{4}$$

Among them,

b: the width of sealing groove

c_b: the tolerance of sealing groove, $c_b = 0.15$ mm

Through input parameters $h = 1.9$ mm, $d = 2.62$ mm, combining formula (1) and formula (2), we can find $b = 2.84$ mm. Considering the machined error, we can calculate the width of the seal groove $b \pm c_b = 2.84 \pm 0.15$ (mm).

The conductive rubber strip surrounds the cover of the chassis and forms a conductive rubber seal. According to the rubber industry manual [6] and the mechanical design manual [7], the amount of compression of the conductive rubber seal is $\varepsilon = (d-h)/d = 0.27$, which meet $\varepsilon_{min} \leq \varepsilon \leq \varepsilon_{max}$.

2. Work out the Diameter of Fixing Screws

$$E = 2 \times (1 + \mu) \times G. \tag{5}$$

$$F = (5/6) \times (\sqrt{d/h} - h/d) \times E. \tag{6}$$

$$F_c = F + (\mu/(1 - \mu)) \times F. \tag{7}$$

$$P = F_c/16. \tag{8}$$

Among them,

E: The elastic modulus of rubber;
F: The pre-pressure sealing force of the conductive rubber seal;
F_c: The sealing pressure when the chassis frame and chassis cover are fully sealed;
P: The tightening force of each screw

It is assumed that 16 screws are used to fix the chassis cover and the chassis frame. According to the width and depth of the seal groove obtained in Formula (1), Table 1 and Formula (5)–Formula (8), it is determined that P = 0.87 MPa.

For each screw, the following formula (9), formula (10) should be satisfied.

$$\sigma_s \leq [\sigma_s]. \tag{9}$$

$$\sigma_s = P/(\pi d_{scew}^2/4). \tag{10}$$

Among them,
d_{scew}: the diameter of the screw.

From the input parameter P = 0.87 MPa, Table 1 and Formula (9) and Formula (10), dscew $\geq$ 1.05 mm are obtained.

According to the manual of fasteners, the screw diameters that meet the seal and connection strength requirements are 2.5 mm, 3 mm, 4 mm, and so on. Considering the frame size limit, screws with a diameter of 3 mm or 4 mm should be used.

Table 2. The design parameters of some type reinforced crate are shown below.

Structure Parameter	The sealing groove		Screw	
	Depth $h \pm c_h$/mm	Width $b \pm c_b$/mm	Number	Diameter/mm
Value	1.9 ± 0.15	2.84 ± 0.15	16	M3 or M4

In order to ensure that the sealing strip has a suitable amount of compression, it needs designing a gap at the outermost edge between the frame and the cover. Combined with the above analysis and calculation, the specific sealing structural dimensions of the crate frame and the cover are as shown in Fig. 6 in mm.

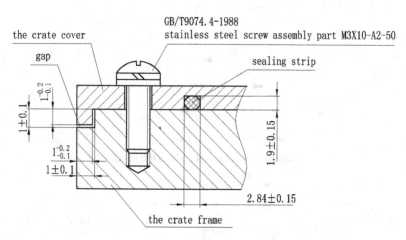

Fig. 6. The sealing structural dimensions between the aluminum alloy frame and the cover is shown above.

3.2.2   Sealing Design Between Connector and Crate Panel

The connector includes a socket, a chassis ground, a signal ground, an indicator light, a power switch, a USB interface, etc. The sealing between the connector and the reinforced chassis panel is mainly achieved through a seal gasket and a sealant. The following takes the sealed design of the socket as an example, and proposes specific sealing measures for the connector of the certain type of reinforced computer and the chassis panel.

The socket is usually installed on the panel of the chassis. The installation method of the socket includes installing from the outside to the inside and installing from the inside to the outside. They can select the corresponding installation method according to the user's needs and the actual project. a and b in Fig. 7 show the installation structure from.

In Fig. 7,

A: the socket square size, in mm;

D: the socket mounting diameter, in mm.

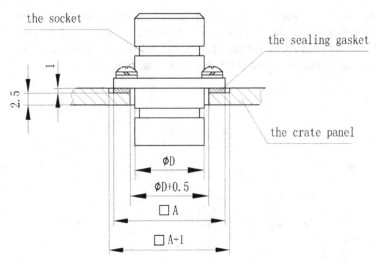

a) Installing from the outside to the inside

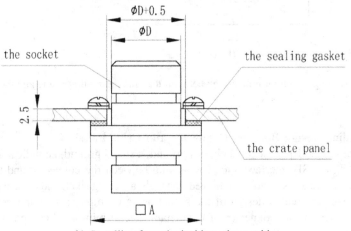

b) Installing from the inside to the outside

Fig. 7. The sealing structure of aviation socket installation is shown above.

According to the model specification of the connector, a suitable gasket can be quickly selected from the shared library of the gasket. The structure of the socket gasket is shown in Fig. 8.

In Fig. 8,

B: the socket mounting hole spacing size, in mm.

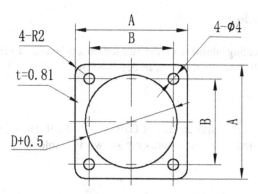

Fig. 8. The structure of the socket gasket is shown above.

A certain type sealing gasket shared library is shown in Table 3.

Table 3. A certain type sealing gasket shared library.

Serial number	Drawing number	A/mm	B/mm	D/mm	Socket type	Installation method	
						Installing from the outside to the inside	Installing from the inside to the outside
1	XXXX-0001	24	17 ± 0.15	Φ17	XXXX-01	√	
2	XXXX-0002	27	20 ± 0.15	Φ20.5	XXXX-02	√	
3	XXXX-0003	29	22 ± 0.15	Φ24	XXXX-03	√	
4	XXXX-0004	31	24 ± 0.15	Φ27	XXXX-04		√
5	XXXX-0005	34	26 ± 0.15	Φ31	XXXX-05		√
6	XXXX-0006	37	28 ± 0.15	Φ33	XXXX-06		√
......	......	......	......	......	......	......	......

In addition to the above two types of sealing design, if some sealing requirements are high or it is not convenient to install the sealing material, a moisture absorbing agent such as color changing silicone and a moisture absorbing plate may be attached, or an appropriate surface protection may be provided, such as the entire housing static spray plastic, etc., which is to achieve effective sealing.

4 Test Verification

To check out the sealing abilities of the reinforced computer, a series of tests were accomplished. It will describe the tests in detail below.

4.1 Rain Test

According to the relevant requirements of GJB150.8A-2009 Part 8 [8], the waterproof performance was tested. The test records are shown in Table 4.

Table 4. The rain test records.

Test detection conditions	Test indexes	Test results
(1) In the power-on state (2) A nozzle is installed in the surface of the chassis for receiving rain of 0.55 m^2 (3) The nozzle is 500 mm away from the surface of the test case (4) The nozzle pressure is 400 kPa (5) The raindrop diameter is 2 mm (6) The test time is 40 min per face	After the test cabinet is restored to normal temperature under normal atmospheric conditions, check the following items: (1) No damage to the appearance (2) No power failure, power failure, black screen and program error after power-on	Passed

4.2 Electromagnetic Compatibility Test

According to the relevant requirements of GJB151B-2013 [9], the tests of CE101, CE102 and RE102 had been achieved. The test results are shown in Fig. 9 a, b and c, which show that the crate meets the requirements of electromagnetic compatibility.

4.3 Vibration Test

According to the relevant requirements of GJB150.16A-2009 Part 16 [10], the module level stress screening test has been completed. The test results are shown in Fig. 10. After the test, all the fasteners are in good condition and we did not find any damage in the structural parts. It can be concluded that the crate satisfies the vibration and shock conditions.

Through the tests above, it proved that this type of reinforced computer meets GJB requirements. At the same time, it further verified this reinforced method is feasible.

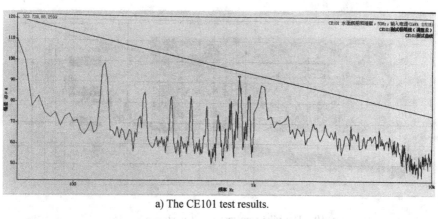

a) The CE101 test results.

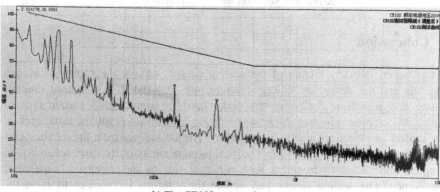

b) The CE102 test results.

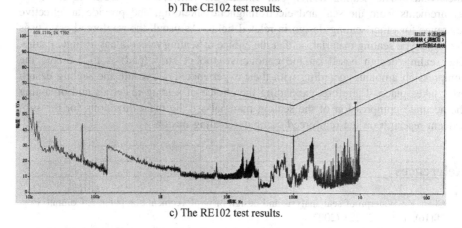

c) The RE102 test results.

Fig. 9. The CE101, CE102 and RE102 test results are shown above.

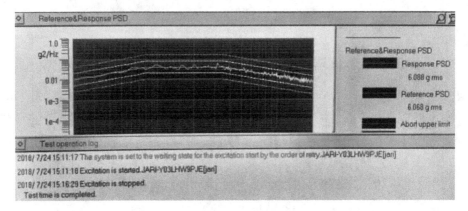

Fig. 10. The vibration test result is shown above.

5 Conclusion

In this paper, two key factors of the sealing design, namely the choice of sealing materials and the design of sealing structure, are analyzed. It is proposed that the sealing design scheme for computers under harsh environment. A certain type of reinforced computer adopting the sealing scheme has withstood routine tests, such as rain shower and electromagnetic compatibility. All the indexes meet the requirements of the national military standard. The sealing scheme improves the reliability of computer under harsh environment, such as humid, salt fog and strong electromagnetic interference. The sealing design can enable the reinforced computer to meet the requirements from the seal and electromagnetic shielding, and provide an effective reference for other sealing design in related fields. As usual, the reinforced crate uses the same type sealing material, so that the choice of sealing material has a single nature. The sealing design based on the conductive rubber strip (pad) is to estimate the compression amount, according with their experience. As a result, the sealing design error takes place. Therefore, expanding the choice of sealing materials and obtaining the accurate compression of the sealing material are the main directions for the subsequent research on the reinforced computer sealing design.

References

1. Chen, Z.: Waterproof seal analysis and design of reinforcement computer. J. Comput. Eng. **28**(10), 191–192, 223 (2002)
2. Tao, Z.: Conductive rubber materials for EMI and RFI shielding. J. World Rubber Ind. **29** (3), 47–50 (2002)
3. Fang, K., Bai, S., et al.: Characteristics and applications of EMI/RFI thermoplastic conductive elastomers. J. Saf. Electromagn. Compat. (1), 41–44 (2007)
4. Xie, S.: Research and development of flexible graphite and its composite sealing materials. J. Chem. Equip. Anti-Corros. **4**, 51–52 (2004)
5. Xian, F.: Research status of conductive adhesives. J. Bond. **22**(5), 37–38 (2001)

6. Li, M., Zhang, Q.: Rubber Industry Handbook, 3rd edn. Chemical Industry Press, Beijing (2012)
7. Cheng, D.: Mechanical Design Manual, 6th edn. Chemical Industry Press, Beijing (2016)
8. GJB150.8A-2009 Laboratory environmental test methods for military materiel-Part 8: Rain test. S. Beijing. Military Standards Publication and Distribution Department, General Armament Department (2018)
9. GJB151B-2013 Electromagnetic emission and susceptibility requirements and measurements for military equipment and subsystems. S. Beijing. Military Standards Publication and Distribution Department, General Armament Department (2018)
10. GJB150.16A-2009 Laboratory environmental test methods for military materiel-Part 16: Vibration test. S. Beijing. Military Standards Publication and Distribution Department, General Armament Department (2018)

An Independent VGA Controller Based on SOPC with Three Pixel-Mapped Schemes

Zerun Li[✉], Yande Jiang, and Yang Guo

College of Computer, National University of Defense Technology,
Changsha, China
li_zr@foxmail.com

Abstract. As a standard display interface, VGA (Video Graphics Array) has been widely used. In this paper, we propose an independent VGA controller, and the CPU (Central Processing Unit) does not need to control and transmit data, which can save hardware resource and enhance data processing speed, compared to the regular VGA design. Specifically, the controller consists of a synchronizing module, a memory module, and a palette module. We implement three pixel-mapped schemes, including bit-mapped scheme, block-mapped and object-mapped scheme, compared with the traditional mapping scheme. Their signal activities are 5.00×10^7, 1.67×10^7, 3.33×10^7 and 5.67×10^7 respectively which measure the display efficiency of the VGA controller. Their synthesized registers are 2348, 2412, 2560 and 2072, which reflect different resource utilization. Our functional simulations and logic syntheses prove that the proposed VGA controller design has strong flexibility, short design cycle, and low production cost under the provided circumstances of application.

Keywords: VGA · FPGA · SOPC · Embedded system

1 Introduction

SOPC (System on Programmable Chip) can realize the main function of the system on an independent FPGA (Field Programmable Gate Array) development board [1]. SOPC integrates memory, logic unit, I/O interface, central processor, bus interface, and other system design necessary functional modules into a PLD (Programmable Logic Device), and consists of a programmable logic system [2]. The design of SOPC is very flexible and its processor system can also be programmed, cut, upgraded, expanded, maintained easily and can be programmed for both software and hardware [3].

The VGA interface is one of the most important interface to a computer monitor and has been used since the age of the bulky CRT (Cathode Ray Tube) display. It is still used today and also known as the D-sub interface. Apart from HDMI (High Definition Multimedia Interface), VGA can also display images of

W. Xu et al. (Eds.): NCCET 2018, CCIS 994, pp. 16–25, 2019.
https://doi.org/10.1007/978-981-13-5919-4_2

the 1080P to achieve higher resolution [4]. The VGA video signal is decomposed into RGB (Red, Green, Blue) three primary colors and HV (Horizontal and Vertical) line field signals, so the transmission loss is quite small [5]. Although liquid crystal displays can receive digital signals directly, many products use VGA interfaces in order to match the VGA interface graphics cards. There is more and more demand for displaying the process result in real time as the fast development of embedded system, especially as the development of high speed image processing [6–8].

Compared to the regular VGA design, the proposed design does not require central processing unit to control and transmit the data, which can save the expense of hardware and enhance the speed of data processing. It can be widely used in the domain of video display. FPGA is free to design, so we choose to use FPGA to control VGA interface. The controller consists of a synchronizing circuit, a memory module and a palette circuit. The synchronizing circuit can support three different mapping schemes to accelerate the graphic display [9]. According to the Avalon bus control protocol and VGA synchronous timing standards, RGB signals, a horizontal synchronization signal and a vertical synchronizing signal are allocated in a reasonable way. The design is able to not only control display data easily and efficiently, but also be capable of functions extensions.

The remaining of this paper is structured as follows. Section 2 presents the basic components of the designed VGA controller. Section 3 demonstrates the results of function simulation and performance comparisons. Section 4 discusses the whole design of the modules. Finally, Sect. 5 gives some concluding remarks.

2 System Components

The designed VGA controller generates the synchronization signal and outputs the data of pixels to screen continuously. We use Avalon bus protocol to transfer the data controlling color display. This bus allows users to connect the peripherals easily and configure the SOPC easily. We develop a VGA controller and software driver with the display resolution of 640×480. The hardware part consists of a VGA synchronization circuit, a controller based on SRAM (Static Random Access Memory) dual-port video memory, and a palette circuit. The software section includes the driver for reading and writing video memory, as well as the basic program to get the image from the BMP (Bitmap) format file. Figure 1 depicts the controller and the coupling relation with the colorful displayer via control signals and color signals.

There are three different mapping schemes to generate the pixel units from the memory: bit-mapped scheme, block-mapped scheme, and object-mapped scheme.

With regard to the bit-mapped scheme, the signal $pixel\_x$ and $pixel\_y$ can generate the position index for the graphic units. The synchronization circuit constantly updates the screen and writes the relevant data to video memory. A retrieval circuit reads video memory continuously and assigns RGB signal

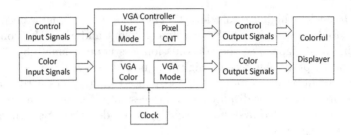

Fig. 1. Controller components and input output signals

data. For a resolution of 640×480 display, there are about $310\,kB$ (640×480) pixel units on a screen to show different pixels [10], which needs $38.4\,kB$ ($640 \times 480 \times 1/8$) space of the memory. The need for 8-bit and 12-bit color display are $310\,kB$ ($640 \times 480 \times 8/8$) and $461\,kB$ ($640 \times 480 \times 12/8$), respectively.

The block-mapped scheme can decrease the demand for the memory performance. In this scheme, a series of data comprise a block and each block is treated as a display unit. For example, an 8×8 pixel square (64 pixels) can be defined as a block. Such a screen, made up of 640×480 pixels, consists of 80×60 blocks and also requires only 4800 words (80×60). The bit width of a word depends on the number of block patterns [11]. For example, if there are 256 block modes, each word should be 8 bits and the block memory size is $4.8\,kB$ ($4800 \times 8/8$), which is called screen memory. Assuming that the VGA uses 8-bit color format, each 8×8 block pattern requires 64 bytes, and all 256 patterns require $16\,kB$. As a result, the overall memory requirement is about $21\,kB$, which is much smaller than $310\,kB$ for the bit-mapped scheme.

The object-mapped scheme uses simple object to display patterns. This scheme, combining and implementing the other two schemes together, can generate different parts of a screen. For instance, the bit-mapped scheme can be used to generate the background, and object-mapped scheme is used to display the main objects. We can also use the bit-mapped scheme to provide one part of the screen and the block-mapped scheme to create another part of the screen [12].

The system is mainly composed of a RAM (Random Access Memory) control module, a time synchronization module and a palette module [13]. The interface diagram is demonstrated in Fig. 2. The whole system has no intervene with graphic processing unit, synchronizes the display information and output color data independently.

2.1   The Synchronization Unit

The synchronization circuit (named VGA_sync circuit in this paper) of VGA interface generates timing signals and synchronizing signals. The two signals are decoded from the internal counter, and the two output signals of the counter are $pixel\_x$ and $pixel\_y$. The signal $pixel\_x$ and $pixel\_y$ represent the relative position of the scan and actually indicate the location of the current pixel.

The vga_sync circuit also produces the video_on signal, indicating whether or not to display it.

In the ideal case, the clock rate of the synchronization circuit should be the same as the pixel rate, for a 640×480 VGA display with a pixel rate of about 25 MHz. In this case, the synchronization circuit can be realized by two special counters: the module 800 counter, used for tracking horizontal scanning, and the module 525 counter for tracking vertical scanning.

If the system clock rate is different from the pixel rate, it is usually necessary to create a separate clock domain for the video system. As the design in this paper uses a 50 MHz quartz oscillator on the development board, the system clock rate is twice the pixel rate. Instead of creating a single 25 MHz clock domain, which complicates the timing, it is better to produce a 25 MHz enabling symbol that enables or pauses the count. This symbol can also be sent to the p_tick port as an output signal to coordinate the operation of the pixel generation circuit.

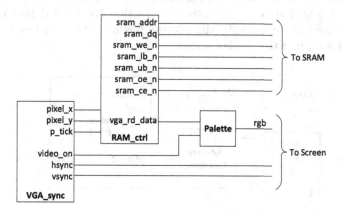

Fig. 2. VGA controller modules interfaces

2.2   The Memory Control Unit

From the bit-mapped scheme point of view, each pixel in the screen is mapped directly to a memory word, and the signal *pixel_x* and *pixel_y* form the pixel address. The system is composed of video RAM memory, and its schematic diagram is shown in Fig. 3. Video memory contains two ports: the VGA port and the host port. The VGA port is marked as *address2* and *data2*, which can be read continuously and beneficial for VGA operation. The pixel address is obtained by the signal *pixel_x* and *pixel_y*, which receive the color information corresponding to the pixel and specify the current coordinate in the screen. The host port, labeled as *address1* and *data1*, connects to the controller. The controller writes information of pixels to the memory and updates the displayed graphics. When it comes to overlapping operations, we may occasionally need to perform reading operations.

The actual performance of video memory depends on the type of physical memory device used in the system. A true dual port memory chip can be used, or a single port memory chip and a multiplexing circuit are used to simulate dual port access. Considering the cost and availability of dual port storage systems, we often adopt the latter methodology.

In a single port implementation, the VGA port and the host port access the same address and data bus of the memory chip. Additional multiplexing and addressing circuits are used to coordinate operations. In order to avoid the graphical display of burr and noise, VGA ports usually have priorities. When video display is closed, the controller can perform the write operation. The other method is double buffering, in which two memory banks are used, one for VGA ports and the other for the controller to write data. Two memory banks operate concurrently and switch roles when a storage body is filled with new data. The scheme actually multiplies the bandwidth of memory, which acts as a real dual port memory. Other similar methods can also be used to simulate dual-port operations. Figure 3 shows a common construction for a RAM controller and emphasizes the interaction with the address bus and the data bus to transfer the original data into the display screen.

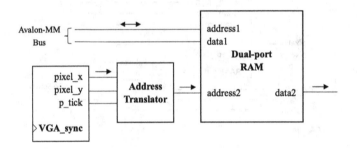

Fig. 3. RAM controller module

2.3   The Palette Unit

The design of VGA controller uses 8 bits for a pixel: 3 for red, 3 for green, and 2 for blue. Assuming the data is $d_7d_6d_5d_4d_3d_2d_1d_0$, the data bits responsible for displaying the red, green and blue are $d_7d_6d_5$, $d_4d_3d_2$ and d_1d_0 respectively. The development board needs 8-bit data bits for each color beam, and three color beams require 24 bits of color depth. We need to convert 8-bit color data of a palette circuit into 24-bit color data output. The easiest way to do this is to use the data bits of the 8-bit color data as the high efficient bit of the 24-bit color output, and copy the low efficient bits. Another more complex solution is to use a color lookup table. In this scheme, the 8-bit input color data is the address of the table which contains 24-bit color data. The 8-bit address corresponds to 256 units in the table, such that the 24-bit colors can catch up to 256. In other words, you can use 24 bits of color in a single image, but we can only use

256 colors in the 4096 possible colors. The size of the lookup table is 256×24 (6144). Many image usage packages contain a palette lookup table that can be invoked according to the actual needs.

3   Function Simulation and Performance Comparisons

The VGA display control system is embedded into the computer in a standardized and effective manner, and the rational circuit conception is realized in the EDA tool. Schematic design input method and hardware description language (HDL) circuit design text is a common design input method in IC design field.

In this design, we use the synchronization circuit, video memory controller, and the module of the palette circuit to realize the RTL (Register Transfer Level) circuit writing of the discrete module [14]. In addition, a package circuit can be added to the video controller to create a SOPC component. It contains three interfaces, one Avalon-MM interface from the device interface functioning as the host port for interacting with the host; a clock input interface for system clock; a conduit interface for the I/O signal of SRAM. The packaged video controller contains additional logics for address decoding, multi-channel data distribution, and appropriate enabling signals.

3.1   Simulation Results

In the Modelsim, the timing sequence of the VGA synchronization signal is simulated in the RTL simulation, and the simulation timing results are shown as Fig. 4. When the row coordinate in the picture above becomes 799, the row coordinate signal will be set to zero and the column coordinate will be 2. At this time, the second row pixel will be scanned. This is a detailed example for the bit-mapped scheme. The length of line synchronization signals sequence is greater than that of the screen opening signals. This phenomenon is consistent with 800 clocks cost by synchronization signal and 640 clocks spent by screen open signal. When the column coordinate becomes 524, the column coordinate is set to zero and the screen completes a refresh process.

The bit-mapped scheme requires all the pixels to display based on the clock edge, so the color and coordinate data are incoherent and independent to display every display datum in a single time period, compared to the other two schemes. Otherwise, the block-mapped scheme allows blocks of display data to transfer continuously without the restrain of the clock edge and contributes to coherent display mode with continuous data output. Furthermore, the object-mapped scheme mixes the benefits of the first two schemes as it supports the high-definition pixel display with the bit-mapped scheme and the high-efficiency data transfer with the block-mapped scheme. But this allocation method for display is quite complex of all three display schemes and may result in display irregularity sometimes.

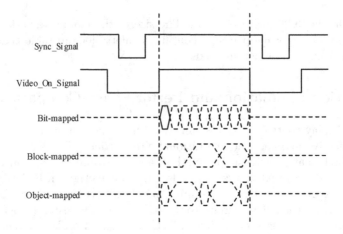

Fig. 4. Synchronization sequence diagram

3.2   Performance and Comparison

The design for three innovated display schemes is independent and reliable for specific applied environment. Compared to primitive VGA controller, the proposed design presents more display mapping modes to appeal to different implementation environment. The VGA controller can be employed in several systems which have video output and support variable mapping schemes to accelerate the display speed compared with the traditional VGA display system [15]. In this section, we propose a FPGA-based system which uses VGA controller as a functional module to display visual data in three mapping display mode. This system plays a role as a remote surveillance system.

The novel VGA controller is not in need of central processing unit to transfer the data for display, which may spare some cost for hardware and increase the speed of data processing. This efficient design can be extensively implemented in the domain of video display without looking up the instant VGA information, while other VGA controllers tend to control the color signals in a monotonic way without the use of independent VGA submodules [5]. FPGA is compatible to various designs and we choose to utilize FPGA to control VGA interface. The design can not only control display data easily and efficiently, but also be capable of functions extensions.

We realize the synthesis of the function modules presented below with Quartus II and observe the overall performance. Moreover, we compare the three mapping schemes with register amounts after compilation, signal amounts and signal activity, as shown in Table 1. The signal amounts affect the complication and the power consumption of the whole system. The block-mapped scheme has two more signals than bit-mapped scheme, including block starts signal and block ends signal. Besides, object-mapped scheme implements bit starts signal and bit ends signal more than block-mapped scheme. The signal activity here indicates the average signal reversal amounts in one second time at 50 MHz clock frequency and the higher signal activity results in greater dynamic power consumption for transistors. The increase in signal amounts can result in more register amounts and synthesized areas.

Table 1. Differences between three display schemes

Scheme	Register amounts	Signal amounts	Signal activity ($\times 10^7$)
Bit-mapped	2348	10	5.00
Block-mapped	2412	12	1.67
Object-mapped	2560	14	3.33
Traditional mapping	2072	10	5.67

4   Discussion

In this paper, we have presented efficient hardware architecture for VGA monitor controller which has a high potential to be used in Altera FPGA-based systems. The highlighted feature makes the design suitable for several FPGA devices and is able to meet different requirements of targeted applications. Using FPGA to control the VGA interface has the advantages of hardware integration and overcoming the disadvantages of large size, difficulty in modifying the architecture, and poor system compatibility. The image information is stored by RAM, which is easy to write RGB trichromatic information, and the image content is displayed according to FPGA. The real-time control of video display based on VGA protocol is realized, which is of great practical significance to the realization of various miniaturized devices and portable embedded systems.

The whole video controller system is composed of a synchronous circuit, a video memory controller circuit, and a color palette circuit. The three basic components can deal with the normal transactions while displaying videos. The resources cost is decreased to a low level and the design achieves low energy use, which relies on the specific design based on SOPC method. The transistors are generated by the experimental platform and cater to many kinds of requirements. This paper presents a practical method to transfer the different color data and synchronize the display lines and rows. However, it fails to be compatible with all FPGA development boards. The compatibility for this design will be under evaluation. Moreover, it may increase the difficulty on setting up the system and selecting the appropriate pixel-mapped schemes. The raise of signal activities causes higher consuming power. And the expansion of synthesized areas may result in more resource utilization. Our experiment results show that the proposed method generates display functions with good subjective quality in terms of the objects' spatial consistency and temporal motion continuity. It also avoids overloaded components and compensates for insufficient available pixels.

5   Conclusion

In this design, the VGA controller based on FPGA development board could be employed to display colorful pixels efficiently. The VGA controller based on SOPC can send data to the screen directly through the used interface. Three pixel-mapped schemes were implemented to accelerate the display rate of the videos. The feasibility of system design, the overall architecture of the hardware description language code, and the development tools affected the performance of the control system. From the perspective of the wide application of VGA interface in flat panel display field, the popularity of this flexible design method combined with FPGA has surged. Our simulation results prove that this system is stable, flexible, short in design period, low in expense, and has certain external expansibility, which clearly suggests the display system with VGA interface opens a promising avenue towards the display market prospect.

References

1. Tormo, D., Monmasson, E., Idkhajine, L., Blasco-Gimenez, R.: Embedded real-time simulator implementations of electromechanical systems using system-on-chip devices. In: Electrimacs (2017). https://hal.archives-ouvertes.fr/hal-01799852
2. Perez, K.G., Yang, X., Scott-Hayward, S., Sezer, S.: Feature study on a programmable network traffic classifier. In: IEEE International System-On-Chip Conference, pp. 108–113 (2017). https://doi.org/10.1109/socc.2016.7905446
3. Luo, Z.J., Zhang, W.N., Liu, L.W., Xie, S.T., Zhou, G.F.: Portable multi-gray scale video playing scheme for high-performance electrowetting displays. J. Soc. Inf. Disp. 24(6), 345–354 (2016). https://doi.org/10.1002/jsid.444
4. Pfeifle, F.: Real-time signal processing on field programmable gate array hardware. In: Bader, R. (ed.) Springer Handbook of Systematic Musicology. SH, pp. 385–417. Springer, Heidelberg (2018). https://doi.org/10.1007/978-3-662-55004-5_20
5. Zhang, Y., Lu, K., Gao, Y.: Fast image matching algorithm based on affine invariants. J. Cent. South Univ. 21(5), 1907–1918 (2014). https://doi.org/10.1007/s11771-014-2137-7
6. Zhang, H.B., Pan, J.C., Zeng, D.J.: Video graphics array interface switch apparatus. US, US8321621B2 (2012)
7. Hu, H.: Testing sysytem and method for video graphics array port, US, US20140244195 (2014)
8. Gurevich, K.L.: Apparatus and methods for video graphics array (VGA) virtualization in system exploiting multiple operating systems, US, US20060036775 (2006)
9. Zhao, T., Li, T., Han, B., Sun, Z., Huang, J.: Design and implementation of software defined hardware counters for SDN. Comput. Netw. 102, 129–144 (2016). https://doi.org/10.1016/j.comnet.2016.03.004
10. Tissot, J.L., Tinnes, S., Durand, A., Minassian, C., Robert, P., Vilain, M., Yon, J.: High-performance uncooled amorphous silicon video graphics array and extended graphics array infrared focal plane arrays with 17-µm pixel pitch. Opt. Eng. 50(60), 409–421 (2011). https://doi.org/10.1117/1.3572155
11. Endoh, T., Tsutomu, S., Yamazaki, T., et al.: Uncooled infrared detector with 12µm pixel pitch video graphics array. In: Infrared Technology and Applications XXXIX International Society for Optics and Photonics (2013). https://doi.org/10.1117/12.2013690

12. Waldvogel, B., Schulz, H., Behnke, S.: Dense real-time mapping of object-class semantics from RGB-D video. J. Real-Time Image Process. **10**(4), 599–609 (2015)
13. Kim, I.H., Choi, J.S., Yun, J.L., Nam, J.Y., Ha, Y.H.: Design and implementation of multimedia functional module for digital TV. IEEE Trans. Consum. Electron. **50**(3), 962–967 (2004). https://doi.org/10.1109/tce.2004.1341707
14. Sivasathya, S.: Design of VGA monitor controller in FPGA using on chip embedded array RAM. Int. J. Technol. Eng. Syst. **6**(1), 27–31 (2004). https://www.ijcns.com
15. Bharathi, M., Yogananth, A.: Design of VGA monitor control using Altera FPGA based system. Int. J. VLSI Embed. Syst. **5**, 866–890 (2014). http://ijves.com

An Inter-Layer-Distance Based Routing Algorithm for 3D Network-on-Chip

Tong Zou[1], Chengyi Zhang[1], Xuefeng Peng[2], and Yuanxi Peng[1(✉)]

[1] School of Computer, National University of Defense Technology, Changsha, China
TongZou94@163.com, pyx@nudt.edu.cn
[2] School of Electronic Information, Hunan Institute of Information Technology, Changsha, China

Abstract. The three-dimensional Network-on-Chip (3D NoC) has been proposed to resolve the complex on-chip communication issues in multi-core systems by using die stacking technology in recent years. It is more difficult to guarantee performance in 3D NoC system than 2D because of stacking dies and the unequal thermal conductance of different logic layers. To ensure the system performance and availability, we proposes an Inter-Layer-Distance based Routing (ILDR) algorithm, which distributes the traffic according to the inter-layer-distance from source node to destination node. We simultaneously consider the buffer status and node temperature of neighbors on path to determine the horizontal route of the next hop. The simulation results show that the proposed ILDR algorithm can apparently reduce network latency and improve network throughput in different experimental traffic patterns. Although the energy consumption is increased, the Energy delay product (EDP) is reduced, so ILDR is a power-efficient solution for 3D NoC.

Keywords: Inter-layer distance · 3D NoC · Routing algorithm

1 Introduction

With Moore's Law, the complexity of system-on-chip (SoCs) increases sharply, system designers are facing unprecedented challenge in on-chip interconnect design. Due to the lack of scalability and predictability, traditional bus-based communication methods cannot be adapted directly in SoC [1]. In recent years, NoC has been proposed as an on-chip communications solution to provide better scalability, performance and modularity for the MP-SOC architecture [2]. In addition, to lower power consumption and to decrease size, three-Dimensional Network-on-Chip (3D NoC) was proposed. Compared with the bus architecture and 2D NoC, 3D NoC have a large number of advantages, including smaller

Supported by the Research Fund of State Key Laboratory of High Performance Computing, National University of Defense Technology, P.R. China. Under Grant No. 201612-01, and HGJ National Key Project with grant 2017ZX01028103.

W. Xu et al. (Eds.): NCCET 2018, CCIS 994, pp. 26–37, 2019.
https://doi.org/10.1007/978-981-13-5919-4_3

layout footprint, shorter physical distances and hops, and more directions for each router [3]. Here are some research results on NoC. Chameleon [4] proposes a heterogeneous Multi-NoC design, which exploits power saving opportunities at different levels of granularity simultaneously. HMMesh [5] present a hybrid Multi-NoC design architecture, and leverages CMesh network to respect its power efficiency at low network utilization.

Thermal is an extremely severe issue in 3D NoC attributing to die stacking, longer heat dissipation path and larger power density. The thermal characteristics is different from each other in stacking dies of 3D structure. The bottom layer tends to be at the lowest temperature because it is close to the heat sink. In contrast, the top layer tends to be at the highest temperature [6].

Most of the previous works try to distribute the traffic evenly in each layer. Actually, owing to the longer heat dissipation path and the varying cooling efficiency in vertical direction, even with a balanced traffic distributed on the network, the performance cannot be guaranteed optimally yet. Based on the inter-layer-distance and considering both cooling efficiency and performance, we propose a novel algorithm called ILDR. ILDR calculates the inter-layer-distance (ILD) from source node to destination node. If the absolute value of ILD is not greater than $ILD_{threshold}$, our routing algorithm routes the packet at current layer horizontally in priority, then sending to the destination node in vertical direction. Otherwise, the routing algorithm routes the packet to the layer which is closer to the bottom layer. In other words, if the source node layer is farther to bottom layer than to the destination node, the algorithm priority routes the packet to the destination layer in the vertical direction and then routes it horizontally to the destination node. On the contrary, the algorithm routes the packet to the projective destination in the same layer (the node that has the same X and Y coordinates in the source layer with the destination node) and then routes to the destination node vertically. Although this algorithm always makes the traffic imbalance, since the bottom layer is close to the heat sink and the heat dissipation is shorter, the algorithm can still achieve a high performance.

The rest of the paper is organized as follows: Sect. 2 presents previous research related to this study, Sect. 3 describes the proposed ILDR algorithm, Sect. 4 illustrates the simulation results and Sect. 5 concludes the paper.

2   Related Work

2.1   Turn Models and Neighbors-on-Path (NOP) Selection Strategy

Since the turn model [7] was proposed, it become widespread to design deadlock-free routing algorithms. It is quite cost-efficient and easy to implement, especially for networks without virtual channels. However, Chiu [8] found that the routing algorithms based on turn model generate uneven routing adaptability several years later. To address this issue, the odd-even turn model, which prohibits different turns in odd and even columns, was proposed. Based on the turn model and the odd-even turn model, many adaptive routing algorithms have been proposed.

Neighbors-on-Path (NOP) [9] is a selection strategy proposed for indecision occurring when the routing function returns several admissible output channels. The main aim is to allocate the channels allowing the packets to be routed to their destination along a path that is as free as possible of congested nodes. NOP selection strategy using a score mechanism, the score of a candidate destination is increased for each neighbor-on-path with available space in a no-reserved input buffer. Finally, the channel with the higher score is selected.

2.2 Mean Time to Throttle (MTTT) Routing Index

Traditional selection strategies determine the routing path based on the traffic information, which may deliver most of the packets to congestion region and then results in huge performance impact. To work out this problem, Kuo et al. proposed a novel thermal-aware routing index called Mean Time To Throttle (MTTT) [10]. MTTT means the remaining active time before the router being throttled by the run-time thermal managements (RTM) and can be repressed as:

$$MTTT = \frac{T_{threshold} - T(t)}{Temperature \quad Comsumption \quad Rate}. \tag{1}$$

Where $T_{threshold}$ denotes the temperature threshold to trigger run-time thermal managements (RTM). $T(t)$ is current temperature at time t. And Temperature Consumption Rate represents the rate of change of temperature in a timing interval which can be expressed as:

$$\frac{dT(t + \Delta t_s)}{dt} = \frac{dT(t)}{dt} \times e^{-\frac{1}{RC}}. \tag{2}$$

The RC parameter denotes the thermal resistance and thermal conductance, respectively.

2.3 Transport Layer Assisted Routing (TLAR) Algorithm and Topology Aware Adaptive Routing (TAAR) Algorithm

Thermal is a significant issue in the 3D NOC design, so several researchers have paid attention to thermal-aware routing algorithms. Chao et al. [11] presented a Transport Layer Assisted Routing (TLAR) algorithm in 2011. They used the topology information to assist the determination of routing in this algorithm. TLAR was composed of two parts: lateral routing algorithms in the horizontal layer and downward routing in the vertical layer. According to the difference of the intra-layer routings, there were three algorithms been proposed on account of the TLAR framework, called Downward-Lateral Adaptive-Deterministic Routing (DLADR), Downward-Lateral Deterministic Routing (DLDR) and Downward-Lateral Adaptive Routing (DLAR).

Although TLAR algorithm effectively improves performance, it is prone to cause the traffic congestion in the bottom of logic layer. For more balanced traffic, Chen et al. [12] proposed the TAAR algorithm. The TAAR algorithm uses cascaded routing for more path diversity while using queuing analysis theory to balance the traffic in the vertical direction. As a result, the routing computational complexity increases the hardware overhead of TAAR algorithm accordingly.

3 Algorithms Design

As mentioned above, thanks to the longer heat dissipation path and the varying cooling efficiency in the vertical direction, even with a balanced traffic distributed on the network, the performance cannot be guaranteed optimally. To ensure the system performance and availability, this work proposes an Inter-Layer-distance based Routing (ILDR) algorithm. Besides, we also consider the logic layer-distance from source node to destination node, buffer status and node temperature of neighbors on path simultaneously.

3.1 Routing Design

The flow chart of the ILDR is shown in Fig. 1, where Src and Dst represent source and destination nodes respectively. Dt is the projective destination which is the node that has the same X and Y coordinates with the destination node in source layer, and St is the projective source which is the node that has the same X and Y coordinates with the source node in destination layer. If the inter-layer-distance from Src to Dst is less than $ILD_{threshold}$, the routing algorithm first routes the packet in the horizontal layer to the projective destination node Dt, and then send it to the destination node in the vertical direction (Up or Down). If the inter-layer-distance is greater than $ILD_{threshold}$, the routing mechanism will be divided into two cases. If Src is farther to the bottom layer than Dst, we first route the packet to St in the destination layer by vertical path, then route to the destination by horizontal path. If Src is closer to the bottom layer than Dst, in this case, we first route the packet in the horizontal layer to Dt, and then route to the destination node in the vertical direction.

Table 1 shows the detail traffic load distribution of the algorithm when $ILD_{threshold} = 1$ in 8*8*4 3D mesh NoC, where layer3 acts as the bottom layer (close to the heat sink layer). The number from "0" to "3" represents which layer is used to routes the packet in horizontal direction, either the source node layer or the destination node layer, depending on the inter-layer-distance. For instance, if a packet needs to be routed from layer0 to layer1, the inter-layer-distance is less than 1, so the horizontal layer used to route is "0". If the transmission is between layer0 and layer2, the horizontal layer used to route is "2", because layer2 is closer to the heat sink layer. The last column of the table shows the traffic load ratio of layer0, layer1, layer2 and layer3 is 2:3:5:6.

For better understanding, we show an example in Fig. 2. The two groups, Src1 to Dst1, Src4 to Dst4, are the absolute value of the inter layer distance less than 1, so first pass in the source node layer, and then passed vertically to the destination node. Src2 to Dst2, Src3 to Dst3, the absolute value of the inter

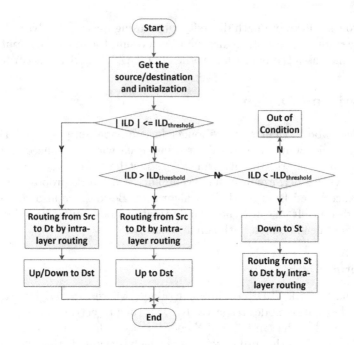

Fig. 1. Flow chart of the ILDR algorithm.

Table 1. Detailed traffic load distribution ($ILD_{threshold} = 1$)

Src \ Dst	Layer0	Layer1	Layer2	Layer3	Traffic Load Ratio
Layer0	0	0	2	3	2
Layer1	1	1	1	3	3
Layer2	2	2	2	2	5
Layer3	3	3	3	3	6

layer distance between the two groups is greater than 1, so the transfer in the horizontal direction is preferentially performed in the layer close to the heat sink layer.

$ILD_{threshold}$ is a very significant parameter in our algorithm. In the $8 * 8 * 4$ 3D mesh NoC, we set $ILD_{threshold} = 1$. Actually, the value of $ILD_{threshold}$ can be adjusted according to the actual number of NoC layers. As shown in Table 2, when $ILD_{threshold} = 0$, the traffic load ratio is 1:3:5:7, which means that the traffic load among the layers is particularly unbalanced. Traffic in the bottom layer is too large and the upper layer is too small, causing traffic congestion at the bottom layer and thus affect the overall performance. On the other hand, as the Table 3 shows, when $ILD_{threshold} = 2$, the traffic load ratio is 3:4:4:5, and only a small fraction of traffic at the top layer are transferred to the bottom, achieving no performance improvement. After the experiment, we chose $ILD_{threshold} = 1$

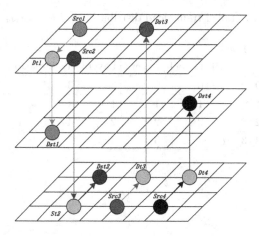

Fig. 2. Examples of ILDR algorithm.

for NoC with 4 layers. When the number of NoC layers changes, we can adjust the value of $ILD_{threshold}$ to achieve maximum performance improvement. For example, in $8*8*8$ 3D mesh NoC, we can set the value of $ILD_{threshold}$ to 3 or 4.

3.2   Intra-layer Routing

The intra-layer routing is a widely applied Odd-Even routing algorithm, which has been proved a deadlock-free algorithm in 2D mesh NoC. In vertical direction, extra channel is affiliated to avoid deadlock. As shown in Fig. 3, we utilize vertical channel 1 to route packet which is transferred from horizontal direction to vertical orientation. When the packet transmission path is form vertical to horizontal, another channel works. Note that it is impossible for a packet to turn twice in a vertical direction with our routing algorithm. Therefore, there is no cyclic dependency and the routing algorithm is deadlock-free.

Table 2. Detailed traffic load distribution ($ILD_{threshold} = 0$)

Src	Dst				
	Layer0	Layer1	Layer2	Layer3	Traffic load ratio
Layer0	0	1	2	3	1
Layer1	1	1	2	3	3
Layer2	2	2	2	3	5
Layer3	3	3	3	3	7

Table 3. Detailed traffic load distribution ($ILD_{threshold} = 2$)

Src	Dst				
	Layer0	Layer1	Layer2	Layer3	Traffic load ratio
Layer0	0	0	0	3	3
Layer1	1	1	1	1	4
Layer2	2	2	2	2	4
Layer3	3	3	3	3	5

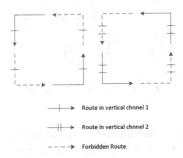

Route in vertical chnnel 1

Route in vertical chnnel 2

Forbidden Route

Fig. 3. Turns in vertical directions.

We combine the NOP with MTTT to determine the route of the next hop, and harness the following objective function to evaluate the routing condition of each neighbor node.

$$S_i = \alpha \frac{S_{NoP}}{B_l} + \beta \frac{MTTT}{(T_{threshold} - T_A)}. \tag{3}$$

Where S_i denotes the Score of the neighbor node in direction i which is one of North, South, East, West in 2D mesh. S_{NoP} is the score computed by NOP score mechanism. B_l denotes the buffer length of each node. MTTT is the mean time to throttle as discussed before. $T_{threshold}$ is the temperature threshold and T_A denotes the ambient temperature. α and β represent the weights for the two objectives. The direction with highest score will be selected at last.

4   Experimental Results and Analysis

We compare our ILDR algorithm with TLAR-DLADR [11] and TAAR [12] in *Average Latency*, *Energy Consumption*, *Throughput* and *Energy Delay Product* (EDP). Access Noxim simulator [13], combining Noxim simulator and HotSpot simulator, and adopts the power model of Intel's 80-core processor, is used for this evaluation. Related parameters for the simulation are shown in Table 4. In order to decrease the simulation time, we set the initial temperature at 85 °C and set the packet size larger than buffer size.

Table 4. Parameters for simulation

ID	Parameter	Value
1	Packet size	8 flits
2	Buffer size	4 flits
3	Simulation time	10^6 cycles
4	Warm up time	10^4 cycles
5	α, β	0.75, 0.25
6	Mesh size	8 * 8 * 4
7	Traffic patterns	Random, Shuffle, Transpose1
8	Temperature threshold	115 °C
9	Initial temperature	85 °C

When implementing the proposed routing algorithm on the simulator, we execute the simulations on a 8 * 8 * 4 mesh network. We have run three simulations with different synthetic traffic patterns which use the poisson process for modeling the temporal variation of traffic. With random traffic, a node sends a packet to each other node with the same probability. In transpose traffic, a node (i, j) only sends packets to a node (N-1-j, N-1-i), where N is the size of the mesh [14,15]. In shuffle traffic, the source node with node number $\{s_i | s_i \in \{0,1\}, i \in [0, n-1]\}$ sends a packet to the destination node whose node number is $\{s_{i-1} \mod n \mid s_{i-1} \in \{0,1\}, i \in [0, n-1]\}$. The comparison results of the average latency, total energy consumption, throughput and EDP at random, transpose and shuffle traffic patterns are illustrated in Figs. 4, 5 and 6.

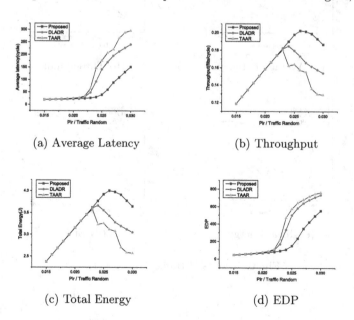

(a) Average Latency

(b) Throughput

(c) Total Energy

(d) EDP

Fig. 4. Results of traffic random.

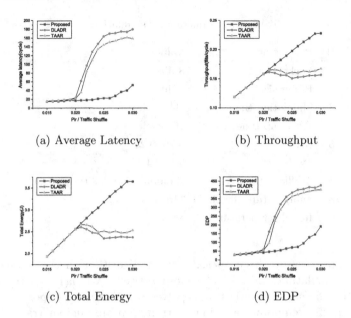

(a) Average Latency   (b) Throughput

(c) Total Energy   (d) EDP

Fig. 5. Results of traffic shuffle.

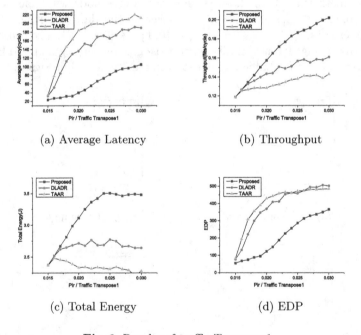

(a) Average Latency   (b) Throughput

(c) Total Energy   (d) EDP

Fig. 6. Results of traffic Transpose1.

Experiments shows that comparing with TAAR and TLAR-DLADR algorithms, our algorithm reduces the network latency and improve network throughput on any traffic patterns in different degrees and shuffle benefits mostly. It can be attributed to our uncomplicated algorithm for routing computation, the transmission delay is lower than other algorithms. Additionally, even though the proposed algorithm allocates more traffics to the layers located closer to the bottom layer, they are close to the heat sink and have shorter heat dissipation path, as a result, the network throughput still stays well. However, the added channel in vertical direction leads to an increase in hardware complexity that ultimately increases total energy consumption. For evaluating the average latency and total energy at the same time, we use the energy delay product (EDP) metric for performance evaluation. We found that the EDP of the algorithm is still better than the other two algorithms, which means that our algorithm is more effective.

In order to understanding of the performance improvement more intuitively, we have listed the detailed simulation data when Packet Injection Rate (PIR) = 0.025 in the Table 5. As can be seen from the table, compared with the DLADR

Table 5. Detailed simulation data for PIR = 0.025

Metrics	Traffic patterns	Proposed ILDR	DLADR	TAAR
Average latency	Random	39.0259	140.948	176.291
			(+72.31%)	(+77.86%)
	Transpose1	81.8089	165.559	204.176
			(+50.59%)	(+59.93%)
	Shuffle	22.4499	163.56	144.33
			(+86.27%)	(+84.44%)
Throughput	Random	0.19776	0.179515	0.163867
			(−9.23%)	(−17.14%)
	Transpose1	0.18649	0.156884	0.138203
			(−15.87%)	(−25.89%)
	Shuffle	0.19756	0.150618	0.161018
			(−23.76%)	(−18.49%)
Total energy	Random	3.91901	3.55471	3.25433
			(−9.29%)	(−16.96%)
	Transpose1	3.50581	2.77286	2.31256
			(−20.91%)	(−34.04%)
	Shuffle	3.1769	2.34537	2.51263
			(−26.17%)	(−20.91%)
EDP	Random	152.94289	501.0293	573.7091
			(+69.47%)	(+73.34%)
	Transpose1	286.80646	459.0719	472.1693
			(+37.52%)	(+39.26%)
	Shuffle	71.32109	383.6087	362.6479
			(+81.41%)	(+80.33%)

algorithm and the TAAR algorithm, the ILDR algorithm reduces the average delay by 50.59%–86.27% and improves the throughput by 9.23%–25.89%. Although the total energy consumption has increased by 9.29%–34.04%, the EDP is decreased by 37.52%–81.41%.

5   Conclusion

In this paper, we proposed an Inter-Layer-distance based Routing algorithm, which use the logic layer-distance from source node to destination node as a metric to allocate traffic load. By comparing with other algorithms, the proposed ILDR can reduce the network latency and improve network throughput. Despite the increasement in total energy consumption, the algorithm's EDP is still better than the other two algorithms. That is to say, the proposed algorithm is effective to maintain a high performance.

References

1. Micheli, G.D., Benini, L.: Network on chip: a new paradigm for systems on chip design. In: Design, Automation and Test in Europe Conference and Exhibition, pp. 418–419. IEEE (2002)
2. Pavlidis, V.F., Friedman, E.G.: 3-D topologies for networks-on-chip. In: SOC Conference, pp. 285–288. IEEE (2006)
3. Chen, K.C., Chao, C.H., Lin, S.Y., Wu, A.Y.: Traffic- and Thermal-Aware Routing Algorithms for 3D Network-on-Chip (3D NoC) systems. In: Palesi, M., Daneshtalab, M. (eds.) Routing Algorithms in Networks-on-Chip, pp. 307–338. Springer, New York (2014). https://doi.org/10.1007/978-1-4614-8274-1_12
4. Wu, J., Dong, D., Liao, X., Wang, L.: Chameleon: Adaptive energy-efficient heterogeneous network-on-chip. In: IEEE International Conference on Computer Design, pp. 419–422. IEEE (2015)
5. Wu, J., Dong, D., Wang, L.: HM-Mesh: energy efficient hybrid multiple network-on-chip. In: International Symposium on Computer, Consumer and Control, pp. 404–407. IEEE (2016)
6. Jheng, K.Y., Chao, C.H., Wang, H.Y., Wu, A.Y.: Traffic-thermal mutual coupling co-simulation platform for three-dimensional Network-on-Chip. In: International Symposium on VlSI Design Automation and Test, pp. 135–138. IEEE (2010)
7. Glass, C.J., Ni, L.M.: The turn model for adaptive routing. In: International Symposium on Computer Architecture, pp. 278–287. IEEE (1998)
8. Chiu, G.M.: The odd-even turn model for adaptive routing. IEEE Trans. Parallel Distrib. Syst. 11(7), 729–738 (2000)
9. Ascia, G., Catania, V., Palesi, M., Patti, D.: Neighbors-on-path: a new selection strategy for on-chip networks. In: Embedded Systems for Real Time Multimedia, pp. 79–84. IEEE (2006)
10. Kuo, C.C., Chen, K.C., Chang, E.J., Wu, A.Y.: Proactive Thermal-Budget-Based Beltway Routing algorithm for thermal-aware 3D NoC systems. In: International Symposium on System on Chip, pp. 1–4. IEEE (2013)
11. Chao, C.H., Yin, T.C., Lin, S.Y., Wu, A.Y.: Transport layer assisted routing for non-stationary irregular mesh of thermal-aware 3D network-on-chip systems. In: SoC Conference, pp. 284–289. IEEE (2011)

12. Chen, K.C., Lin, S.Y., Hung, H.S., Wu, A.Y.: Topology-aware adaptive routing for non-stationary irregular mesh in throttled 3D NoC systems. IEEE Trans. Parallel Distrib. Syst. **24**(10), 2109–2120 (2013)
13. Access Noxim. http://access.ee.ntu.edu.tw/noxim/index.html
14. Ascia, G., Catania, V., Palesi, M., et al.: Implementation and analysis of a new selection strategy for adaptive routing in networks-on-chip. IEEE Trans. Comput. **57**(6), 809–820 (2008)
15. Zeng, L., Pan, T., Jiang, X., Watanabe, T.: An efficient highly adaptive and deadlock-free routing algorithm for 3D network-on-chip. IEICE Trans. Fundam. Electron. Commun. Comput. Sci. **E99**(A.7), 1334–1344 (2016)

Impact of Temperature Characteristics on High-Speed Optical Communication Modules

Tengyue Li[1(✉)], Libing Liu[2], Yifan Song[3], and Mingche Lai[2]

[1] School of Information Science and Engineering, Ocean University of China, Qingdao, China
litengyue0532@163.com
[2] School of Computer Science, National University of Defense Technology, Changsha, China
[3] GEOMAR Helmholtz Centre for Ocean Research Kiel, Wischhofstr. 1-3, 24148 Kiel, Germany

Abstract. This paper presents a method to evaluate the impact of temperature characteristics on vertical cavity surface emitting laser (VCSEL) module. As one of the core modules in the optical communication system, the performance of VCSEL strongly influences the communication quality of the high-speed optical communication system. However, it is difficult to directly analyze the temperature change of VCSEL. In order to solve this problem, batches of laser sources have been integrated into the optical communication module, the physical properties of the laser beams then can be easily measured at different temperatures (low temperature −5 °C, room temperature 25 °C and high temperature 70 °C). By analyzing the wavelength, ext. ratio and the margin of eye diagram of these laser beams, we calculate the percentage value which referrers to an engineering experience standard value as the evaluator, to describe the quality of the optical communication system. The performance of communication quality is evaluated under different parameters, including amplitude, emphasis, mode and bias etc. Several tests have been preceded which all obtained the satisfactory results.

Keywords: Temperature characteristics · Vertical cavity surface emitting laser Optical communication modules

1 Introduction

With the developing of high performance computing technologies, various high-speed optical networks are widely used in the field of high-performance computer. As a core part of optical interconnect networks, optical communication module plays an important role in high-speed data communication applications [1, 2]. In the optical communication data transmission, 850 nm vertical cavity surface emitting laser (VCSEL) shows a desirable performance with the advantages of high modulation rate, low power consumption and easy packing, especially suitable for short-range local area network such as high-performance computers and data centers [1, 3, 4].

© Springer Nature Singapore Pte Ltd. 2019
W. Xu et al. (Eds.): NCCET 2018, CCIS 994, pp. 38–47, 2019.
https://doi.org/10.1007/978-981-13-5919-4_4

The photograph of VCSEL array and transmitting driver chip are shown in Fig. 1. Many optical communication researches have been presented based on VCSELs: By the means of inserting a high-bandgap electron blocking layer, the carrier blocking effect on 850 nm InAlGaAs/AlGaAs VCSELs was theoretically and experimentally investigated by National Chiao-Tung University. With the optimized 850 nm VCSEL devices for high-speed operation under direct modulation, the researchers from Chalmers University of Technology has been achieved to record an optimal oxide aperture diameter [5, 6]. A researcher from Tyndall National Institute presented gain calculations using an 8-band k p Hamiltonian which indicates that the incorporation of 10%. The In-GaAs/AlGaAs QW structure could approximately double the differential gain with the compare to the GaAs/AlGaAs QW structure, with little additional improvement achieved by further increasing the In composition in the QW [7].

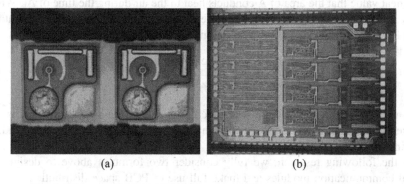

(a)   (b)

Fig. 1. Photograph of (a) VCSEL array and (b) transmitting driver chip.

Many achievements have been achieved in the area of VCSELs. However, the self-heating problem of the device still remains in the short-wavelength and low-power VCSELs. The thermal characteristic parameter is a very strong impact on the semiconductor laser which leads the temperature characteristic test to become particularly crucial [8, 9]. Thus, the test of temperature characteristic needs to be carried out in a stable heat balance system. This paper applied a self-designed thermal closed system which is packaged in the optical modules, to study on the 850 nm VCSELs. The temperature characteristics of the optical modules gave a series data of VCSELs to describe the thermal performance at extreme temperatures [10]. We note that the research method introduced in this paper is designed for 850 nm high-speed optical communication module because it is the most common communication device in data center or high-performance computer. However, it potentially generally more useful because it is based on a principle common to other 850 nm optical communication products.

The remaining part of this paper is organized as follows. In Sect. 2, the thermal model assessment of VCSEL is introduced. Section 3 provides the temperature experiments and data. Section 4 gives the high-speed communication system experiments, which come up with an effective method to overcome the high temperature problem. At the end of the paper, the main conclusion of this paper's work is drawn in Sect. 5.

2   Thermal Model Assessment of VCSEL

In the optical communication modules, GaAs substrate has a Cr/Au photolithographic electrode and VCSEL arrays are sintered on the substrate by solder. In order to have a good heat dissipation performance, GaAs substrate is fixed to the PCB by thermal conductive adhesive. The reserved position is gold-plated and has multiple cooling holes [11]. The whole system is mainly through the air natural convection for heat dissipation, so the calculation formula of conduction heat in the system can be expressed as below:

$$\Delta Q = hA\Delta T\Delta t \tag{1}$$

Where ΔT is the temperature difference between the material in the area and air. ΔQ is the heat value that the area of A conducts heat to the air during the time of Δt. While h is the heat conduction coefficient, it represents the capacity of the material to heat the air under natural heat dissipation. The thermal diffusion equation is shown below.

$$\frac{\partial^2 t}{\partial x^2} + \frac{\partial^2 t}{\partial y^2} + \frac{\partial^2 t}{\partial z^2} + \frac{Q}{\lambda} = \frac{1}{\alpha}\frac{\partial t}{\partial \tau} \tag{2}$$

Where λ is coefficient of thermal conduction, thermal diffusivity of material is α, t represents the temperature of (x, y, z) coordinate, Q is the heat flux at the corresponding coordinates and τ is for time.

In the following research, we fully consider two formulas above to design the optical communication modules and make full use of PCB space distribution.

3   Temperature Experiments and Data Analysis

As it is known that the bandwidth performance of VCSEL degrades at high temperature and corresponds to room temperature at low temperature. By integrating VCSELs into optical communication modules, the wavelength and eye diagram are analyzed respectively in different systems. 21pcs VCSELs are provided by the supplier for verifying the performance. Each optical module has 4 transmitting channels, which is tested in the temperature experiment. All the optical modules are numbered sequentially from 1# to 21#. Figure 2 demonstrates the temperature testing system. Testing instrumentation includes optical spectrum analyzer (OSA) and digital communication analyzer (DCA).

As it is shown in Fig. 2, temperature control system respectively provides constant temperatures low temperature −5 °C, room temperature 25 °C and high temperature 70 °C. The temperature hood is above the optical modules, which is in a sealed environment to make the module in a certain temperature environment. The computer sends control commands to BERT by the I2C. Bit error ration tester (BERT) which is utilized to generate and send high-speed electric signal to the test board. The optical module connects to the test board through the interface and achieves the electro-optical conversion. Optical signal is analyzed by OSA or DCA by using the optical fibers.

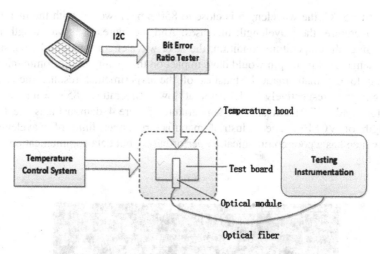

Fig. 2. The temperature testing system.

3.1 Temperature Experiments for the Wavelength

The testing parameters of OSA are shown in Table 1. 21pcs optical modules at different temperatures are tested. The laser wavelength changes with the temperature. Figure 3 illustrates the changes of laser array wavelength in each optical module at different temperatures.

Table 1. The parameters of OSA.

Smplg	SwpAvg	VBW (Hz)	Sm	Intvl
2001pt	2	100	off	off

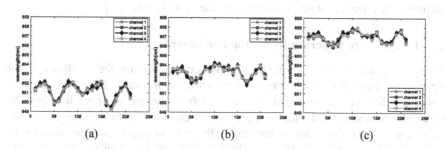

     (a)   (b)   (c)

Fig. 3. Laser wavelength at (a) −5 °C (b) 25 °C (c) 70 °C.

As we can see in the result, the influence of temperature change on the laser is mainly behaved as the drift of wavelength, which may cause the instability of the output like errors and packet loss. The optimal communication wavelength is around

850 nm. At −5 °C, the wavelength is close to 850 nm. However, with the increments of the temperature, the wavelength increases. And the increase in wavelength is not irregular. In each temperature condition, the laser wavelength trends to be consistent. But the change of wavelength would have impact on the quality of the communication. According to the mathematical statistics of the experimental results, the average wavelengths are respectively 851.14 nm at low temperature, 853.23 nm at room temperature and 857.01 nm at high temperature. Figure 4 demonstrates the typical wavelength of VCSEL. The industrial manufacture upper limit of wavelength is 860 nm which has a poor communication performance, but data communication can be still possible.

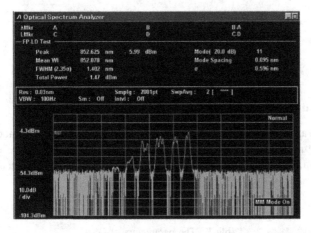

Fig. 4. Typical wavelength of VCSEL (7# at room temperature 25 °C).

The analysis above shows that the wavelengths of some VCSELs are very close to the upper limit (860 nm) at the high temperature. However, as for data transmission acceptable wavelength range (840–860 nm), the yield is 100%.

3.2   Temperature Experiments for the Eye Diagram

The eye diagram is series of digital signals accumulated on the oscilloscope and displayed on Keysight, which contains a bunch of information. The effects of inter-symbol interference and noise can be observed from the eye diagram. It reflects the overall characteristics of the digital signal which can be used to estimate the system performance. Thus, eye diagram analysis is the core of signal integrity analysis for high-speed interconnect systems. In addition, the characteristics of the receiving filter can also be adjusted using this pattern in order to reduce inter-symbol interference and improve the transmission performance of the system. Two key measurements, Margin and Ext. Ratio, are studied in this paper. In the course of industrial production, acceptable Margin of hit ration is 10% at 5e−5 at any temperature. And acceptable Ext. Ratio is between 3 dB and 5 dB at any temperature. These two important parameters have been studied in detail when we teste the optical eye diagram of 21pcs optical communication modules. Figures 5 and 6 illustrate the results.

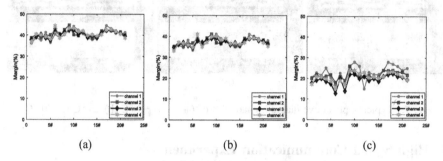

(a)   (b)   (c)

Fig. 5. Margin (%) (5e−5 hit ratio) at (a) −5 °C (b) 25 °C (c) 70 °C.

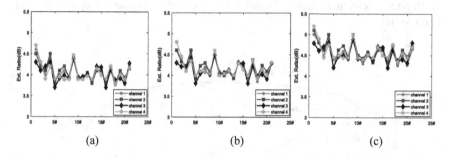

(a)   (b)   (c)

Fig. 6. Ext. Ratio at (a) −5 °C (b) 25 °C (c) 70 °C.

At the high temperature, the margin is mostly between 15% to 25%, which is very crucial for communication system. It is acceptable that the margin at high temp should be above 10%. Even though all the optical modules are acceptable, the performance of them are not desirable at the high temperature. The average Margins from the statistics are 40.53% at low temperature, 37.01% at room temperature and 21.21% at high temperature. Optical eye diagram has a significant decline while the temperature increases. However, there is an opposite tendency in the data for Ext. Ratio. The average Ext. Ratios are 4.05 dB, 4.17 dB and 4.57 dB respect to different temperatures, but some channels of 1#, 4# and 9# are over 5 dB which is unacceptable. Table 2 and Fig. 7 demonstrate the typical examples.

Table 2. The results of typical optical eye diagram channel 3 of 6# at different temperatures.

TEMP (°C)	ER (dB)	Crossing (%)	Jitter-pp (ps)	Jitter-rms (ps)	Rise time (ps)	Fall time (ps)	Margin (%)
−5	3.92	46.3	9.72	1.47	15.82	18.75	43.0
25	4.05	46.4	10.58	1.51	15.48	18.49	37.9
70	4.08	46.8	14.36	2.04	17.72	22.70	12.8

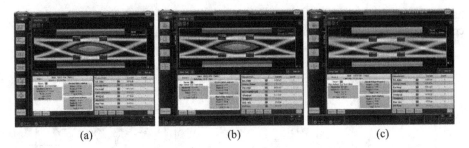

(a)   (b)   (c)

Fig. 7. Typical optical eye diagram channel 3 of 6# at (a) −5 °C (b) 25 °C (c) 70 °C.

4 High-Speed Communication Experiments

After analyzing the performance of VCSEL, we tested the communication quality of optical communication modules. Figure 8 illustrates the diagram of optical communication system.

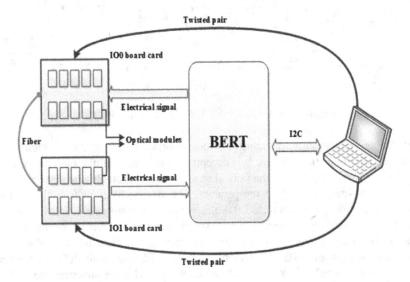

Fig. 8. The diagram of optical communication system.

Pseudo-Random Binary Sequence (PRBS) is used in testing, a pseudo-random sequence containing only 0 and 1, which can be predetermined, and can be repeatedly produced and replicated. Bit Error Ratio Test (BERT) system generates PRBS31 code pattern and transfers the code to IO0 board card by the coaxial cable. Electrical signals are converted into optical signals in optical modules, which on the IO0 board card. Optical modules on IO1 board card get the optical signals through the fiber, which converts the optical signals into electrical signals and transfer back to the BERT.

For comparing the emitted and recovered signals, the error codes and error ratio of the data transmission are calculated. According to the error codes or error ratio, we can evaluate the performance and reliability of optical communication modules. The software on the control computer displays the result of error codes and error ratio. By twisted pair, the control computer monitors the optical communication modules and changes parameter settings real-timely. Figure 9 illustrates the details of channel connection between the optical communication modules.

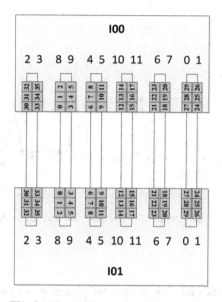

Fig. 9. The details of channel connection.

We select a default plan and a modified plan to test optical signal transmission especially for long working time. The temperature of the operating system increases and eventually stabilizes in a region, which is similar to the high temperature condition. The optical communication modules of a default plan use the parameters recommended by the supplier, while a modified plan uses the parameters adjusted in the laboratory which may lead to a good performance. The process of modified plan is as fellows. First, we applied the control variable method to adjust the most sensitive optical communication module configuration parameters, other parameters remain at their default values. Optical modules are tested in Fig. 8 system after parameters being set. Through reasonable pre-emphasis and post-emphasis collocation, signal to noise is deduced. This is a good way to improve analog noise reduction in analog signal noise processing. We first set the pre-emphasis and post-emphasis optimal parameters, which are the most sensitive parameters, and the effect of other configuration parameters is neglected. Then we fixed the pre-emphasis and post-emphasis parameters and adjusted other parameters (amplitude, equalization and bias) for several tests. Finally, we got a set of final optimal configuration parameters respect to the modified plan. Line chart in

Fig. 10 respectively shows the result of a default plan and a modified plan corresponds to their configuration parameters. The horizontal coordinate represents the test ports and the ordinate indicates the amount of errors.

The communication quality and performance of the BERT system are stable under multiple tests with configuration parameters of modified plan (as is shown in Fig. 10b). Modified plan has a better performance than default plan, which means that the plan overcome the problem of high temperature by adjusting parameters of optical communication modules.

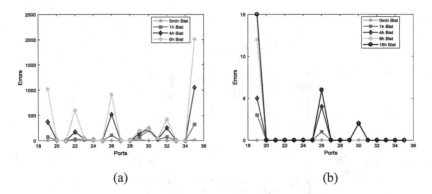

(a)   (b)

Fig. 10. The testing result of (a) default plan and (b) modified plan.

5   Conclusion

Temperature characteristics have significant influences on the optical communication system. The research we carried out in this paper is about the performance of VCSELs at different temperatures. First, 21pcs VCSELs are packaged into optical modules and tested in a temperature testing system. By analyzing the key parameter indicators of wavelength and eye diagram under different temperatures, margin of optical eye diagram has a noticeable decline while the temperature increasing to a higher temperature, which will affect the quality of communication. Then optical communication system is built to test the performance of optical modules for a long working time with a default plan and a modified plan. The temperature of hardware goes up as optical communication system works for a long time. It is similar to high temperature condition in the practical application. After a series of adjusting amplitude, emphasis and bias etc., the modified plan has a better performance than the default plan, which overcomes the problem of VCSEL temperature drift in the communication system. Finally, the research has some reference value for the industrial manufacture of 850 nm VCSEL products.

Acknowledgments. The research is supported by the National Natural Science Foundation of China (No. 61572509), the research is also supported by the National Key Research and Development Plan (No. 2016YFB0200203).

References

1. Rashed, A.N.Z., Nabih, A.: Current trends of high capacity optical interconnection data link in high performance optical communication systems. I. J. Intell. Syst. Appl. **3**, 94–110 (2013)
2. Li, T., Liu, L., Lai, M.: An optimization solution of high performance computer communication quality. In: 21st Annual Conference on Computer Engineering and Technology China Computer Federation (2017)
3. Larsson, A., et al.: High-speed VCSELs for short reach communication. Semicond. Sci. Technol. **26**(1), 014017 (2010)
4. Kuchta, D.M., et al.: A 71-Gb/s NRZ modulated 850-nm VCSEL-based optical link. IEEE Photonics Technol. Lett. **27**(6), 577–580 (2015)
5. Chang, Y.A., et al.: The carrier blocking effect on 850 nm InAlGaAs/AlGaAs vertical-cavity surface-emitting lasers. Semicond. Sci. Technol. **21**(21), 1488–1494 (2006)
6. Westbergh, P., et al.: High-speed 850 nm VCSELs with 28 GHz modulation bandwidth for short reach communication. In: Vertical-Cavity Surface-Emitting Lasers XVII International Society for Optics and Photonics (2013)
7. Gustavsson, J.S., et al.: Optimized active region design for high speed 850 nm VCSELs. IEEE J. Quantum Electron. **46**(4), 506–512 (2009)
8. Zhang, Y., Zhong, J., Zhao, Y., et al.: Temperature characteristics of 850 nm Oxide limited VCSEL. J. Semicond. **26**(5), 1024–1027 (2005)
9. Vanzi, M., Mura, G., Marcello, G., et al.: ESD tests on 850 nm GaAs-based VCSELs. Microelectron. Reliab. **64**, 617–622 (2016)
10. Kao, H.Y., et al.: Comparison of single-/few-/multi-mode 850 nm VCSELs for optical OFDM transmission. Opt. Express **25**(14), 16347 (2017)
11. Tian, K., et al.: Thermal model and simulation of 850 nm VCSEL 4×4 arrays for applications in optical interconnection system. Semicond. Optoelectron. **31**(1), 96–100 (2010)

A Parallel 1-D FFT Implementation Method for Multi-core Vector Processors

Zhong Liu$^{(\boxtimes)}$ and Xi Tian

College of Computer, National University of Defense Technology,
Changsha 410073, China
zhongliu@nudt.edu.cn

Abstract. This paper presents an efficient parallel 1-D FFT implementation method based on the architecture features of multi-core vector processor. It divides the parallel computation of large-point 1-D FFT into the (n-m)-level parallel FFT computation and M-point parallel FFT computation according to the number of data points M that can be accommodated in the global cache (GC). The parallel FFT computation for each stage are performed using a shared DDR data method in (n-m)-level FFT computation. In the M-point parallel FFT computation, a parallel FFT computation method based on the matrix Fourier algorithm is designed, it converts the original M-point 1-D FFT computation into a 2-D FFT computation, and achieves parallel FFT computation using a shared GC data method, which avoids multiple data transfers between GC and AM and reduces data transmission overhead. Merge Column FFT computation with factor matrix multiplication and column FFT computation results in the AM, which further reduces the number of data transfer between AM and GC, and can significantly improve the efficiency of M-point FFT computation. The experimental results on Matrix show that the average speedup of the single-core single-precision 1-D FFT is 8.26 times and the average speedup of the dual-core single-precision 1-D FFT is 6.78 times compared with the TMS320C6678 with the same frequency.

Keywords: Multi-core vector processors
Large-point 1-D Fast Fourier Transform
Matrix Fourier algorithm · Parallel

Discrete Fourier Transform (DFT) is one of the most important algorithms for scientific computing, especially in the field of signal processing systems, such as radar signal processing, underwater acoustic signal processing, spectrum analysis, video image algorithm, speech recognition, etc. With the increasingly prominent problems of power consumption and heat dissipation, energy consumption has gradually become an increasingly important factor affecting high-performance computing systems, and the architecture of the processor is moving toward multi-core, many-core, heterogeneous GPUs, embedded DSPs, etc. How to improve the computational performance of DFT for novel architecture has been a research hotspot [1–7]. The fast Fourier transform (FFT) algorithm proposed by Cooley and Turkey [8] significantly reduces the

Supported by the National Natural Science Foundation of China under Grant No. 61572025.

W. Xu et al. (Eds.): NCCET 2018, CCIS 994, pp. 48–58, 2019.
https://doi.org/10.1007/978-981-13-5919-4_5

computational complexity of the N-point DFT algorithm from the original $O(N^2)$ to $O(Nlog_2N)$. It can achieve high FFT computation performance if the FFT computation data can be stored in the on-chip memory of processors. On the other hand, because the FFT computation data of the same level is not reusable, the computation data needs to be processed multiple times in the processor's storage to complete the computing, thereby greatly reducing the computation performance of the FFT. Therefore, the computational performance optimization of large-point FFTs is very dependent on the layout and migration methods of the data, and it needs to be performed according to the processor architecture characteristics. Goedecker [9] and Karner [10] study how to use FMA instructions to reduce the number of multiply-add operations to optimize FFT computation performance for processors that provide FMA instructions. Liu [11] proposed a vectorization method using FMA to accelerate FFT calculations for FMA structured vector processors. HE [12] proposed a large point FFT optimization method for GPU architecture. FFTW [13] is a widely used FFT math library on general-purpose CPU platforms. It has good portability and can search for optimal FFT implementation based on processor architecture features. Daisuke [14, 15] studied the 1-D parallel FFT implementation of distributed storage. Jongsoo [16] proposed a 1-D FFT implementation method with low communication overhead for Intel's Xeon Phi coprocessor.

1 Matrix Architecture

As shown in Fig. 1, Matrix is a high-performance multi-core vector processor designed for high-density computing. It is designed as Very Long Instruction Word (VLIW) architecture and includes a Scalar Processing Unit (SPU) and a Vector Processing Unit (VPU). The SPU is responsible for scalar task computing and flow control, and the VPU is responsible for vector computing. Matrix includes a complex multi-level

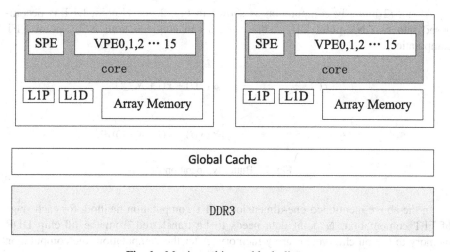

Fig. 1. Matrix multi-core block diagram

storage structure such as scalar register file, vector register file, scalar Level 1 cache, large-capacity on-chip vector array memory (AM), multi-core shared global cache (GC), and external shared DDR3. Matrix provides Fused Multiply-Add (FMA) instructions and its peak performance of single core is up to 100GFLOPS at 1 GHz. It can not effectively unleash Matrix's VLIW pipeline structure, vector computing and multi-level storage characteristics using traditional FFT algorithm, and results in low computing performance. Based on the architectural features of Matrix, this paper presents an efficient large-point parallel one-dimensional FFT implementation method, which can significantly improve the performance of large-point one-dimensional FFT on Matrix.

2   Parallel 1-D FFT Computing Method

The basic principle of the Decimation-In-Frequency (DIF) radix-2 FFT algorithm is as follows. Let x0, ... , xN − 1 be N = 2n points complex numbers. The 1-D DFT is defined by the formula:

$$X(k) = \sum_{i=0}^{N-1} x(i) W_N^{ik} \quad (\mathrm{k} = 0, \ldots \ldots, N-1)$$

Where $0 \leq \mathrm{k} < \mathrm{n}$, $W_N^{ik} = e^{-j(2\pi/N)ik} (j = \sqrt{-1})$ (known as the twiddle factor). Decompose the output sequence X(k) into two sequences by parity, then

$$\begin{cases} X(2k) = \sum_{i=0}^{N/2-1} (x(i) + x(i+N/2)) W_{N/2}^{ik} \\ X(2k+1) = \sum_{i=0}^{N/2-1} ((x(i) - x(i+N/2)) W_N^i) W_{N/2}^{ik} \end{cases} \tag{1}$$

After N/2 butterfly computation as shown in Fig. 2, the N-point DFT is decomposed into two N/2-point DFT. This process can continue until N/2 2-point DFT computation.

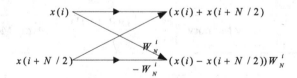

Fig. 2. Butterfly operation

In the above-mentioned one-dimensional FFT computation method, for each stage of FFT computation, N point data needs to be transferred from the off-chip DDR memory to the on-chip vector array memory. After the computation, the computation result is transferred from the on-chip vector array memory to the off-chip DDR memory. In the next stage of FFT computation, repeat the above process until all stages of FFT computation are completed. For large-point FFT, at each stage of FFT computation, because the total computation data far exceeds the capacity of the global cache (GC), the data in the GC is continuously replaced, but there is no hit, and the data transmission time cannot be reduced. The $N = 2^n$ point FFT computation, including n-level FFT butterfly unit calculation, requires 2n data transmissions back and forth. The data transmission time is very expensive; the data transmission time is much longer than the computation time, which results in low overall FFT computation efficiency.

Assume that the global cache (GC) can accommodate $M = 2^m$ point FFT computation data. After the (n-m)-level FFT butterfly unit computation, instead of computing all the FFT butterfly units step by step, 2^{n-m} M-point FFT computations are computed in sequence. In each M-point FFT computation, since the data is completely cached in the GC, it is not necessary to fetch computation data from off-chip DDR memories, which significantly reduces the data transfer time. It can effectively reduce the computation time of the M-point FFT, thus greatly improving the overall FFT computation efficiency. Therefore, the parallel computing of large-point 1-D FFT is divided into parallel computing of the (n-m)-level FFT and parallel computing of the M-point FFT.

2.1   (n-m)-Level Parallel FFT Computation Method

In the (n-m)-level FFT computation, each stage of FFT computation needs to transfer N-point data from the off-chip DDR memory to the on-chip vector array memory AM. Since the computation data are all one-time consumption, the data cached in the GC cannot be reused, and the test data indicates that the transmission time spent for transmitting data from the DDR to the AM is greater than the total computation time of the butterfly computation of each level. So parallel FFT computation is performed using a shared DDR data method, which can reduce the total computation time in the (n-m)-level FFT computation. As shown in Fig. 3, taking the first-stage FFT computation as an example, the core 0 computes the butterfly computation of the first and third 1/4-section data and the core 1 computes the butterfly computation of the 2nd and 4th 1/4-section data. After each stage is computed, the cores synchronize once to ensure data consistency. In the (n-m)-level FFT computation, the amount of data read each time is significantly greater than the length of the vector. Therefore, the data blocks computed by the butterfly unit are all continuously accessed in DDR, which improves the efficiency of DDR data access. The data transmitted to the AM is also a continuous data block, which facilitates vector data access and is easy to be vectorized.

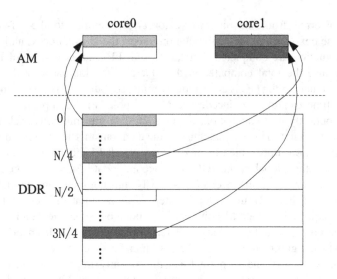

Fig. 3. Parallel 1-level FFT computing based on sharing DDR data

2.2   m-Level Parallel FFT Computation Method

After the (n-m)-level FFT butterfly computation, 2^{n-m} M-point FFT computations need to be computed in turn. In each M-point FFT computation, although the computation data of the M-point FFT can be completely accommodated in the GC, it cannot be fully accommodated in the vector array storage AM, and which requires 2 m data transmission processes. In order to facilitate vector computation and continuous data block transmission to improve FFT computation efficiency, it is still necessary to modify the original computation method. For this reason, the FFT vectorization computation method based on the matrix Fourier algorithm is designed, and the original M-point 1-D FFT is converted into a two-dimensional FFT computation. This method can significantly improve the computational efficiency of the M-point 1-D FFT.

Let $M = RS$, $R = 2r$, $S = 2$ s. The sequence x(i) is grouped into R subsequences of length S, that is, 1-D sequence x(i) is converted into a 2-D array sequence of the following form:

$$
\begin{bmatrix}
x(0) & x(1) & \cdots & x(S-1) \\
x(S) & x(S+1) & \cdots & x(2S-1) \\
\vdots & \vdots & \cdots & \vdots \\
x((R-1)S) & x((R-1)S+1) & \cdots & x(RS-1)
\end{bmatrix}
$$

Let i and k be mapped as follows:

$$\begin{cases} i = Si_1 + i_2, & \begin{cases} 0 \le i_1 \le R-1 \\ 0 \le i_2 \le S-1 \end{cases} \\ k = k_1 + Rk_2, & \begin{cases} 0 \le k_1 \le R-1 \\ 0 \le k_2 \le S-1 \end{cases} \end{cases}$$

Then X(k) can be transformed as follows:

$$\begin{aligned} X(k) &= X(k_1 + RK_2) \\ &= \sum_{i_2=0}^{S-1} \sum_{i_1=0}^{R-1} x(Si_1 + i_2) W_M^{(k_1 + Rk_2)(Si_1 + i_2)} \\ &= \sum_{i_2=0}^{S-1} \left\{ \left[\sum_{i_1=0}^{R-1} x(Si_1 + i_2) W_R^{k_1 i_2} \right] W_M^{k_1 i_1} \right\} W_S^{k_2 i_2} \end{aligned} \tag{2}$$

As can be seen from the above equation, the 1-D FFT computation of M-point can be converted into a computation similar to 2-D FFT. That is, first compute the S R-point column FFT computation by column, then multiply the result of the computation with a factor matrix, then compute the R S-point row FFT computation by row. Where, the computation data of R-point column FFT and S-point row FFT can be accommodated in the AM. It only need to design a suitable data layout method, convenient vector data access and computation, and it can achieve efficient computation efficiency.

In the M-point FFT computation, the parallel FFT computation is performed using the shared GC data method. As shown in Fig. 4, the first computation is the S R-point column FFT computation by column. The core 0 computes the first half of the S/2 R-point column FFT computation, and the core 1 computes the second half of the S/2 R-point column FFT computation. The cores synchronize once before performing row FFT computation to ensure that all data has completed column FFT computation.

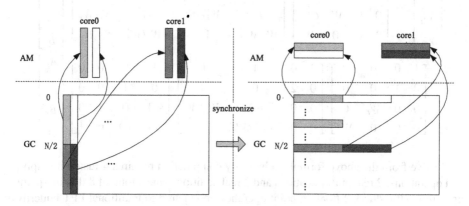

Fig. 4. Parallel M-points FFT computing based on sharing GC data

If directly performing computation according to the above formula (2), you need to complete all column FFT computation before multiplying the result data with a factor matrix. In order to avoid multiple data transmission between GC and AM and reduce data transmission overhead, after the column FFT computation in the AM is computed, the column FFT computation result in this section is multiplied by the factor matrix. It makes the column FFT computation and the column FFT computation result and the factor matrix multiplication only need one traversal computation, and no longer requires multiple data transmission between AM and GC, which improves the computation efficiency of the M-point FFT.

To further overlap the computation time into the data transmission time and reduce the total computation time, a computation method based on the DMA double buffering mechanism is adopted in each stage of the above-mentioned FFT computation, column FFT and row FFT computation.

2.3 FMA Optimized Buttery Computation

The FMA instruction provided by Matrix can further improve the computational efficiency of the FFT butterfly computation. Assume that the two inputs of a butterfly computation of the DIF radix-2 FFT are A and B respectively, the outputs are Y1 and Y2 respectively, the butterfly factor is W, and the subscripts r and i respectively represent the real and imaginary parts of the complex, according to the formula (1), there are

$$\begin{bmatrix} Y_1 \\ Y_2 \end{bmatrix} = \begin{bmatrix} 1 & 1 \\ W & -W \end{bmatrix} \begin{bmatrix} A \\ B \end{bmatrix} = \begin{bmatrix} 1 & \\ & W \end{bmatrix} \begin{bmatrix} 1 & 1 \\ 1 & -1 \end{bmatrix} \begin{bmatrix} A \\ B \end{bmatrix}$$

Expand the formula:

$$\begin{bmatrix} Y_{1i} \\ Y_{1r} \\ Y_{2i} \\ Y_{2r} \end{bmatrix} = \begin{bmatrix} 1 & 0 & 0 & 0 \\ 0 & 1 & 0 & 0 \\ 0 & 0 & W_r & 0 \\ 0 & 0 & 0 & W_r \end{bmatrix} \begin{bmatrix} 1 & 0 & 1 & 0 \\ 0 & 1 & 0 & 1 \\ 1 & -W_i/W_r & -1 & W_i/W_r \\ W_i/W_r & 1 & -W_i/W_r & -1 \end{bmatrix} \begin{bmatrix} A_r \\ A_i \\ B_r \\ B_i \end{bmatrix}$$

$$= \begin{bmatrix} 1 & 0 & 0 & 0 \\ 0 & 1 & 0 & 0 \\ 0 & 0 & W_r & 0 \\ 0 & 0 & 0 & W_r \end{bmatrix} \begin{bmatrix} 2 & 0 & 1 & 0 \\ 0 & 2 & 0 & 1 \\ 0 & 0 & -1 & W_i/W_r \\ 0 & 0 & -W_i/W_r & -1 \end{bmatrix} \begin{bmatrix} 1 & 0 & 0 & 0 \\ 0 & 1 & 0 & 0 \\ -1 & 0 & 1 & 0 \\ 0 & -1 & 0 & 1 \end{bmatrix} \begin{bmatrix} A_r \\ A_i \\ B_r \\ B_i \end{bmatrix}$$

Derive from the above formula, a butterfly computation requires 4 fusion multiply-add operations, 2 real multiplications and 2 real additions, and a total of 8 floating-point operations. It reduces 2 floating point operations compared to traditional FFT butterfly computation.

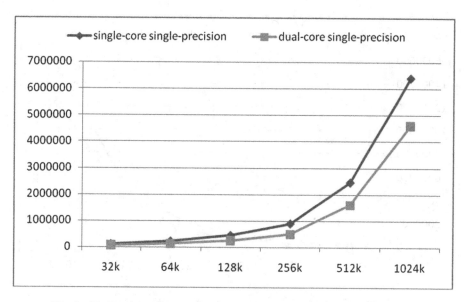

Fig. 5. The computation performance of single-precision 1-D FFT in matrix

3   Performance Testing and Analysis

The parallel 1-D FFT algorithm proposed in this paper was tested and analyzed in the RTL-level test environment of the multi-core vector processor Matrix. The system frequency of Matrix in the test is 1 GHz, the frequency of DDR3 is 1600 MHz, and the single and dual core peak performances are 100GFLOPS and 200GFLOPS, respectively. The single-core and dual-core peak performance of the same frequency TMS320C6678 tested at the same time is 16GFLOPS and 32GFLOPS, respectively. Statistical experimental data is averaged over multiple experiments.

First, as shown in Fig. 5, single-core and dual-core performance of a single-precision 32k, 64k, 128k, 256k, 512k, and 1024k-point radix-2 FFT is tested on Matrix respectively. The speedups from 32k to 1024k are 1.61, 1.69, 1.74, 1.8, 1.53, 1.39, respectively, and the average speedup is 1.63. As shown in Fig. 6, single-core and dual-core performance of a double-precision 32k, 64k, 128k, 256k, 512k, and 1024k-point radix-2 FFT is tested on Matrix respectively. The speedups from 32k to 1024k are 1.66, 1.72, 1.67, 1.48, 1.35, 1.26, and the average speedup is 1.52. It can be seen that when the computed data exceeds the GC capacity (single-precision 256k, double-precision 128k), the computation performance and speedup decreased significantly because of the limited DDR bandwidth.

Second, we compared the single- and dual-core single-precision 1-D FFT performance of the Matrix and TMS320C6678, respectively. As shown in Figs. 7 and 8, the test data shows that the computation time of the single-core single-precision 32k points radix-2 FFT is only 0.11 ms, and the corresponding performance of the TMS320C6678 at the same frequency is 0.915 ms. The performance ratios from 32k to 1024k are 8.29, 8.54, 9.26, 9.85, 7.61, 6.03, respectively, and the average ratio is 8.26.

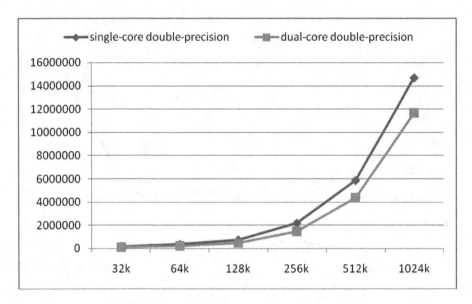

Fig. 6. The computation performance of double-precision 1-D FFT in matrix

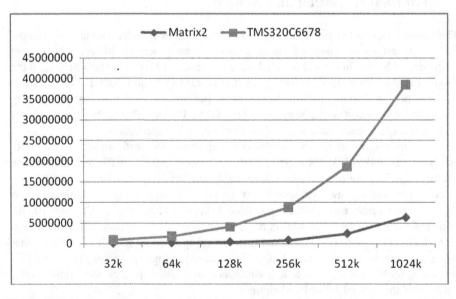

Fig. 7. Performance comparison of single-core single-precision 1-D FFT on matrix and TMS320C6678

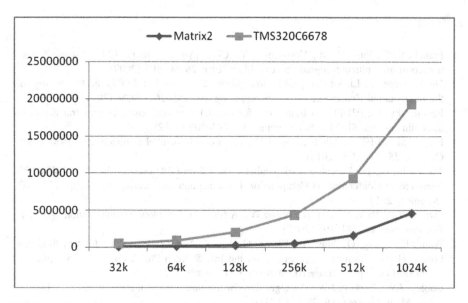

Fig. 8. Performance comparison of dual-core single-precision 1-D FFT on matrix and TMS320C6678

The computation time of the dual-core single-precision 32k points radix-2 FFT is only 0.0686 ms, and the corresponding performance of the TMS320C6678 at the same frequency is 0.478 ms. The performance ratios from 32k to 1024k are 6.97, 7.18, 7.86, 8.72, 5.78, and 4.19, respectively and the average ratio is 6.78. However, the peak performance ratio of the two is 6.25. It shows that the proposed 1-D FFT vector and parallel algorithm have higher computational efficiency and efficiently exploit the computing performance of Matrix.

4   Conclusions

With the rapid development of microprocessor technology, the architecture is becoming more and more novel and complex. The computation performance optimization of large-point FFT depends more on the mining of processor architecture features. The computation performance of large-point FFT is not only related to the processor's peak computational performance, but more importantly depends on the data storage layout and migration method. This paper proposes a large-point parallel 1-D FFT implementation method based on matrix Fourier algorithm for the independently developed vector processor Matrix. Experimental results show that the proposed parallel 1-D FFT implementation method based on multi-core vector processors has significant advantages. It can efficiently exploit the computing performance of multi-core vector processors. Compared with the TMS320C6678 with the same frequency, the average speedup of the single-core single-precision 1-D FFT is 8.26 times, and the average speedup of the dual-core single-precision 1-D FFT is 6.78 times.

References

1. Franchetti, F., Puschel, M., Voronenko, Y., Chellappa, S., Moura, J.M.: Discrete fourier transform on multicore. Signal Process. Mag. IEEE **26**, 90–102 (2009)
2. Gu, L., Siegel, J., Li, X.: Using GPUs to compute large out-of-card FFTs. In: Proceedings of the International Conference on Supercomputing, pp. 255–264. ACM (2011)
3. Pekurovsky, D.: P3DFFT: a framework for parallel computations of Fourier transforms in three dimensions. SIAM J. Sci. Comput. **34**, 192–209 (2012)
4. Pippig, M.: PFFT: an extension of FFTW to massively parallel architectures. SIAM J. Sci. Comput. **35**, 213–236 (2013)
5. Takahashi, D.: Implementation of parallel 1-D FFT on GPU clusters. In: 2013 IEEE 16th International Conference on Computational Science and Engineering (CSE), pp. 174–180, December 2013
6. Tang, P.T.P., Park, J., Kim, D., Petrov, V.: A framework for low-communication 1-D FFT. Sci. Program. **21**, 181–195 (2013)
7. Wang, E., Zhang, Q., Shen, B., Zhang, G., Lu, X., Wu, Q., Wang, Y.: Intel math kernel library. High-Performance Computing on the Intel® Xeon Phi™, pp. 167–188. Springer, Cham (2014). https://doi.org/10.1007/978-3-319-06486-4_7
8. Cooley, J.W., Turkey, J.W.: An algorithm for the machine calculation of complex Fourier series. Math. Comput. **19**, 297–301 (1965)
9. Goedecker, S.: Fast Radix 2, 3, 4, and 5 kernels for fast Fourier Transformations on computers with overlapping multiply-add instructions. SIAM J. Sci. Comput. **18**(6), 1605–1611 (1997)
10. Karner, H., Auer, M., Ueberhuber, C.W.: Multiply-add optimized FFT kernels. Math. Model. Methods Appl. Sci. **11**(01), 105–117 (2001)
11. Liu, Z., Chen, H., Xiang, H.V.: Vectorization of accelerating fast fourier transform computation based on fused multiply-add instruction. J. Natl. Univ. Def. Technol. **37**(2), 72–78 (2015)
12. HE, T., Zhu, D.: Design and implementation of large-point 1D FFT on GPU. Comput. Eng. Sci. **35**(11), 34–41 (2013)
13. Frigo, M., Johnson, S.G.: The design and implementation of FFTW. Proc. IEEE **93**(2), 216–231 (2005)
14. Takahashi, D.: A parallel 1-D FFT algorithm for the Hitachi SR8000. Parallel Comput. **29**(6), 679–690 (2003)
15. Takahashi, D., Uno, A., Yokokawa, M.: An implementation of Parallel 1-D FFT on the K computer. Int. Conf. High Perform. Comput. Commun. **248**(4), 344–350 (2012)
16. Park, J., Bikshandi, G., Vaidyanathan, K., Tang, P.T.P., Dubey, P., Kim, D.: Tera-scale 1D FFT with low communication algorithm and Intel® Xeon Phi™ coprocessors. In: Proceedings of SC13: International Conference for High Performance Computing, Networking, Storage and Analysis, vol. 31, no. 12, p. 34. ACM (2013)

The Analysis and Countermeasures of Mobile Terminal RE or RSE Problem

Liangliang Kong[(✉)] and Lin Chen

The College of Engineering,
Shanghai Polytechnic University, Shanghai 201209, China
{llkong, chenl}@sspu.edu.cn

Abstract. Considering the electronic product stability and personal safety, most countries strictly formulate a lot of EMC compulsory certification standards in the field of information technology. However, during the authentication testing of the mobile terminals, the problem of Radiated Emission (RE) or Radiated Spurious Emission (RSE) occurs often and it is usually difficult to be solved. In this paper, reasons that result the RE and RSE problems of mobile terminals are analyzed at first. The architecture of related test system is introduced. A new method to solve the problems is proposed. And then, detailed experimental countermeasures and process are illustrated to solve the problem. Finally, some design guidance for RE/RSE problem is concluded. This paper has shown that our method is an effective way to eliminate or decrease the probability of RE/RSE problem for mobile terminal design.

Keywords: Mobile terminal · RE · RSE · EMC

1 Introduction and Background

It is usually that engineers apply high speed microprocessor in the electronic products, but these digital circuits running in the product will produce strong electromagnetic emission to other circuits of itself or other devices. So it may cause bad stability or failure to pass EMC (Electro Magnetic Compatibility) authentication [1]. In consideration of the electronic product stability and personal safety, most countries formulated a lot of EMC compulsory certification standard in the field of information technology [2, 3].

For mobile communication terminals, EMC tests mainly include: CE (Conducted Emission), RE (Radiated Emission), CSE (Conducted Spurious Emission), RSE (Radiated Spurious Emission), CS (Conducted Susceptibility), RS (Radiated Susceptibility), EFT/B (Electrical Fast Transient Burst), de-sensitivity problem, and etc. In the process of certification test, RE and RSE fail occurs often and it is usually difficult to be solved. It will not affect the stability of the mobile terminal, ignored easily in the early develop stage, but it usually occurs in the product certification test. The mainly reason

This work has been supported by the Discipline of Computer Science and Technology of Shanghai Polytechnic University (Grant No. XXKZD1604).

for it is insufficient design considerations in early development stage. And it is difficult and time-consuming to be rectified in authentication test stage. Finally, it will affect the market plan of the product at last. So we can conclude that solving and avoiding the RE/RSE problem is very important for the research and development of mobile terminals.

2 Theoretical Analysis

2.1 RE/RSE Analysis

RE (Radiated Emission) test is mainly measure the radiated electromagnetic wave energy of the mobile terminal, which is plugged in the charger. The Chinese standard define that the test frequency range of GSM communication mode is 30 MHz–6 GHz, and the other communication mode tests are 30 MHz–1 GHz, but the European standard is 30 MHz–6 GHz for all modes of mobile phones.

RSE (Radiated Spurious Emission) test is mainly test the radiated energy of harmonic component, non-harmonic components and parasitic components of communication radio wave [4, 5]. The measuring frequency range is 30 MHz–4 GHz, and the test settings and limits are slightly different according to the communication band. The details can be found in the 3GPP test specification.

Fig. 1. EMC 3 factors

Both RE test and RSE test are belong to the EMC test. EMC means that in the electromagnetic environment, the equipment can work well, but can't be interfered by other devices, at mean time, it also does not interfere other devices working. The generation of EMC problem is often dealt with from the three factors: interference source, jamming path and risk sensitive device (see Fig. 1). Lack of any one of three factors does not cause an EMC problem, so the solution of the EMC problem can start from these three aspects and only need to deal with one at sometimes. The EMC problem includes two aspects: electromagnetic interference (EMI) and electromagnetic sensitivity (EMS). EMI is the interference to other devices or systems; EMS is the work capability to tolerate other interference [1, 2].

2.2 Test System

RE/RSE authentication test system diagram is showed on the Fig. 2. In addition to software configuration and testing methods, the obvious difference between RE test and RSE test is that the RE test need to plug the charger, but RSE does not need. Taking the test system as a whole, the interference source is the device under test (DUT), the jamming path is space radiation, and the interfered device is the EMC measuring system. Among them, the equipment, measuring antenna and microwave chamber are the standard configuration of the authentication system. Except running abnormally, it cannot be rectified, so solving the RE and RSE problems must be considered from the terminal side. From the jamming path, the interference may be radiated through the communication antenna, and it may be also radiated through the PCB trace or the internal connector line of the terminal or the external charger connector line [6–9].

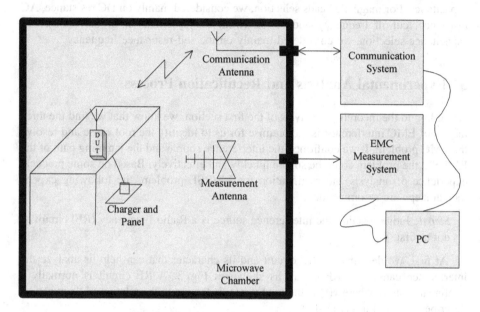

Fig. 2. The RE/RSE certification test system

2.3 Countermeasures

If we could weaken or eliminate any one of the three factors of EMC, the EMC problem cannot be generated. Therefore, the optimization of EMC performance is within these three aspects. The common optimization method of RE/RSE performance is listed as below:

1. Reduce the working voltage, current or power of the interference source.
2. Change the working frequency of the interference source, so that it does not produce interference wave of the corresponding test frequency.
3. The spread spectrum technology which does not affect the source working performance can be applied also.
4. Add resistor, inductor, magnetic bead and common mode inductor between the interference source and the sensitive device, can weaken or block the corresponding interference signal.
5. Add capacitors, RC filter, LC filter, EMI device and special filter, can weaken or block the corresponding interference signal also.

6. On the jamming path, we should strengthen isolation and shielding also, which include shielding cover, shielding box, shielding line, protecting the PCB signal line by use GND shielding [7, 8], and so on.

The means list above, 1–3 is based on weakening interference sources signal, and the 4–6 is the diverting or blocking of EMI signals based on the jamming path.

By the way, the selection of all kinds of EMC elements is also an experience technology. We described briefly two kind of universal elements: magnetic beads and capacitance. For magnetic beads selection, we considered mainly on DC resistance, AC resistance, cut-off frequency and so on (from the specification of the book). For capacitance selection, we considered mainly on the self-resonance frequency.

3   Experimental Analysis and Rectification Process

According to the theoretical analysis of the first section, we know that we find the three factors of EMC interference is the premise for us to identify the root cause and resolve the EMC problem. If we confirmed the interference source and the jamming path of the RE/RSE, the problem could be solved quickly and effectively. Based on some practical experience of analysis and rectification for RE/RSE problem, the following experimental steps are recommended.

Step 1. Judge whether the interference source is a Radio Frequency (RF) circuit or not at first.

At first, we describe the RF circuit and its character that can help us analyze the interference caused by RF circuit as shown in Fig. 3. A RF circuit is normally a nonlinear system, where $y(t)$ is the output, $x(t)$ is the input, the relation of them can be described by the Eq. (1) [10].

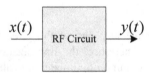

Fig. 3. The RF circuit

$$y(t) = c_1 x(t) + c_2 x^2(t) + c_3 x^3(t) + \dots \tag{1}$$

Assume $x(t)$ is a sine wave single tone, $x(t) = A\cos(\omega t)$, we can get $y(t)$ in the following express.

$$y(t) = \frac{c_2 A^2}{2} + \left(c_1 A + \frac{3c_3 A^3}{4}\right)\cos(\omega t) + \frac{c_2 A^2}{2}\cos(2\omega t) + \frac{c_3 A^3}{4}\cos(3\omega t) + \dots \tag{2}$$

Assume $x(t)$ is two signal, $x(t) = A_1 cos(\omega_1 t) + A_2 cos(\omega_2 t)$, we can also get $y(t)$ expression of $cos(m\omega_1 \pm n\omega_2)$, where m, n is the signed integer number [10].

In Eq. (2), $10 \, log\left(\frac{c_2 A^2}{2}\right) = 20 \, log\left(\frac{c_2 A}{2}\right)$ and $10 \, log\left(\frac{c_3 A^3}{4}\right) = 30 \, log\left(\frac{c_3 A}{4}\right)$. So, if the amplitude of input signal changes λ dB, the harmonic amplitude will change 2λ dB and the third harmonic will change 3λ dB. In the other word, the harmonic signals' amplitude in dB is also multiple of the input signal's amplitude.

Whether the interference is the radiation of the radio frequency circuit or not, can be judged by experience at first. The interference signal below 500 MHz is generally not produced by the radio frequency circuit, but the interference signal which frequency is integer multiple of the communication frequency and its amplitude in dB is also multiple of the useful RF signal, is usually generated by the RF circuit. Of course, there are exceptions, non-harmonic signals may also be generated by RF circuits, such as intra-band and out-band mixing interference which can be described by expression of $cos(m\omega_1 \pm n\omega_2 \pm \cdots)$, side band interference caused by incorrect timing of RF switch (see Fig. 4, RE test results of a GSM900 frequency band). So in addition to experience judgment, it is also necessary to observe the interference signal changing by reducing the power of the terminal or setting to the idle state or even closing the transmit circuit or changing the communication channel.

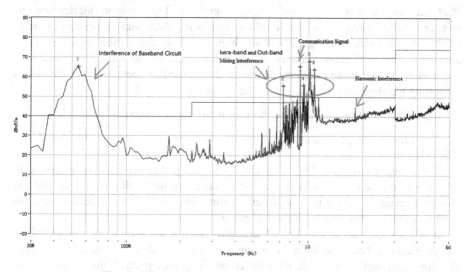

Fig. 4. RE test result of GSM900 band of a telephone

If the interference frequency changes with the communication channel of the terminal, or the amplitude of the interference decreases with the communication power, the interference source can be preliminarily determined by the RF circuit, and then the Step 2 is continued. Conversely, if it does not change due to the change of channel and transmission power, it can be basically determined as interference of other circuits, and we can jump to Step 3.

Step 2. Determinate whether it is the radiation of the communication antenna or not on second.

Whether it is the radiation of antenna or not can be judged by adding attenuator or filter to the interface between communication antenna and RF circuit.

If the power at the interference frequency point is smaller after added the attenuator or filter, it means that the interference is the radiation of the communication antenna [11], so we can jump to Step 5, and conversely, the interference of the RF circuit may be radiated through other circuits, and the Step 3 is continued.

Step 3. Determine which function of the circuit is radiated again.

One by one, remove the functional circuit with the components of the metal lead or plug, in order to determinate which part of the circuit is the interference source. For mobile phones, there is usually charger (RE test), Speaker, Receiver, Microphone, LCD, battery, GPS antenna, Bluetooth antenna, and various interface sockets and so on. For wireless fixed telephones, there is usually charger (RE test), handle, hand-free Microphone, hand-free speaker, LCD, HOOK key, battery and so on. If a component is removed, the RE/RSE problem is solved or the amplitude of interference is reduced, and we can jump to Step 5. If it is not found, continue Step 4.

Step 4. Further locate the interference source on the PCB circuit.

To analyze the problem continually, we need to localize the interference source on PCB with near-field RF probe and spectrum analyzer. The common interference circuits are DC/DC circuits, all kinds of circuit power supplies, amplifier circuits, clocks, DSP, audio and other analog circuits and high-speed circuits. In the shielding room, after the mobile terminal powered on and communicated, we can use the magnetic field probe to detect the strong interference area, and then use the electric field probe to find the strong interference position, record the result, go to Step 5.

Step 5. Further test to determine the root interference source.

According to the previous analysis results, after dealing with it, we continue do the RE/RSE test.

If the antenna is judged to be radiated source by the Step 2, it is necessary to continue to check the metal parts near the antenna in the shell (remove or add the absorbing material for the test). After eliminating the interference of the structure, we need to solve the problem from the RF circuit.

If in Step 3, 4, we judged that a functional circuit is the source, we can add filters (series magnetic bead and shunt capacitance etc.) or shielding scheme (using copper skin for wrapping) according to the interference frequency point. If the solution is not clear the problem thoroughly, after added the strongest weak interference means, we can jump to Step 4 to continue to find the root interference sources and other strong interference sources. Because it is undeniable that sometimes there are more than one interference sources or more than one jamming path.

Step 6. Rectification on the interference source or the jamming path.

Based on the experiment bellow, we can basically identify the source of interference or the jamming path, and use the common method mentioned in the second section to continue the experiment to solve the RE/RSE problem directly.

Different interference sources or jamming paths will bring different corrective means. The processing of various situations is listed as follows:

Case One. If the interference signal is radiated by the antenna and reflected by the structure, we can deal with the structural parts, such as attaching wave absorbing material, removing metal coating, and grounding [11].

Case Two. If the interference signal is radiated by the antenna, but not reflected by the structure, we can do conducted spurious emission test at first. If the margin to limit of spurious emission is not enough, we can adjust the PA output matching circuit, RF parameters, RF filter or filter to the RF power supply, and replaced with better spurious performance elements. If the margin is sufficient and the interference frequency is far away from the working frequency, we can add the filter to the antenna port, and change the antenna shape, and adjust its matching circuit when it is just a little over the limit. Of course, when the transmitting power is high enough, it can also reduce power properly, but that must be kept enough margins for the 3GPP test speciation.

Case Three. If the interference signal is radiated by the functional circuits, we can shield it by add grounding shielding, series inductor/magnetic bead/EMI filter, magnetic ring and shunt capacitor.

Case Four. If the interference signal is directly radiated by the circuit on the PCB, we can add a copper skin shielding, a series of inductors/magnetic beads, and a shunt capacitor, or reduce the interference power, or change the working frequency through software (such as reducing the working voltage, using the spread frequency technology, etc.) [6–9].

When we selected one of all the above means, the productivity and cost of the production should be considered, so that the products can be authenticated at the same time without losing their competitiveness.

4 Design Considerations for RE/RSE

After completed RE/RSE problem analysis and rectification, we need to consider how to rectify it in mass production. Although there are various countermeasures for improvement, time consumption is often unavoidable. For example, we should modify the PCB in order to add the series inductor, the shunt capacitance, and the EMI filter. In the same way, if the structure component causes the problem, it is not only possible to modify the PCB, but also possible to redesign the structure mold. And so on, we will take a fixed time cycle using all these countermeasures to deal with the problems, so it will delay the time to market of products and even lose valuable orders. Therefore, we should pay more attention to the matters improving RE/RSE performance in design. Some design recommendations for RE/RSE could be list as following:

- In the early design time, it is the first thing that we place the antenna and the functional components, and reduce interference between each other as much as possible, and ensure good grounding design of the metal structure.
- For using the component with metal lead, we can add EMI compatible circuit design to the interface on the PCB, and string the magnetic ring to the component leads line. We can use EMI compatible circuit such as stringing the resistor and

shunting the capacitor on the hook key, stringing the EMI device to the LCD, stringing the magnetic beads and shunting the capacitor to the audio interface, adding magnetic rings to the charger line and the USB line, etc. [12].

- Recommend to weaken the mutual interference by placing far away from each other between high speed digital circuits, analog circuits and RF circuits [13].
- Adding the shielding box around the strong interference circuit or the sensitive circuit is also recommended.
- Choosing the suitable element of better performance in harmonics emission and spurious suppression (PA, duplexer).
- Optimized the trace and adding the filter to the chip power supply, especially the RF power, is recommend [6, 8, 13].
- Branching the baseband circuit and RF circuit power in the root source on the PCB trace line [9], and adding series bead, is recommend also.
- Minimizing the current loop of power supply is also a good mean.
- Adding the matching resistance (22 Ω to 51 Ω) on the output end of high speed signal bus, clock signal and so on, is also necessary sometimes. And the NC (Not Connected) bypass capacitor can be added in design also, which can be normally changed to several pF to 10 uF if need.
- The clock line, RF line and other sensitive lines on the top or bottom of the PCB, maybe act as the antenna of interference signal. So we should shield them by adding ground wire or plane around them.
- Due to space constraints, if the strong interference signal line or sensitive line cannot be wrapped by grounding, we can layout them as far as possible to the other lines and keep them unparallel. If it is impossible to avoid, we need comply with the 3W principle.
- Paving copper plane on the periphery of the board and connect it to GND net, can reduce unnecessary radiation.

5   Conclusions

This paper describes and analyzes the generation mechanism of RE and RSE problems of mobile terminals at first. And then detailed experimental countermeasures and process is given to solve the problems. Finally, some design guidance for the RE/RSE problem is concluded. This paper provides a method for solving the RE/RSE problem of mobile terminals, so that we can avoid the problem as much as possible in the design, and can solve these problems in an effective way during the certification testing.

References

1. Gu, H.Z., Ma, S.W.: PCB Electromagnetic Compatibility Technology – Design and Practice, 1st edn. Tsinghua University Press, Beijing (2004). (in Chinese)
2. Dhia, S.B., Ramdani, M., Sicard, E.: Electromagnetic Compatibility of Integrated Circuits: Techniques for Low Emission and Susceptibility, 1st edn. PHEI Press, Beijing (2015). Translated by Wang H., et al. (in Chinese)

3. Dahlman, E., Parkvall, S., Sköld, J.: 4G LTE/LTE-Advanced for Mobile Broadband, 1st edn. Southeast University Press, Nanjing (2012)
4. Audone, B., Colombo, R.: Measurement of radiated spurious emissions with the substitution and field strength test methods. In: IEEE International Symposium on Electromagnetic Compatibility, pp. 353–357. IEEE Press, New York (2016)
5. Yu, Q.: Radiated spurious emissions measurement by substitution method. In: IEEE International Symposium on Electromagnetic Compatibility, pp. 159–164. IEEE Press, New York (2010)
6. Zhang, Y., Ye, S., Zhang, J., Yao, Y.: Review of conducted noise suppression method for power electronic and electrical equipment. Trans. China Electrotech. Soc. 32(14), 77–86 (2017) (in Chinese)
7. Patra, K., Dhar, S., Gupta, B.: Analysis of arbitrarily curved microstrip lines for radiated emission. IEEE Trans. Electromagn. Compat. 60(3), 572–579 (2018)
8. Sayegh, A.M., Jenu, M.Z.B.M., Sapuan, S.Z., Dahlan, S.H.B.: Analytical solution for maximum differential-mode radiated emissions of microstrip trace. IEEE Trans. Electromagn. Compat. 58(5), 1417–1424 (2016)
9. Shin, D., Kim, N., Lee, J., Park, Y., Kim, J.: Quantified design guides for the reduction of radiated emissions in package-level power distribution networks. IEEE Trans. Electromagn. Compat. 59(2), 468–480 (2017)
10. Li, Z.Q., Wang, Z.G.: Radio Frequency Integrated Circuits and System, 1st edn. CSPM Press, Beijing (2008). (in Chinese)
11. Azpurua, M.A., Pous, M., Silva, F.: A single antenna ambient noise cancellation method for in-situ radiated EMI measurements in the time-domain. In: IEEE International Symposium on Electromagnetic Compatibility, pp. 501–506. IEEE Press, New York (2016)
12. Koo, T.W., Lee, H.S., Yook, J.G., Yoo, K., Cheon, J., Lee, S.Y.: Radiated spurious emission reduction using parasitic element for mobile applications. In: IEEE International Symposium on Electromagnetic Compatibility, pp. 760–764. IEEE Press, New York (2014)
13. Khorrami, M.A., Dixon, P., Arien, Y., Song, J.: Effective power delivery filtering of mixed-signal systems with negligible radiated emission. IEEE Electromagn. Compat. Mag. 5(4), 128–132 (2016)

Robust Option Pricing Under Change of Numéraire

Guyue Hu$^{(\boxtimes)}$ and Weixia Xu

State Key Laboratory of High Performance Computing (HPCL),
College of Computer, National University of Defense Technology,
Changsha, People's Republic of China
cindy.guyuehu@outlook.com

Abstract. In this paper, we consider the problem of option pricing from the perspect of minimax algorithm, an online learning framework. We introduce numéraire, which is a unit of account in economics, to the market dynamic as a multi-round game between two players: the investor and the nature. In this way, we are able to apply the online learning framework namely minimax algorithm in game theory. We model the repeated games between the investor and the nature as a price process under different numéraires, thus permit arbitrary choice of numéraire, and study this model under no arbitrage condition of a complete market. We also relax the constraint of convex payoff functions in previous works by characterizing the explicit mixed-strategy Nash equilibrium in a single-round game, and then generalize this result to multi-round games.

Keywords: Online learning · Minimax · Numéraire

1 Introduction

Contracts like options have been used for risk management from the time of Ancient Romans, Grecians, and Phoenicians. The first reputed option buyer was the ancient Greek mathematician and philosopher Thales of Miletus [14]. An option is a contract which gives the buyer, or the holder of the option, the right, but not the obligation, to buy or sell an underlying asset at a specified strike price on a specified future date. The seller has the corresponding obligation to fulfill the transaction, to sell or buy, if the buyer exercises the option [11]. An option that provides the owner the right to buy at a specific price is referred to as a call option, and likely an option that provides the right of the owner to sell at a specific price is referred to as a put option.

A European call option on a risky asset gives the buyer the right but not the obligation to buy a risky asset on a pre-specified expiration date T, at a pre-specified strike price K. For example, a $T = 2$-year call option on Alibaba with a strike price $K = 210$ dollars gives the buyer the right to buy an Alibaba share from the seller for a price 210 dollars in 2-year's time. We denote the Alibaba stock price at time t by S_t. If the price of one Alibaba share is greater than

W. Xu et al. (Eds.): NCCET 2018, CCIS 994, pp. 68–82, 2019.
https://doi.org/10.1007/978-981-13-5919-4_7

210 dollars in the end of the second year, the holder will choose to execute his option, and gain a payoff of $(S_T - K)$. Otherwise, the holder will not execute his option, so the payoff is 0. Thus time T the payoff of the European call option is given by:

$$\max\{S_T - K, 0\} \tag{1}$$

"What is value of such an option today?" is a fundamental question in finance. Black and Scholes [3] published their path breaking paper on this topic in 1973, and led to a boom of option trading in financial markets. Their work was later recognized by the 1997 Nobel Prize. They show that one can replicate the payoff of an option by a dynamic trading strategy of the underlying assets, and they provide an exact current value (price) of the option. Black and Scholes model assumes: (1) the stock price follows a geometric Brownian motion (GBM), which is a continuous time version of random walk; and (2) the underlying assets, i.e. stock and risk-free bond, can be traded continuously.

These assumptions are important limitations of the Black and Scholes model. In practice, the behaviour of stock price is not consistent with the GBM, and both the trading and stock path are time-discrete. Since Black and Scholes, there has been many research results (e.g. [7,8,17]) in extending their results to different stochastic processes. Some recent works (e.g. [1,2,6,15]) relax the stochastic assumption of stock price process and consider the option pricing as a regret minimization problem in learning theory.

2   Related Work and Our Contributions

2.1   Arbitrage Pricing Theory and Standard Binomial Model

The arbitrage pricing theory (APT) is developed by American economist Stephen Ross in the mid-1970s [18]. By APT, the axim of pricing any asset or financial derivative in a market is "there should be no arbitrage opportunities in a complete market". Stephen Ross states that if there exist arbitrage opportunities in a portfolio of two or more assets, at least one of them is mispriced.

Using the no arbitrage condition, Cox et al. [5] developed binomial option pricing model. The binomial pricing model traces the price evolution of underlying assets (e.g. the stock) in discrete time. This is done by means of a binomial lattice (Fig. 1) for a number of time steps between the valuation and expiration dates. Each node in the lattice represents a possible prices of the underlying assets at a given point of time.

It is assumed that the underlying asset will move up or down by a specific factor $(1 + u)$ or $(1 + d)$ per level of the nodes in the tree. Without loss of generality we assume $u > d$. For example, if S_0 is the current price, in the next time period the price will either be $S_1^u = (1 + u)S_0$ or $S_1^d = (1 + d)S_0$. Notice that, under no arbitrage assumption, u and d in the standard binomial model described above should satisfy $u < r < d$, where r is the risk-free interest rate [10].

In the binomial pricing model, valuation is performed iteratively, starting at each of the leave nodes representing the possible prices on the expiration date, and then working backwards through the tree towards the root node representing the price on valuation date. The value computed at each node is the value of the option at that point in time.

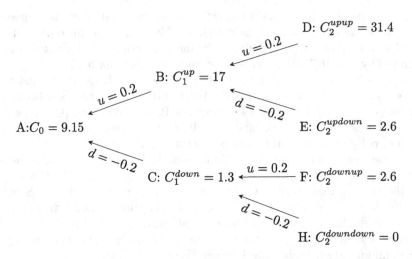

Fig. 1. The backward pricing tree of a binomial model for European call option. The number of period $t = 2$, striking price $K = 55$, the starting stock price $S_0 = 60$, and the probability of stock price going up is $p = 0.5$ at each node.

2.2   Numéraire and Forward Price Process

The numéraire is a basic standard by which value is computed. It provides a common benchmark relative to which the worths of various goods and services can be measured. In a monetary economy, we usually consider money as the numéraire. However, there is nothing stopping us from choosing other strictly positive priced assets as the numéraire.

Formally, a numéraire, denoted as G_t, is any strictly positive asset price process, i.e., with payoff $G_t > 0$ and initial price $G_0 > 0$. The numéraire G can be any asset, or any strictly positive portfolios (linear combinations of base assets), or even derivatives. The quantity

$$V_t \equiv \{\frac{A_t}{G_t}\}_{t \geq 0} \tag{2}$$

is called the value process of asset A discounted by numéraire G.

Several previous works (e.g. [9,12]) take numéraire into account when pricing options, especially exotic options. The work of Brigo et al. [4] considered change of numéraire as a response to smiling effect.

2.3   Learning Theory in Option Pricing Problems

To consider the option pricing as a problem of regret minimization, or a minimax game in learning theory is a recent progress in the literature. Relaxing the stochastic process assumption on stock price is the main advantage of this consideration.

In Mansour's work "Learning, regret minimization and option pricing" (2007) [15], the idea of regret minimization is related to the option pricing problem, which is interpreted as an online learning task.

By defining a generic algorithm under this frame work, DeMarzo et al. find the (generic) upper bound of the European call option price, and verify empirically that the generic upper bound is qualitatively and quantitatively similar to the Black and Scholes model [6].

Some more recent studies on this topic are from Abernethy et al. In their work (2012) [2], Abernethy et al. prove when the risk-free interest rate $r = 0$, the upper bound of value of the minimax game converges to Black and Scholes model in the limit, i.e. when $n \to \infty$. They also explicitly find the hedging strategy under which this upper bound can be achieved (2013) [1].

However, two limitations in the works of Abernethy et al. are: (1) Their approach of finding the upper bounds is difficult to generalize to a more realistic case when the risk-free interest rate $r > 0$; and (2) they do not show the lower bound, which is equally important as the upper bound in finding the option price.

2.4   Our Contributions

We address the two limitations in the previous works. We use a binomial tree following the sprit of Cox to model the backward discrete pricing process of options. This naturally leads to a game theoretical interpretation: from the leaves to the root, for two children nodes, we solve the single round game by explicitly find the mixde-strategy Nash equilibrium, and the value of their parent node is the value of this game; This process is back propagated until the value of the root node is calculated, which is the option price at the valuation time t_0. Different risk-free interest rate r can be flexibly adapted to our model and pack propagation process, and the lower bound can also be found by changing the buy/sell position in our game.

Other contributions in our work includes: (1) We prove that the lower bound meets the upper bound in every single round game, thus the option price calculated by our model is robust; (2) Finding the mixed-strategy Nash equilibrium in a single round game does not depends on the convexity of the payoff function, which means the payoff function could be any function in our model; and (3) We add numéraire to the model, and by changing the numéraire we prove the robustness of our model; Our model could also be generalized to other derivatives by using different payoff functions and numéraires.

3 Our Model

3.1 No Arbitrage Condition in Multi-round Hedging Game

As a concrete example, we consider a multi-round hedging game to replicate the value of a European call option, and the underlying asset is a stock S. Assume n decision makings occur at $t = \{0, T/n, ..., (n-1)T/n\}$, although this equal division is not necessary. Denote $S_t \equiv S_{t-1}(1 + \xi_t)$, $B_t \equiv B_{t-1}(1 + r)$, and C_t as the value of the European call option at t. Also assume the numéraire is the bond, i.e. $G = B$.

Consider the following buy portfolio of the investor: (1) At time $t = 0$, The investor buys a share of option, and spends C_0. At time $t = n$, the investor sells the option and gains payoff $g(S_n, K) = g(S_0 \cdot \prod_{t=1}^{n}(1 + \xi_t), K)$; and (2) To hedge his position, the investor makes a sequence of n short sells of stock. For $t = 1, 2, ..., n$, at time $t - 1$, short sells Δ_t of stock; at time t, buys and returns the stock and gains a profit of $-(\xi_t - r)\Delta_t$. Notice that we absorb the investor's randomized decision into a single variable Δ_t.

The payoff of the buy portfolio $\mathcal{V}_0(buy)$, under numéraire $G = B$, is made up of the cost of buying the option $-C_0$, the present value of the option payoff $g(S_n, K)$, and gains/losses from hedging:

$$\mathcal{V}_0(buy) := -C_0 + B_0\left(-\sum_{t=1}^{n} \frac{(\xi_t - r)\Delta_t}{B_t} + \frac{g(S_n, K)}{B_n}\right) \tag{3}$$

Consider the investor acts his optimized sequence of decision against the worst-case stock price fluctuation, and the no arbitrage condition in his or her buy portfolio is:

$$V_0^r(buy) := -C_0 + B_0 \cdot \max_{\Delta_t} \min_{\xi_t \in \mathcal{U}}\left(-\sum_{t=1}^{n} \frac{(\xi_t - r)\Delta_t}{B_t} + \frac{g(S_n, K)}{B_n}\right) \leq 0 \tag{4}$$

because $V_0^r(buy)$ is the payoff guarantee the investor can get with his or her optimal strategy (no matter how nature acts), thus if $V_0^r(buy) > 0$ the investor can obtained non-negative payoff in all possible future states and positive payoff in some possible future states from a self-financing portfolio mentioned in Sect. 2.1, i.e. there is arbitrage opportunity. So we must have $V_0^r(buy) \leq 0$ in (4).

By rearranging (4), we can get the lower bound of C_0:

$$L_0 = G_0 \cdot \max_{\Delta_t, t \in [n]} \min_{r_{gt}, r_{at}, t \in [n]}\left(-\sum_{t=1}^{n} \frac{(r_{at} - r_{gt})\Delta_t}{G_t} + \frac{g(G_n, A_n)}{G_n}\right) \tag{5}$$

Similarly, we consider the sell portfolio of the investor: (1) time $t = 0$, The investor sells a share of option, with a gain of C_0. At time $t = n$, the investor is charged the payoff of the option $g(S_n, K) = g(S_0 \cdot \prod_{t=1}^{n}(1 + \xi_t), K)$; and (2) To hedge his position, the investor makes a sequence of n investments in the stock. For $t = 1, 2, ..., n$, at time $t - 1$, invest Δ_t in stock; at time t, sells the stock and gains a profit of $(\xi_t - r)\Delta_t$. Similar to the lower bound, we have the upper bound of C_0:

$$U_0 = G_0 \cdot \min_{\Delta_t, t \in [n]} \max_{r_{gt}, r_{at}, t \in [n]} (-\sum_{t=1}^{n} \frac{(r_{at} - r_{gt})\Delta_t}{G_t} + \frac{g(G_n, A_n)}{G_n}) \qquad (6)$$

The adversary nature must be restricted in this model. Otherwise, as Merton states [16], one can only bound the price C_0 of European call option by the current stock price S_0 and the strike price K as $\max\{0, S_0 - K\} \leq C_0 \leq S_0$.

In this work, we model the uncertainty of price process by a binomial model following the spirit of [5]. Because both the numéraire and the asset can be risky set, instead of model the fluctuation of a single asset, we adopt a binomial model of the relative fluctuation rate defined as $c_t = \frac{r_{at} - r_{gt}}{1 + r_{gt}}$, where a represents the asset and g represents the numéraire.

We model $c_t \in \mathcal{U}$, and $\mathcal{U} = \{\alpha, \beta\}$, with no arbitrage condition $\beta < 0 < \alpha$. Although most of our analysis is not dependent on the choice of α and β, readers should keep in mind that α and β should be quadratically bounded by the number of rounds n. One such bound in [13] is $\mathcal{U} = [-\underline{k}/\sqrt{n}, \overline{k}/\sqrt{n}]$, where $\underline{k}$ and $\overline{k}$ are some positive constant.

4 Upper Bound and Lower Bound in Our Model

4.1 Upper Bound in a Single Round Game

In this section, we explicitly solve the upper bound of option (or some other derivative) price in a single round game by address the mixed-strategy Nash equilibrium. We start by set $n = 1$ in (6):

$$U_0 = G_0 \cdot \min_{\Delta} \max_{r_g, r_a} (-\frac{(r_a - r_g)\Delta}{G_1} + \frac{g(G_1, A_1)}{G_1}) \qquad (7)$$

For simplicity of the expression, we use Δ, r_g, and r_a instead of Δ_1, r_{g1}, and r_{a1} in (7).

In this single round case, the investor needs only to decide Δ, the amount of the underlying asset to hold for hedging, and the nature decides r_g and r_a. Because the process of finding the lower bound is similar to finding the upper bound, we focus on analysing the upper bound.

Theorem. Consider a single round game. For a numéraire G and an asset A, and a derivative with payoff $C_1 = g(G_1, A_1)$. G_0 and A_0 are known, and $G_1 = G_0(1 + r_g)$, $A_1 = A_0(1 + r_a)$. Assume $c \in \{\alpha, \beta\}$, where c is the relative fluctuation rate defined by $c = \frac{r_a - r_g}{1 + r_g}$. The upper bound U_0 derivative price satisfies:

$$U_0 = G_0 \cdot \min_{P} \max_{Q} \mathbb{E}_{\Delta \leftarrow P} \mathbb{E}_{c \leftarrow Q} \{-c\Delta + G_0 \cdot \frac{g(G_1, A_1)}{G_1}\} \qquad (8)$$

$$= G_0 \cdot \mathbb{E}_{c \leftarrow Q^{g*}} [\frac{g(G_1, A_1)}{G_1}] \qquad (9)$$

where Q^{g*} is given by

$$q_\alpha^* = \frac{-\beta}{\alpha - \beta} \tag{10}$$

$$q_\beta^* = \frac{\alpha}{\alpha - \beta} \tag{11}$$

and P^* satisfies:

$$\mathbb{E}_{\Delta \leftarrow P^*}[\Delta] = \frac{G_0}{G_1} \cdot \frac{C_1^\alpha - C_1^\beta}{\alpha - \beta} \tag{12}$$

Where C^α is the payoff $g(G_1, A_1)$ when $c = \alpha$, and C_1^β is payoff $g(G_1, A_1)$ when $c = \beta$.

The proof of this theorem uses the mixed-strategy Nash Equilibrium in game theory.

Definition. In a two-player zero-sum game, a mixed strategy profile $\pi^* = P^* \times Q^*$ is called a mixed-strategy Nash equilibrium if for any mixed strategy P of the row player and any mixed strategy Q of the column player:

$$\mathbb{E}_{r \leftarrow P^*} \mathbb{E}_{c \leftarrow Q}[\ell(r, c)] \leq \mathbb{E}_{r \leftarrow P^*} \mathbb{E}_{c \leftarrow Q^*}[\ell(r, c)] \leq \mathbb{E}_{r \leftarrow P} \mathbb{E}_{c \leftarrow Q^*}[\ell(r, c)] \tag{13}$$

Lemma. In a two-person zero-sum game, the row player can choose from $\mathcal{R} = \{r^{(1)}, .., r^{(N)}\}$, and the column player can choose from $\mathcal{C} = \{c^{(1)}, ..., c^{(M)}\}$. Let $\pi^* = P^* \times Q^*$ be a mixed-strategy Nash equilibrium, where $P^* = (p^{*(1)}, ..., p^{*(N)})$ and $Q^* = (q^{*(1)}, ..., q^{*(M)})$, then for the row player:

(i) If $p^{*(u)} > 0$ and $p^{*(v)} = 0$

$$\mathbb{E}_{c \leftarrow Q^*} \ell(r^{(u)}, c) \leq \mathbb{E}_{c \leftarrow Q^*} \ell(r^{(v)}, c) \tag{14}$$

(ii) If $p^{*(u)} > 0$ and $p^{*(w)} > 0$

$$\mathbb{E}_{c \leftarrow Q^*} \ell(r^{(u)}, c) = \mathbb{E}_{c \leftarrow Q^*} \ell(r^{(w)}, c) \tag{15}$$

and for the column player:
(iii) If $q^{*(u)} > 0$ and $q^{*(v)} = 0$

$$\mathbb{E}_{r \leftarrow P^*} \ell(r, c^{(u)}) \geq \mathbb{E}_{r \leftarrow P^*} \ell(r, c^{(v)}) \tag{16}$$

(iv) If $q^{*(u)} > 0$ and $q^{*(w)} > 0$

$$\mathbb{E}_{r \leftarrow p^*} \ell(r, c^{(u)}) = \mathbb{E}_{r \leftarrow P^*} \ell(r, c^{(w)}) \tag{17}$$

Proof of Lemma. We start proof of (i) by contradiction. If (14) does not hold, we must have,

$$\sum_{j=1}^{M} q_j^* \cdot \ell(r^{(u)}, c^{(j)}) > \sum_{j=1}^{M} q_j^* \cdot \ell(r^{(v)}, c^{(j)}) \tag{18}$$

recall by definition, the expected loss of row player under mixed-strategy Nash equilibrium is

$$\mathbb{E}_{r\leftarrow P^*}\mathbb{E}_{c\leftarrow Q^*}[\ell(r,c)] = \sum_{i=1}^{N}\sum_{j=1}^{M} p^{*(i)}q^{*(j)}\ell(r^{(i)},c^{(j)})$$

$$= \sum_{i\notin\{u,v\}}\sum_{j=1}^{M} p^{*(i)}q^{*(j)}\ell(r^{(i)},c^{(j)})+$$

$$p^{*(u)}\sum_{j=1}^{M} q^{*(j)}\ell(r^{(u)},c^{(j)}) + p^{*(v)}\sum_{j=1}^{M} q^{*(j)}\ell(r^{(v)},c^{(j)})$$

$$= \sum_{i\notin\{u,v\}}\sum_{j=1}^{M} p^{*(i)}q^{*(j)}\ell(r^{(i)},c^{(j)}) + p^{*(u)}\sum_{j=1}^{M} q^{*(j)}\ell(r^{(u)},c^{(j)})$$

$$(19)$$

The last line follows the assumption $p^{*(v)} = 0$ in (i).

If we define P' by swapping $p^{*(u)}$ and $p^{*(v)}$, i.e., $p^{'(u)} = p^{*(v)}$, $p^{'(v)} = p^{*(u)}$, and $p^{'(i)} = p^{*(i)}$ for $i \notin \{u,v\}$. The expect loss of row player under $\pi' = p' \times q'$ is:

$$\mathbb{E}_{r\leftarrow P'}\mathbb{E}_{c\leftarrow Q'}[\ell(r,c)] = \sum_{i=1}^{N}\sum_{j=1}^{M} p^{'(i)}q^{'(j)}\ell(r^{(i)},c^{(j)})$$

$$= \sum_{i\notin\{u,v\}}\sum_{j=1}^{M} p^{'(i)}q^{'(j)}\ell(r^{(i)},c^{(j)})+$$

$$p^{'(u)}\sum_{j=1}^{M} q^{'(j)}\ell(r^{(u)},c^{(j)}) + p^{'(v)}\sum_{j=1}^{M} q^{'(j)}\ell(r^{(v)},c^{(j)})$$

$$= \sum_{i\notin\{u,v\}}\sum_{j=1}^{M} p^{*(i)}q^{*(j)}\ell(r^{(i)},c^{(j)}) + p^{*(v)}\sum_{j=1}^{M} q^{*(j)}\ell(r^{(v)},c^{(j)})$$

$$<\mathbb{E}_{r\leftarrow P^*}\mathbb{E}_{c\leftarrow Q^*}[\ell(r,c)] \qquad (20)$$

The forth line follows the swap of $p^{*(u)}$ and $p^{*(v)}$, and the last line follows (18) and (19). Inequality (20) contradicts with the definition of mixed-strategy Nash equilibrium (13), which finishes the proof of (i).

Next we prove (ii) by contradiction. If (15) does not hold, we must have,

$$\sum_{j=1}^{M} q_j^* \cdot \ell(r^{(u)},c^{(j)}) \neq \sum_{j=1}^{M} q_j^* \cdot \ell(r^{(w)},c^{(j)})$$

Without loss of generality, assume

$$\sum_{j=1}^{M} q_j^* \cdot \ell(r^{(u)},c^{(j)}) > \sum_{j=1}^{M} q_j^* \cdot \ell(r^{(w)},c^{(j)}) \qquad (21)$$

By definition, the expected loss of row player is

$$\mathbb{E}_{r \leftarrow P^*} \mathbb{E}_{c \leftarrow Q^*}[\ell(r,c)] = \sum_{i=1}^{N} \sum_{j=1}^{M} p^{*(i)} q^{*(j)} \ell(r^{(i)}, c^{(j)})$$

$$= \sum_{i \notin \{u,w\}} \sum_{j=1}^{M} p^{*(i)} q^{*(j)} \ell(r^{(i)}, c^{(j)}) +$$

$$p^{*(u)} \sum_{j=1}^{M} q^{*(j)} \ell(r^{(u)}, c^{(j)}) + p^{*(w)} \sum_{j=1}^{M} q^{*(j)} \ell(r^{(w)}, c^{(j)})$$

$$(22)$$

If we define p' by moving the probability from $p^{*(u)}$ to $p^{*(w)}$, i.e. $p'^{(u)} = 0$, $p'^{(w)} = p^{*(u)} + p^{*(w)}$, and $p'_i = p_i$ for $i \notin \{a,b\}$. then the expected loss of row player under $\pi' = p' \times q'$ is

$$\mathbb{E}_{r \leftarrow P'} \mathbb{E}_{c \leftarrow Q'}[\ell(r,c)] = \sum_{i=1}^{N} \sum_{j=1}^{M} p'^{(i)} q'^{(j)} \ell(r^{(i)}, c^{(j)})$$

$$= \sum_{i \notin \{u,w\}} \sum_{j=1}^{M} p'^{(i)} q'^{(j)} \ell(r^{(i)}, c^{(j)}) +$$

$$p'^{(u)} \sum_{j=1}^{M} q'^{(j)} \ell(r^{(u)}, c^{(j)}) + p'^{(w)} \sum_{j=1}^{M} q'^{(j)} \ell(r^{(w)}, c^{(j)})$$

$$= \sum_{i \notin \{u,w\}} \sum_{j=1}^{M} p^{*(i)} q^{*(j)} \ell(r^{(i)}, c^{(j)}) +$$

$$p^{*(u)} \sum_{j=1}^{M} q^{*(j)} \ell(r^{(w)}, c^{(j)}) + p^{*(w)} \sum_{j=1}^{M} q^{*(j)} \ell(r^{(w)}, c^{(j)})$$

$$< \mathbb{E}_{r \leftarrow P^*} \mathbb{E}_{c \leftarrow Q^*}[\ell(r,c)]$$

$$(23)$$

Inequality (23) contradicts with the definition of mixed-strategy Nash equilibrium (13), which finishes the proof of (ii).

The proof of (iii) and (iv) is similar to the prove of (i) and (ii). This finishes the proof of lemma.

Proof Theorem. By definition, P^* and Q^* are the mixed strategy of investor (row player) and nature (column player) under mixed-strategy Nash equilibrium.

Using the result (ii) in lemma, We have

$$q^*(-\alpha \cdot \Delta^{(1)} + G_0 \cdot \frac{C_1^\alpha}{G_1}) + (1 - q^*)(-\beta \cdot \Delta^{(1)} + G_0 \cdot \frac{C_1^\beta}{G_1})$$

$$= q^*(-\alpha \cdot \Delta^{(2)} + G_0 \cdot \frac{C_1^\alpha}{G_1}) + (1 - q^*)(-\beta \cdot \Delta^{(2)} + G_0 \cdot \frac{C_1^\beta}{G_1}) \qquad (24)$$

$$= ...$$

$$= q^*(-\alpha \cdot \Delta^{(N)} + G_0 \cdot \frac{C_1^\alpha}{G_1}) + (1 - q^*)(-\beta \cdot \Delta^{(N)} + G_0 \cdot \frac{C_1^\beta}{G_1})$$

which leads to (10) and (11)

Using the result (iv) in lemma 2, we have

$$- \alpha \cdot \mathbb{E}_{\Delta \leftarrow P^*}[\Delta] + G_0 \cdot \frac{C_1^\alpha}{G_1} = -\beta \cdot \mathbb{E}_{\Delta \leftarrow P^*}[\Delta] + G_0 \cdot \frac{C_1^\beta}{G_1} \qquad (25)$$

which leads to (12). This finishes the proof of Theorem.

Several inferences can be concluded from Theorem: (1) We do not make any assumption on the payoff function $g(.)$, thus we relax the convex assumption of payoff functions in previous works; (2) The current value (price) of the derivative is the expectation of the current value of payoff $g(.)$; (3) Because the regret is a linear function of Δ, the optimal randomized decision of the investor can be absorbed into a single value $\Delta^* = \mathbb{E}_{\Delta \leftarrow P^*}[\Delta]$; and (4) Acting his or her optimal randomized decision, i.e. best hedging strategy, the investor is, in fact, indifferent about the action of Nature (i.e. don't care if the stock price goes up or goes down).

4.2 Lower Bound in a Single-Round Game

In a single-round game, the lower bound of the option price C_0:

$$L_0 = G_0 \cdot \max_\Delta \min_{r_g, r_a} \left(-\frac{(r_a - r_g)\Delta}{G_1} + \frac{g(G_1, A_1)}{G_1} \right) \qquad (26)$$

Following the same analysis as in Sect. 4.1, we can conclude the lower bound

$$L_0 = G_0 \cdot \mathbb{E}_{c \leftarrow Q^{g*}} \left[\frac{g(G_1, A_1)}{G_1} \right] \qquad (27)$$

where Q^{g*} is given by

$$q_\alpha^* = \frac{-\beta}{\alpha - \beta} \qquad (28)$$

$$q_\beta^* = \frac{\alpha}{\alpha - \beta} \qquad (29)$$

Notice that through the lens of game theory, as long as the loss function $R = -\frac{(r_a - r_g)\Delta}{G_1} + \frac{g(G_1, A_1)}{G_1}$ stays the same, the preference of the players (min or max) does not actually affect the mixed-strategy Nash equilibrium, or expected loss under the mixed-strategy Nash equilibrium.

By comparing (9) and (27) we can conclude that $L_0 = U_0$, or in other words that in a single round game the lower bound meets the lower bound. This conclusion does not depend on any assumption of the payoff function g(.).

Hence the option price in a single-round game is given by:

$$C_0 = G_0 \cdot \mathbb{E}_{c \leftarrow Q^{g*}}[\frac{g(G_1, A_1)}{G_1}] \tag{30}$$

where Q^{g*} is given by

$$q_\alpha^* = \frac{-\beta}{\alpha - \beta} \tag{31}$$

$$q_\beta^* = \frac{\alpha}{\alpha - \beta} \tag{32}$$

4.3   Option Pricing in Multi-round Game

Now we generalize the lower bound and the upper bound in a multi-round game.

For a $n \geq 2$ round game, the upper bound (6) can be rewritten in the following dynamic program:

$$U_n = g(G_n, A_n) \tag{33}$$

$$U_{t-1} = \min_{\Delta_t} \max_{c_t} \{-c_t \Delta_t + \frac{G_{t-1}}{G_t} U_t\} \tag{34}$$

Similarly, the lower bound (5) can be rewritten as:

$$L_n = g(G_n, A_n) \tag{35}$$

$$L_{t-1} = \max_{\Delta_t} \min_{c_t} \{-c_t \Delta_t + \frac{G_{t-1}}{G_t} L_t\} \tag{36}$$

Where (33) and (35) are the boundary cases.

Because $U_n = L_n = g(G_n, A_n)$, we can conclude

$$C_n = g(G_n, A_n) \tag{37}$$

By backward induction, if we have $U_t = L_t = C_t$, by the linear program (34) and (36), we have

$$U_{t-1} = \min_{\Delta_t} \max_{c_t} \{-c_t \Delta_t + \frac{G_{t-1}}{G_t} C_t\}$$

$$L_{t-1} = \max_{\Delta_t} \min_{c_t} \{-c_t \Delta_t + \frac{G_{t-1}}{G_t} C_t\}$$

Using the results (9) and (27) of single round game, we have

$$C_{t-1} = U_{t-1} = L_{t-1} = G_{t-1} \mathbb{E}_{c \leftarrow Q^{g*}}[\frac{C_t}{G_t}]$$

where Q^{g*} is given by

$$q_\alpha^* = \frac{-\beta}{\alpha - \beta} \tag{38}$$

$$q_\beta^* = \frac{\alpha}{\alpha - \beta} \tag{39}$$

which means the lower bounds meet the upper bounds in every round of the game.

When the time segment n is finite, because it is feasible to calculate the boundary case in the leaf nodes of the binomial tree, the worst case complexity of this binomial pricing model is $O(2^n)$, however, when binomial tree is combined, the complexity of the binomial pricing model is $O(n^2)$.

5   Our Model Under Different Numéraires

Our model we employ allows arbitrary choice of numéraire. This feature is especially important when we are generalizing to more complex derivatives such as exotic options. As an example, we still use European stock options in a single round game to show that our pricing model is robust under different numéraires.

For an European call option with underlying asset stock S, the numéraire can be either the bond or the stock $G \in \{S, B\}$. The payoff function is $g(S_1) = \max\{S_1 - K, 0\}$. Assume the initial price $B_0 = K(1 + r)^{-1}$, and S_0 are given, and $S_1 = S_0(1 + \xi)$, $B_1 = (1 + r)B_0$. We also assume $\xi \in \{u, d\}$ following the standard binomial model. For simplicity, we consider a single round game.

When the numéraire is the bond $G = B$, by definition

$$c = \frac{S_1/B_1}{S_0/B_0} - 1 = \frac{\xi - r}{1 + r} \tag{40}$$

The condition $\xi \in \{u, d\}$ is equivalent to

$$c \in \{\frac{u - r}{1 + r}, \frac{d - r}{1 + r}\} \tag{41}$$

so we have

$$\alpha^{(B)} = \frac{u - r}{1 + r} \tag{42}$$

$$\beta^{(B)} = \frac{d - r}{1 + r} \tag{43}$$

By theorem, $Q^{(g=B)*}$ is given by

$$q_\alpha^{(B)*} = \frac{-\beta^{(B)}}{\alpha^{(B)} - \beta^{(B)}} = \frac{r - d}{u - d} \tag{44}$$

$$q_\beta^{(B)*} = \frac{\alpha^{(B)}}{\alpha^{(B)} - \beta^{(B)}} = \frac{u - r}{u - d} \tag{45}$$

So the option price C_0 is given by

$$C_0 = B_0 \cdot \mathbb{E}_{Q^{(g=B)*}}[\frac{g(S_1)}{B_1}]$$

$$= \frac{1}{1+r}(q_\alpha^{(B)*} \cdot g(S_1^u) + q_\beta^{(B)*} \cdot g(S_1^d)) \qquad (46)$$

$$= \frac{1}{1+r}(\frac{r-d}{u-d}g(S_1^u) + \frac{u-r}{u-d}g(S_1^d))$$

When the numéraire is the stock, or $G = S$, by definition

$$c = \frac{S_1/B_1}{S_0/B_0} - 1 = \frac{r-\xi}{1+\xi} \qquad (47)$$

The condition $\xi \in \{u, d\}$ is equivalent to

$$c \in \{\frac{r-d}{1+d}, \frac{r-u}{1+u}\} \qquad (48)$$

so we have

$$\alpha^{(S)} = \frac{r-d}{1+d} \qquad (49)$$

$$\beta^{(S)} = \frac{r-u}{1+u} \qquad (50)$$

By theorem, $Q^{(g=S)*}$ is given by

$$q_\alpha^{(S)*} = \frac{-\beta^{(S)}}{\alpha^{(S)} - \beta^{(S)}} = \frac{(u-r)(1+d)}{(u-d)(1+r)} \qquad (51)$$

$$q_\beta^{(S)*} = \frac{\alpha^{(S)}}{\alpha^{(S)} - \beta^{(S)}} = \frac{(r-d)(1+u)}{(u-d)(1+r)} \qquad (52)$$

Notice that when the numéraire is the stock, $c = \alpha$ actually corresponds to stock price goes down, so the option price C_0 is given by

$$C_0 = S_0 \cdot \mathbb{E}_{Q^{(g=S)*}}[\frac{g(S_1)}{S_1}]$$

$$= (q_\alpha^{(S)*} \cdot \frac{g(S_1^d)}{1+d} + q_\beta^{(S)*} \cdot \frac{g(S_1^u)}{1+u})$$

$$= (\frac{(u-r)(1+d)}{(u-d)(1+r)} \frac{g(S_1^d)}{1+d} + \frac{(r-d)(1+u)}{(u-d)(1+r)} \frac{g(S_1^u)}{1+u}) \qquad (53)$$

$$= \frac{1}{1+r}(\frac{r-d}{u-d}g(S_1^u) + \frac{u-r}{u-d}g(S_1^d))$$

Comparing (46) and (53), it can be concluded that the choice of numéraire does not affect the option pricing. In other words, our model is robust under change of numéraire.

6   Summary and Outlook

We have presented a robust option pricing model as Minimax game under the no arbitrage assumption. By doing so, we are able to apply the classic game theory method of Nash Equilibrium, and calculate the lower bound and upper bound in a single round game. We further show that the lower bound and upper bound converge to a single price under the no arbitrage assumption, and generalize this conclution to multi-round games by mathematical induction. Another important feature of our model is that it does not depend on the convexity of the payoff function. Finally, we us European call option as an example to show that our model has the flexibility of changing Numéraire. Future work could (1) apply the online learning framework to more complex financial derivatives like exotic options, (2) consider the generalization of the model when the number of time segments goes to infinity.

References

1. Abernethy, J., Bartlett, P.L., Frongillo, R., Wibisono, A.: How to hedge an option against an adversary: Black-Scholes pricing is minimax optimal, pp. 2346–2354 (2013)
2. Abernethy, J., Frongillo, R.M., Wibisono, A.: Minimax option pricing meets Black-scholes in the limit. In: Proceedings of the Forty-fourth Annual ACM Symposium on Theory of Computing, pp. 1029–1040. ACM (2012)
3. Black, F., Scholes, M.: The pricing of options and corporate liabilities. J. Polit. Econ. **81**, 637–654 (1973)
4. Brigo, D., Mercurio, F.: Interest Rate Models - Theory and Practice: With Smile. Inflation and Credit. Springer, Heidelberg (2007). https://doi.org/10.1007/978-3-540-34604-3
5. Cox, J.C., Ross, S.A., Rubinstein, M.: Option pricing: a simplified approach. J. Financ. Econ. **7**(3), 229–263 (1979)
6. DeMarzo, P., Kremer, I., Mansour, Y.: Online trading algorithms and robust option pricing. In: Proceedings of the Thirty-eighth Annual ACM Symposium on Theory of Computing, pp. 477–486. ACM (2006)
7. Eraker, B.: Do stock prices and volatility jump? Reconciling evidence from spot and option prices. J. Financ. **59**(3), 1367–1403 (2004)
8. Eraker, B., Johannes, M., Polson, N.: The impact of jumps in volatility and returns. J. Financ. **58**(3), 1269–1300 (2003)
9. Geman, H., El Karoui, N., Rochet, J.C.: Changes of numeraire, changes of probability measure and option pricing. J. Appl. Probab. **32**, 443–458 (1995)
10. Van der Hoek, J., Elliott, R.J.: Binomial Models in Finance. Springer, New York (2006). https://doi.org/10.1007/0-387-31607-8
11. Hull, J.C.: Options, Futures & Other Derivatives. Prentice Hall, Upper Saddle River (2009)
12. Jamshidian, F.: An exact bond option formula. J. Financ. **44**(1), 205–209 (1989)
13. Lam, H., Liu, Z.: Robust dynamic hedging
14. Sander, M.: Bondesson's representation of the variance gamma model and Monte Carlo option pricing (2008)

15. Mansour, Y.: Learning, regret minimization and option pricing. In: Proceedings of the 11th Conference on Theoretical Aspects of Rationality and Knowledge, pp. 2–3. ACM (2007)

16. Merton, R.C.: Theory of rational option pricing. Bell J. Econ. Manag. Sci., 141–183 (1973)

17. Pan, J.: The jump-risk premia implicit in options: evidence from an integrated time-series study. J. Financ. Econ. **63**(1), 3–50 (2002)

18. Ross, S.A.: The arbitrage theory of capital asset pricing. J. Econ. Theory **13**(3), 341–360 (1976)

Numerical Simulation Study on Heat Exchange Effect of Open Computer

Xiangci Meng[(✉)]

The Computer Department, Jiangsu Automation Research Institute,
Lianyungang, China
mengxiangci_hrbeu@163.com

Abstract. This article conducts a thermal simulation analysis of an open computer. Through the simulation results, the module structure and the chassis structure are optimized. And verify the reliability of thermal design of the chassis. It provides reference for thermal simulation analysis and thermal optimization design of other similar electronic devices.

Keywords: Natural convection · Chassis · Thermal simulation
Optimal design

1 Introduction

With the continuous advancement of science and technology, electronic equipment, especially the field of military electronic systems, is becoming integrated and miniaturized, and the degree of integration of computer systems has increased at an unprecedented rate [1, 2]. Large-scale integrated circuits are commonly used in circuit design, and the functions of independent devices and modules have become increasingly complex, resulting in an increase in output power. A large amount of electrical energy is converted into heat energy, resulting in high heat flux and heat accumulation effects. The reliability of power devices is closely related to their temperature. It has been pointed out in the report that 55% of failures in electronic devices are caused by temperature, and the reliability of semiconductor devices is reduced by 50% for every 10 °C increase in temperature [3–6]. In the design process of computer products, designers need to consider the chassis structure and thermal design together to realize the collaborative design of the structure and thermal control.

Thermal design of electronic devices is based on three types of heat transfer: heat conduction, thermal convection, and thermal radiation. With the upgrading of computer hardware and the development of software integration technology, the use of numerical methods for thermal analysis of electronic devices has become the main means of thermal design of electronic devices. Compared with traditional thermal analysis methods, numerical simulation technology can effectively reduce design costs and shorten design time [7, 8]. The designer grasps the weak points in the design that are prone to problems and evades the design risks so as to increase the success rate of the products [9–11]. This paper adopts Icepak software with high precision and fast calculation speed to perform thermal design and thermal simulation analysis on an open

W. Xu et al. (Eds.): NCCET 2018, CCIS 994, pp. 83–90, 2019.
https://doi.org/10.1007/978-981-13-5919-4_8

chassis. The conclusion of this paper provides a reference for the thermal design and thermal simulation of this type of equipment.

2 Numerical Model

2.1 Chassis Structure and Module Structure

As shown in Fig. 1, the module of the open computer adopts the plug-in structure design. The external dimensions of the chassis (L × W × H) are 365 mm × 286 mm × 212 mm. The entire chassis consists of 2 power modules, 1 network module, 2 data exchange modules, 1 storage module, 5 waterproof modules, and 1 electrical connector module. The 12 module plugs are placed parallel to the inside of the chassis. The total heat consumption is 213 W. The heat dissipation components are shown in Table 1.

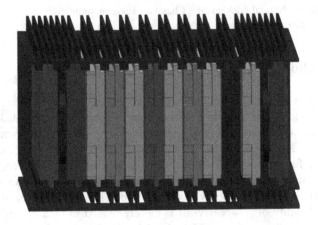

Fig. 1. Computer structure

Table 1. Power consumption table

Module	Quantity	Slot number	Power consumption (W)		
			CPU	Whole board	Total
Power module	2	2, 12		20	213
Network module	1	6		38	
Data module	2	4, 8	35	45	
Storage module	1	10	35	45	
Waterproof module	5	3, 5, 7, 9			
Electrical connector module	1	1			

The main heat dissipation methods of the open computer studied in this paper are natural convection heat transfer and heat radiation. For the entire computer, due to the non-compulsory heat dissipation method, the heat dissipation of the modules in the chassis is difficult. After the components are heated, they are transferred to their own cold plate mold through the thermal pad, and then the heat is transferred to the edge of the module through its own cold plate and heat conduction structure, and then trans- mitted to the side wall of the chassis through the locking device, finally through the cooling fins of the side plate of the chassis. Through the analysis of the heat dissipation conditions of the internal modules of the chassis, it can be seen that there are two main factors affecting the heat dissipation performance from the thermal conduction of the electrical components from the module to the side plates, the natural convection of the external walls of the side plates and the air: Thermal conductivity of module cold plate and heat-conducting structure/natural convection heat dissipation performance of cooling fins and external air; Thermal path as shown in Fig. 2.

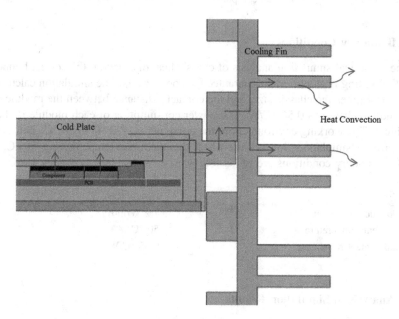

Fig. 2. The cooling path of the computer

2.2   Computational Models and Grids

For the open computer studied in this paper, the finite volume method is used for numerical calculation. In order to increase the efficiency of simulation and calculation, the chassis should be simplified first. Local details such as screws, nuts, fillets, mounting holes, etc. that have little effect on heat dissipation are ignored.

Based on the simplification of the model, the whole machine needs to be meshed. This chassis cooling simulation mesh adopts Mesh-HD mesh type that is provided by

Icepak. This grid can meet the calculation requirements. In addition, the cooling fins and module models have been refined to increase simulation accuracy, as shown in Figs. 3 and 4.

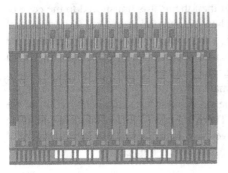

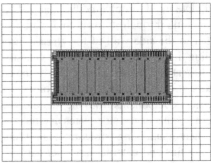

Fig. 3. Simplified model of open computer

Fig. 4. Computational mesh

2.3   Boundary Conditions

For the numerical simulation analysis of chassis heat dissipation, the correct boundary condition setting is an important guarantee for good results. The simulation calculation domain is 4 times the chassis size, and the contact resistance between the module cold plate and the chassis is 0.56 °C/W. The power consumption of each module is shown in Table 1. The working environment of the computer is −20 °C to 50 °C. This article only performs simulations for the case where the maximum temperature is 50 °C. The specific boundary conditions are set as follows:

	Parameters
Heat-conducting gasket	7.2 W/m·K
Environment temperature	50 °C
Thermal contact resistance	0.56 °C/W

2.4   Analysis of Simulation Results

The final simulation results are shown in Figs. 5 and 6.

Figure 5 shows the open computer temperature cloud diagram; Fig. 6 shows the temperature distribution of the local module.

From the open computer temperature cloud diagram in Fig. 5, it can be seen that the internal maximum temperature is 98.98 °C when the operating conditions are stable. At the same time, it can be seen from Fig. 6 that the highest temperature region is the CPU of the data module. The junction temperature of this CPU is 95 °C, so the temperature is too high, which seriously affects the normal operation of the computer and requires optimization and improvement of the structure.

Fig. 5. The temperature of the computer

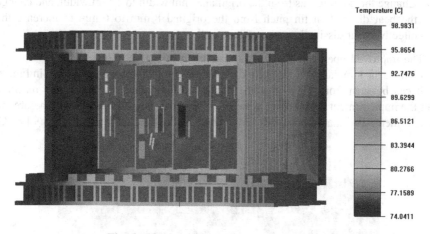

Fig. 6. The local temperature of the module

The temperature distribution of the chassis is analyzed and the following conclusions are drawn based on the analysis results:

(a) As can be seen from the temperature distribution of the heat dissipating fins in Fig. 5, the temperature of the fins corresponding to slot 7 is 83.5 °C. The temperature of corresponding fins in slot 8 is 86.2 °C, and the difference between them is 3 °C. This is because slot 7 corresponds to a power-free waterproof module, and slot 8 corresponds to a high-power data module. However, the existence of a temperature difference of 3 °C also indicates that the heat conduction path of the slot board on the chassis is unreasonable, thereby affecting the heat transfer between the adjacent heat dissipation fins.

(b) It can be seen from Fig. 6 that the CPU temperature of the data module is too high. According to the principle of heat exchange, it can be seen that the chassis and the outside air are cooled by the natural convection heat transfer method. The heat dissipation of this heat exchange method has a large relationship with the heat transfer area. Increasing the heat dissipation effect of the whole machine while changing the heat transfer path is the key to lowering the temperature.

3   Optimization Measures

According to the simulation results, we optimized the chassis as follows:

(a) Open the corresponding slot with high power consumption, and the corresponding slot of the waterproof module does not turn on. This will not only ensure that the heat of the high-temperature main board can be transferred to the outside of the chassis through convection heat transfer, but also optimize and improve the heat transfer path.
(b) Change the cooling fins from the original 3 mm width to 2 mm width, and change the heat dissipation fin pitch from the original 8 mm to 6 mm to increase the effective heat dissipation area of the cooling fins.

The improved open chassis structure is shown in Fig. 7.

Finally, the simulated temperature distribution can be improved as shown in Fig. 8.

It can be seen from Fig. 9 that the maximum temperature of the whole machine after the improvement is 94.85 °C, which is 4 °C lower than the temperature before the improvement. The maximum CPU temperature of the module at this time is 94.8 °C.

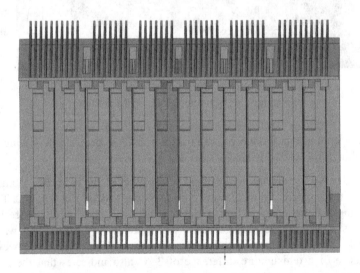

Fig. 7. Schematic diagram of the optimized chassis

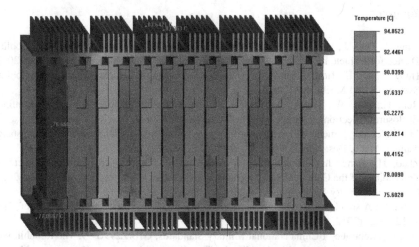

Fig. 8. The temperature of the complete machine after improvement

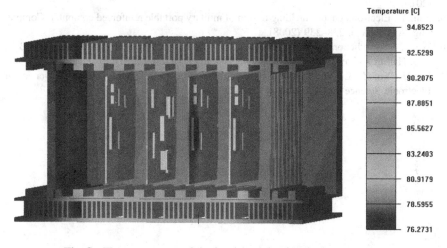

Fig. 9. The temperature of the local module after the improvement

4 Conclusion

This paper optimizes the design of a computer through numerical simulation. By changing the thermal conduction structure of the chassis and the heat dissipation area to enhance the heat dissipation of the computer, increasing the area of the heat dissipation fins can effectively increase the heat dissipation of the computer. The maximum temperature of the computer was reduced from the original 98.98 °C to 94.8 °C, and the CPU can work stably in a safe environment.

References

1. Tang, J., Guo, J., Hou, C., Cheng, Z., Wei, J., Zheng, R.: Research on Secondary Cooling Device for Vehicle-mounted Electronic Equipment. Electro-Mechanical Engineering (2007)
2. Hu, J., Chen, E., Hou, C., Jiang, Y., Zhong, G.: Design of Vehicle Radar Liquid Cooling System - Fluid Machinery (2006)
3. Ren, H., Liu, W., Huang, J., Hong, D.: Icepak Based Thermal Design of Confined Enclosures. Electronic Science and Technology (2015)
4. Li, K., et al.: Structural design and dynamics simulation for anti-adverse circumstance cabinet. Mech. Des. Manuf. 9(9), 35–37 (2012)
5. Zhao, H., Jiang, J.: The construction design about a military ruggedized cabinet. In: Proceedings of the Conference on Mechanical and Electrical Engineering for the Year 2005. Electronic Industry Press, Nanjing (2005)
6. Yuan, L.: A small cabinet structure and strengthening protection design. Mod. Manuf. Eng. 7, 123–125 (2012)
7. People's Republic of China National Military Standards, GJB/Z299B-99. The Reliability of Electronic Equipment Design Handbook. The General Armament Department Military Standard Publishing Unit, Beijing (1999)
8. Hui, L.: Reinforced VXI Test Chassis Development. Harbin Institute of Technology, Harbin (2010)
9. Sun, Y.: Electromagnetic shielding design of military portable reinforced computer. Comput. Eng. Appl. 44(1), 238–239 (2008)
10. Wang, S.: Prediction Research on Shielding Effectiveness of Electronic Equipment Box, p. 3. Harbin University of Science and Technology, Harbin (2010)
11. Lu, H., Yu, Z., Li, W.: Engineering Electromagnetic Compatibility. Xi'an University of Electronic Science and Technology Press, Xi'an (2012)

A High-Matching Low Noise Differential Charge Pump for PLL

Hengzhou Yuan and Yang Guo[✉]

College of Computer, National University of Defense Technology,
Deya Str. 109, Changsha 410073, People's Republic of China
guoyang@nudt.edu.cn

Abstract. This paper presents a high matching charge pump with low noise. Two pairs of charge pumps in differential structure alleviate charge sharing and improve static mismatch. This simple structure with minimum number of transistors can reduce the noise of CP. A differential low amplitude buffer stage is proposed to reduce the dynamic mismatch of CP. A 3.125 GHz PLL is implemented with the proposed charge pumps in 65 nm CMOS process. In simulation, the proposed CP achieved good static mismatch and dynamic mismatch in a dynamic range larger than half VDD. The noise simulated at 1 kHz achieved −227 dB. The reference spur measured at 25 MHz was lower than −51.5 dBc. The test results show the good performance of proposed CPPLL.

Keywords: PLL · Charge pump · Low noise

1 Introduction

There are strict requirements of both jitter and power consumption in SerDes (Serializer-Deserializer) [1] system and it is essential to make PLL [2–8] meet those requirements with low voltage and low mismatch in clock data recovery. As Fig. 1 shows, in a conventional charge pump the UP and DN pulses from the PFD drive switch transistors connected in series with current sources and convert the voltage pulses to current pulses in equal width. The current is integrated by the loop filter, the output voltage modulates the oscillating frequency of VCO (Voltage Controlled Oscillator).

Any difference between the charging and discharging currents of conventional charge-pump will lead to static phase offset and dynamic jitter, known as reference spur. There are two kinds of mismatch exist in charge pump. Static mismatch is caused by the leakage current and the channel length modulation effect. These two kinds of mismatch will lead to static phase error and high ripple on the control voltage even when the loop is locked. The PLL output will be modulated by the ripple and cause a reference spur. In frequency synthesis, the spur caused by CP is the dominant source.

There is another problem with the conventional CP. When PLL is locked, assume one switch is off, the voltage difference across its current source will become zero. For example, when UP is zero, the voltage of node A1 equals to VDDA and makes Iup equal to zero. When the UP signal arrives again, the switch connects node Out to VDDA creating an unwanted transient ripple and leads the spur of VCO output.

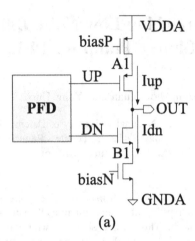

Fig. 1. Conventional change pump

Several circuit technologies are introduced to reduce current mismatch. Static mismatch improvements have been obtained by employing cascode structure [9] or gain boosting technology [10] to increase CP output resistance. The pseudo-cascode structure and bulk biasing technology [11] are adopted to increase output impedance for better current matching. A charge pump with dual compensation circuits is design to achieve better matching [12]. These two methods increase power consumption and are not suitable for low voltage because of cascade transistors.

To achieve better noise performance of CP, a differential CP is designed by using a flicker-noise-free resistor instead of a transistor [13]. An SSCP with reverse leakage compensation technology [14] is proposed to reduce spur level in wideband PLL. However, the operational amplifier used in these proposed charge pumps would introduce flicker noise which is considered as noise source. A new reference-spur elimination architecture is proposed to reduce the spur of PLL, but the structure is complex and consumes large areas [15]. Other alternative technologies which will reduce the noise of CP in systematic level of PLL [16] are not discussed in this paper.

2   Charge Pump Design and Simulation

In this paper, we propose a differential charge pump that improves current matching without sacrificing the output dynamic range via differential low-amplitude input buffer stage. As shown in Fig. 2, compared to conventional differential change pump, the proposed CP has a low amplitude input buffer to minimize the input swing. To minimize noise, the minimum number of transistors is used. No operational amplifier exists in the proposed charge pump therefore flicker noise is avoided.

Meanwhile, the proposed charge pump is especially suitable for low power consumption system because no cascode structure is used. Two current sources are used to constitute one charge pump. Two overdrive voltages are essential to make the current

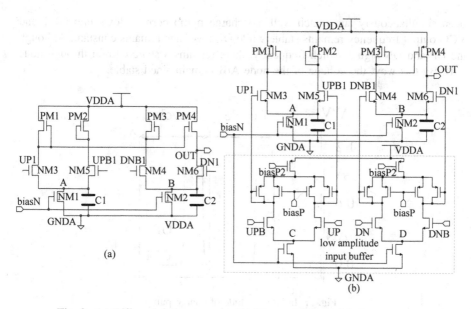

Fig. 2. (a) Differential change pump (b) Proposed differential charge pump

source transistors in the saturation region. Our charge pump only needs one current source which leads to low voltage drop and adaptability to low voltage application.

To improve the static mismatch, the proposed CP uses differential structure of two pairs of charge pump to alleviate the charge sharing in conventional charge pump. The tail current source can be designed quite identically.

$$I_{NM1d} = I_{NM2d} \tag{1}$$

$$I_{NM1d} = I_{NM3d} = I_{PM1d} + I_{PM1g} + I_{PM4g} = I_{PM1d} + C_1\frac{du}{dt} + C_2\frac{du}{dt} \tag{2}$$

$$I_{mis} = \frac{I_{PM4d} - I_{NM2d}}{I_{NM2d}} = \frac{I_{PM2d} - I_{NM2d}}{I_{NM2d}} = -\frac{C_1\frac{du}{dt} + C_2\frac{du}{dt}}{I_{NM2d}} \tag{3}$$

Where INM1d, INM3d and IPM1d are the drain currents of the corresponding transistors, IPM1g and IPM4g are the gate currents of corresponding transistors. As can be expressed in (1), (2) and (3), to reduce transient dynamic mismatch, small voltage variation of drain of PM1 transistor can reduce the I_{mis}. The differential low amplitude buffer stage is designed to reduce amplitude of CP. The UP and DN signals are split into four signals. UPB and DNB are the inversion signals of UP and DN. Instead of directly input, the full rail-to-rail amplitude UP/UPB/DN/DNB into CP, the differential low amplitude buffer stage will reduce the swing of output signals. Compared with black line(UP) in Fig. 3, the swing of red line (UP1) signal is reduced. When UP1 and DN1 equal high, the NM3 and NM6 are both opened, and the current mirror would replicate the current of PM1 to PM4. Ideally, when the charging and discharging paths open simultaneously and match well, no charge pump current flows into OUT and VCO output frequency remains stable while OUT voltage remains constant. Although the UP and DN signal switch frequently, there remains a static current through node A/B. By this way, the voltage of the node A/B is maintained stable.

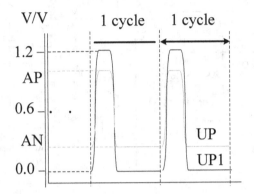

Fig. 3. Input amplitude of charge pump

The UP1/UPB1 and DN1/DNB1 cannot switch at the same time otherwise it will reduce the stability of node A/B. To alleviate the transient disturbance in the drain of current source, capacitors are connected between the drain of NM1/NM2 and GND. These two capacitors (dummy transistors) can be placed beside the tail current.

There remains the trading off between the static mismatch, dynamic mismatch and noise performance. To reduce the dynamic mismatch, the length of the transistor should be small. However, the smaller length will cause an increased static mismatch. While length becomes smaller, its 1/f noise performance becomes worse. Because of the low-pass character of reference spur and noise CP of PLL, the bandwidth of PLL is limited which lead to noise performance degradation in PLL.

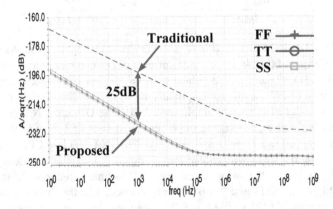

Fig. 4. Output noise of CP

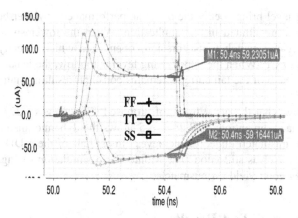

Fig. 5. Dynamic mismatch

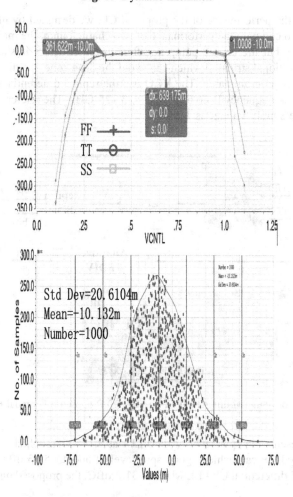

Fig. 6. State mismatch of corners and Monte Carlo

Small swing level brings better the dynamic performance however both lower and upper swing level are limited in this application. When the lower swing level is too low, it will force the switch transistors into open state which directly damage the normal function of CP. When the upper swing level is too low, the leakage current will be high since the sum of the tail currents remains constant, resulting static mismatch of the CP of PLL.

Figure 4 shows that the noise figure of proposed CP achieves −227 dB at 1 kHz, 25 dB smaller than conventional CP. Figure 5 shows the dynamic mismatch of CP. In Fig. 6, the static mismatch under 1% achieves almost half of the VDD voltage while the dynamic mismatch is still good. The Monte Carlo simulation of Fig. 6 shows the structure features good yield on mismatch.

3   Simulation and Test Results

To demonstrate the performance of the proposed CP, we designed two PLL in 65 nm CMOS process to compare the performance of two charge pump, the main block of the PLL is the same, but the charge pump is different, the structure is shown in Fig. 7. The PFD use traditional structure which can avoid the dead zone, the divider is consists of DFFs, and it is programmable. The VCO use the replica differential ring structure. The PLL generates frequency from 625 MHz to 3.125 GHz. The reference frequency is 25 MHz and the supply voltage is 1.2 V.

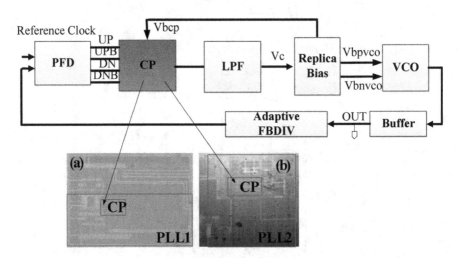

Fig. 7. (a) Conventional differential CP in PLL (b) Proposed differential CP in PLL

Figure 8 presents the spur level of the PLLs at 3.125 GHz which shows the PLL with the proposed CP can achieve good spur level of about −51.5 dBc. Compared to the conventional differential CP PLL which is 31.2 dBC, the proposed one can improve about 20 dB.

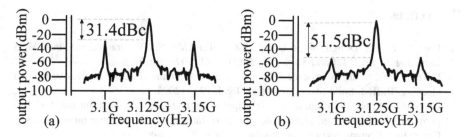

Fig. 8. (a) PLL output spectrum in conventional CP (b) PLL output spectrum in proposed CP

Figure 9 presents the phase noise of the proposed charge pump PLLs, it can achieve good phase noise about −100.5 dBc/Hz @100 kHz, the integrated RMS jitter is about 2.75 ps from 1 kHz to 20 MHz.

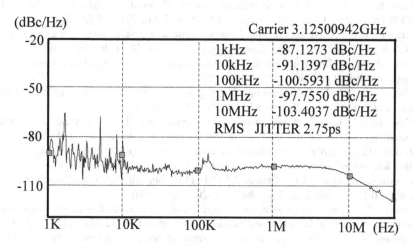

Fig. 9. Phase noise of proposed CPPLL

4   Conclusion

A highly matched charge pump with low noise character is designed for PLL. It achieves low spur level and phase noise. The test results show the good performance of the charge pump PLL.

Acknowledgments. This research was supported by National Natural Science Foundation of China Program (No. 61772540).

References

1. Lee, J., et al.: Design of 56 Gb/s NRZ and PAM4 SerDes transceivers in CMOS technologies. IEEE J. Solid State Circ. **50**(9), 2061–2073 (2015)
2. Loke, A.L.S., et al.: A versatile 90-nm CMOS charge-pump PLL for SerDes transmitter clocking. IEEE J. Solid State Circ. **41**(8), 1894–1907 (2006)
3. Bhardwaj, M., et al.: Design of a wide output range and reduced current mismatch charge pump PLL with improved performance. In: 2016 International Conference on Advances in Computing, Communications and Informatics, pp. 2644–2649 (2016)
4. Schober, S., et al.: A 1.25 mW 0.8–28.2 GHz charge pump PLL with 0.82 ps RMS jitter in all-digital 40 nm CMOS. In: 2015 IEEE International Symposium on Circuits and Systems (ISCAS), pp. 549–552 (2015)
5. Goyal, B., et al.: Design of charge pump PLL using improved performance ring VCO. In: 2016 International Conference on Electrical, Electronics, and Optimization Techniques, pp. 3254–3258 (2016)
6. Dhar, D., et al.: Analysis of the effect of PFD sampling on charge-pump PLL stability. In: 2018 IEEE International Symposium on Circuits and Systems, pp. 1–5 (2018)
7. Zhao, B., et al.: Supply-noise interactions among submodules inside a charge-pump PLL. IEEE Trans. Very Large Scale Integr. (VLSI) Syst. **23**(4), 771–775 (2015)
8. Zhao, B., et al.: A spur suppression technique using an edge-interpolator for a charge-pump PLL. IEEE Trans. Very Large Scale Integr. (VLSI) Syst. **20**(5), 969–973 (2015)
9. Lee, J.-S., et al.: Charge pump with perfect current matching characteristics in phase-locked loops. Electron. Lett. **36**(23), 1907–1908 (2000)
10. Choi, Y.-S., et al.: Gain-boosting charge pump for current matching in phase-locked loop. IEEE Trans. Circ. Syst. II **53**(10), 1022–1025 (2006)
11. Shao, H., et al.: A high-performance charge pump with improved static and dynamic matching characteristic. In: IEEE International Conference on Asic, pp. 1–4 (2016)
12. Zhong, D., et al.: A perfectly current matched charge pump with wide dynamic range for ultra low voltage applications. IEICE Electron. Express **11**(23), 1–6 (2014)
13. Brownlee, M., et al.: A 0.5-GHz to 2.5-GHz PLL with fully differential supply regulated tuning. IEEE J. Solid State Circ. **46**(12), 2720–2728 (2006)
14. Zhang, Z., et al.: Source-switched charge pump with reverse leakage compensation technique for spur reduction of wideband PLL. Electron. Lett. **52**(14), 1211–1212 (2016)
15. Jonsson, F., et al.: Techniques to reduce folding of noise and interferers in PLL charge-pump. In: IEEE International Conference on Electronics, Circuits and Systems, pp. 1067–1070 (2008)
16. Choi, J., et al.: A spur suppression technique using an edge-interpolator for a charge-pump PLL. IEEE Trans. Very Large Scale Integr. (VLSI) Syst. **20**(5), 969–973 (2012)

A 12.5-Gb/s Equalizer with CTLE and a 4-Tap Quarter-Rate DFE in 40 nm Technology

Qing Xu, Jianjun Chen[✉], Yueyue Chen, Bin Liang, Bo Xiong,
Yuan Luo, and Jizuo Zhang

School of Computer, National University of Defense Technology, Deya Str. 109,
Changsha 410073, People's Republic of China
xqysnju@163.com

Abstract. On account of finite channel bandwidth and reflection, receiver cannot receive data accurately resulting from ISI. To satisfy the transmission requirements of PCIE3.1 and Rapid IO3.2, this paper presents a 12.5 Gb/s equalizer based on 40 nm CMOS. It uses Continuous-Time Linear Equalizer (CTLE) and a quarter-baud-rate decision feedback equalizer (DFE) with 4 taps. Finally, the receiver can effectively balance data and restore eye diagram with a channel loss of 28 dB at 12.5 Gb/s. The layout area of equalizer is 0.66 mm^2, and its consumption is 33.08 mW from a 1.1-V supply.

Keywords: Equalizers · DFE · CTLE · ISI · Data eye

1 Introduction

With the increase of transmission rate and transmission distance as well as insufficient bandwidth backplane, the reflection, crosstalk, skin effect and loss during transmission become more and more serious. Inter symbol interference (ISI) cannot be eliminated over recent bandwidth backplane. The received data eye has been closed in many cases, so equalization techniques have been developed in system design, such as Continuous-Time Linear Equalizer (CTLE), Low-Frequency Equalizer, Decision Feedback Equalization (DFE) and so on. The application of these technologies has promoted the transmission of data to higher speed and longer distance.

At present, the international advanced SERDES can operate up to 112 Gb/s with PAM-4 [1, 5] or at 56 Gb/s with NRZ modulation in a single lane [2, 3]. Domestic technology is relatively backward, 12.5 Gb/s SERDES based on PCIE 3.1 and Rapid IO 3.2 protocol was designed in our subject. To meet with the requirements of data eye width and height, this paper describes a circuit with analog equalizer (e.g., CTLE) and nonlinear equalizer (e.g., DFE) at 12.5 Gb/s to effectively utilize the available bandwidth. CTLE is used to adjust the gain in all frequency domains, especially in high frequency. DFE is utilized to further settle the signals resulting from ISI without amplifying noise. The combination of two circuits greatly solves the problem of crosstalk noise and compensates for the attenuation.

© Springer Nature Singapore Pte Ltd. 2019
W. Xu et al. (Eds.): NCCET 2018, CCIS 994, pp. 99–107, 2019.
https://doi.org/10.1007/978-981-13-5919-4_10

The reminder of paper is organized as follows. We introduce the design of the entire equalizer circuit in detail, including schematics and characteristics in Sect. 2. Then, the circuit layout and post-simulation results are described in Sect. 3. Finally, we draw conclusions in Sect. 4.

2 Equalizer Design

2.1 Architecture

Figure 1(a) shows the overall structure of analog equalizer. It is composed of two stages of CTLE, a variable gain amplifier (VGA) and a cml buffer. CTLE controls the high-frequency gain through the source negative feedback capacitor. VGA controls the low-frequency gain by adjusting the source negative feedback resistor. Buffer is the most basic differential amplifier with spectral characteristics as a low-pass filter providing approximately 5 dB of gain over the entire bandwidth. In order to make up more than 20 dB attenuation caused by the channel, the gain of each CTLE needs to reach 6 dB and VGA needs to be adjustable from −3 dB–6 dB.

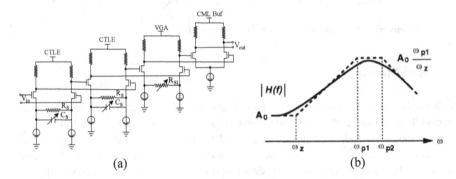

Fig. 1. (a) Analog Equalizer Architecture. (b) CTLE.'s magnitude response.

DFE is a 4-tap structure and consisted of an isolation amplifier, samplers, latches and mux. In order to reduce the clock frequency, we divided clock into four to achieve a quarter-baud-rate receiver. In Fig. 2(a) (shown single-ended for simplicity), this structure uses parallel pipeline technology, including four branches in phase 0°, 90°, 180° and 270, reducing the design difficulty of the CDR circuit and clock buffer. At the beginning of the circuit, the ac-coupled receiver input (from CTLE) is passed to the sampling circuit through the amplifier A1. The amplifier is used to buffer the input data. In addition to providing about 6 dB gain, it also isolates the equalized signal from the channel. The output current from mux and CTLE are summed into a resistive load, producing the equalized signal. Figure 2(b) shows the channel response of DFE. It effectively solves the crosstalk problem of posts-cursor components.

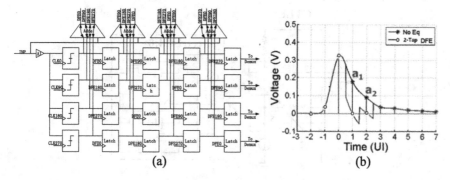

Fig. 2. (a) DFE Architecture. (b) DFE's channel pulse response

2.2   CTLE Design

As is shown in Fig. 3, CTLE uses resistive and capacitive negative feedback techniques by adding parallel resistors and capacitors in the source of the differential amplifier. Most CTLE designs [4, 8] utilize the structure. The introduced source negative feedback adds a zero and a pole, making it similar in spectral characteristics of high-pass filter. The parallel connection of source negative feedback also makes the differential amplifier's high-frequency gain greater than the DC gain. The transfer function of the circuit is

$$G(s) = \frac{g_m R_D}{1 + \frac{g_m R_s}{2}} \frac{1 + s/\omega_z}{1 + s/\omega_{p1}} \frac{1}{1 + s/\omega_{p2}} \tag{1}$$

yields a zero at

$$\omega_z = \frac{1}{R_s C_s} \tag{2}$$

and poles at

$$\omega_{p1} = \frac{1 + g_m R_s/2}{R_s C_s} \tag{3}$$

and

$$\omega_{p2} = \frac{1}{R_D C_L}. \tag{4}$$

Figure 1(b) depicts the frequency response. In order to obtain the best performance, we generally adjust the DC gain by R_s and the high frequency gain by C_s.

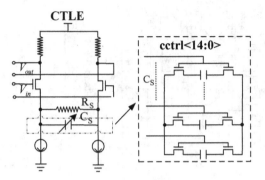

Fig. 3. CTLE schematic.

2.3 VGA Design

The structure of VGA is the same as CTLE. Figure 4(a) shows a degenerated differential pair with a pole at

$$\omega_p = \frac{1}{R_D C_L} \tag{5}$$

and its transfer function is

$$G(s) = \frac{g_m R_D}{1 + \frac{g_m R_s}{2}} \frac{1}{1 + s/\omega_p}. \tag{6}$$

The source degeneration resistor is implemented by NMOS tube operating at linear region. We control the resistance R_s by eight signals, thus control the gain of VGA. In usual, the range of gain is from -3 dB to 6 dB and gradient is about 1 dB. Figure 4(b) illustrates the response.

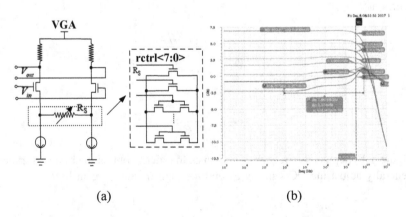

(a)   (b)

Fig. 4. (a) VGA schematic. (b) VGA.'s magnitude response.

2.4   Sampler Design

The sampler is usually composed of a sense amplifier and a latch in most designs [6–8]. To minimize the delay time and satisfy the speed requirements, a new structure of high-speed sense amplifier is applied (Fig. 5). Its outputs are buffered by a pair of clocked inverters and parallel hold latches. The comparator amplifies the signal with a small input amplitude and high speed to an output signal with a swing power supply voltage. Hysteresis is minimized because the comparator is always evaluated and precharged at the level level of clock and changed at the high level. During the precharge state, the clocked inverters isolate comparators from output latches to achieve a full UI of pre-charge time. What's more, the clocked inverters provide the strength to drive the large feedback mux capacitance. The last parallel latches can be chosen as a SR latch or normal auxiliary circuit by the control signal DFECLK. It can increase the hold time of sampling data.

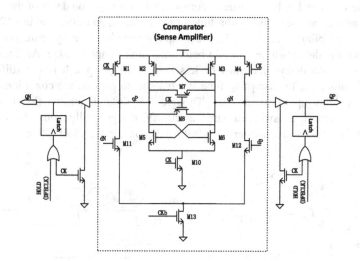

Fig. 5. Sampler schematic.

2.5   Tap Feedback Mux Design

The tap feedback mux is distributed in Fig. 6. They are adders based on current mode circuit and used to multiply the delay signal by the corresponding tap coefficient and subtract the sum of these weights from the currently received signal with inter-symbol interference. Each mux is split into two separated CML branches with four different phase signals. It is necessary to confirm CML clocks are well suited to high data rate transceivers and only one phase of the signals can be turned on at the same time. As a result, the duty cycle of the CML clocks is 25%. DFE coefficient weight is controlled by tail current.

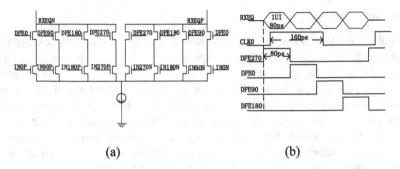

Fig. 6. (a) DFE tap feedback mux schematic. (b) DFECLK response.

2.6 DFE Critical Timing Path

It is necessary to consider DFE timing constraints in practical applications. The critical path timing described in Fig. 7 usually composes the propagation delay of the sampler, the adder as well as the transmission time of the isolation amplifier. Taking 12.5-Gb/s data stream sampling as an example, the sampling time is generally at the data centre location and the data must be returned before the next sampling edge. As a result, the whole propagation delay time must be less than ½ UI (40 ps). It is very difficult to achieve. In this case, the sampling time is advanced to provide the conditions for the propagation delay up to about 1 UI. Though it is difficult for the first tap for its resolution to input signal swings as small as 20 mV, it is generally required to complete the whole data return in a shorter time (80% UI) considering clock jitter.

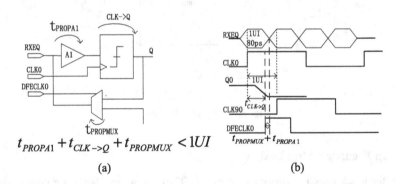

Fig. 7. DFE critical path timing. (a) Delay contributors. (b) Timing diagram.

3 Experimental Results

This section presents simulation results of the design. The final layout of the receiver equalizer is obtained in Fig. 8. Experiments were performed on different lengths of transmission lines and various corners. The transmission channel is constructed with a distributed model RLGC (per-unit-length resistance, inductance, conductance and capacitance) model and its amplitude frequency characteristics are shown in Fig. 9(a). The transmission 12.5 Gbps data is generated by a PRBS (Pseudo Random Sequence), in Fig. 9(b) with the formula $x^7 + x^6 + 1 = 0$. The longest connection '1' in the code stream of PRBS7 is 7 and '0' is 6, which brought more severe inter-symbol interference after transmission and left a design margin for the equalizer. Experiments taken under 6 m with different process corners and results were illustrated in Table 1 as example. It is clearly data width all reached 0.8 UI. Compared with designs [8–10], Table 2 shows the performance of four different equalizers. It is obvious this work is effective, with a small area, low power consumption, and good performance.

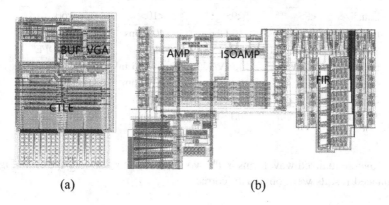

(a)   (b)

Fig. 8. Equalizers' layout. (a) Analog equalizer. (b) DFE.

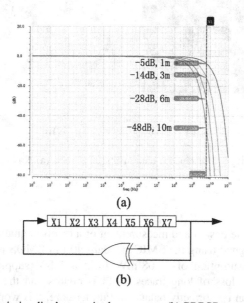

Fig. 9. (a) Transmission line's magnitude response. (b) PRBS7 generator architecture.

Table 1. Experimental results in different corners in 6 m channel.

Type	Corner					
	TT/65 °C/1.1 V		SS/125 °C/0.99 V		FF/125 °C/1.21 V	
	No-Eq	With-Eq	No-Eq	With-Eq	No-Eq	With-Eq
Eye width (ps)	0	68.52	0	70.14	0	67.59
Eye height (mV)	0	316.61	0	331.58	0	185.86

Table 2. Performance summary.

Equalizer	<8>	<9>	<10>	This work
Data rate	6.25 Gbps	10 Gbps	40 Gbps	12.5 Gbps
Structure	CTLE + DFE	CTLE	FFE	CTLE + DFE
EQ power	1.2 V/–	1.6 V/133 mW	1 V/65 mW	1.1 V/33.08 mW
Area	–	0.61 mm^2	0.75 mm^2	0.66 mm^2
Gain	21.3 dB	18 dB	10 dB	28 dB
Technology	0.13-um	0.13-um	65-nm	40-nm

Moreover, equalized waveforms in the worst process corner were shown in Fig. 10. The balanced results were obviously correct.

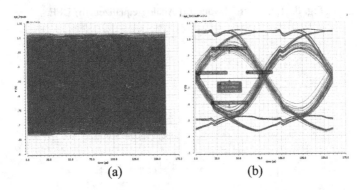

(a)   (b)

Fig. 10. Eye diagram of random data in SS125 corner. (a) No-Eq. (b) With-Eq.

4 Conclusion

This paper presents the design and measurement of a receive equalizer with CTLE and 4-tap DFE. It is designed using the SMIC standard 40 nm CMOS process with area of 0.086 mm^2 and consumption of 33.08 mW from a 1.1-V supply. The design can compensate the high loss of long traces on PCB boards and the 12.5 Gbps data of 28 dB attenuation can be correctly balanced. Furthermore, this work has been verified under different process corner.

The biggest innovation of this paper is to provide the architecture of four-clock sampling, which slows down the pressure of the phase-locked loop clock. This structure lays the foundation for the subsequent study of higher-speed SERDES. What's more, power of this design is relatively low.

References

1. Kim, J., et al.: A 112Gb/s PAM-4 transmitter with 3-Tap FFE in 10nm CMOS. In: ISSCC, pp. 102–104, February 2018
2. Han, J., et al.: A 60Gb/s 288mW NRZ transceiver with adaptive equalization and baud-rate clock and data recovery in 65nm CMOS technology. In: ISSCC, pp. 112–113, February 2017
3. Peng, P.-J., et al.: A 56Gb/s PAM-4/NRZ transceiver in 40nm CMOS. In: ISSCC, pp. 110–111, February 2017
4. Rahman, W., et al.: A 22.5-to-32Gb/s 3.2pJ/b referenceless baud-rate digital CDR with DFE and CTLE in 28nm CMOS. In: ISSCC, pp. 120–121, February 2017
5. Menolfi, C., et al.: A 112Gb/s 2.6pJ/b 8-Tap FFE PAM-4 SST TX in 14nm CMOS. In: ISSCC, pp. 104–106, February 2018
6. Matsui, M., et al.: A 200 MHz 13 mm 2-D DCT macrocell using sense-amplifying pipeline flip-flop scheme. IEEE J. Solid State Circ. **29**(12), 1482–1490 (1994)
7. Nikolic, B., Oklobdzija, V.G., Stojanovic, V., Jia, W., Chiu, J.K., Leung, M.M.: Improved sense-amplifier-based flip-flop: design and measurements. IEEE J. Solid State Circ. **35**(6), 876–884 (2000)
8. Payne, R., et al.: A 6.25-Gb/s binary transceiver in 0.13um CMOS for serial data transmission across high loss legacy backplane channels. IEEE JSSC **40**(12), 2646–2657 (2005)
9 Gondi, S., Razavi, B.: Equalization and clock and data recovery techniques for 10-Gb/s CMOS serial-link receivers. IEEE JSSC **42**(9), 1999–2011 (2007)
10. Momtaz, A., Green, M.M.: An 80 mW 40 Gb/s 7-Tap T/2-spaced feed-forward equalizer in 65 nm CMOS. IEEE JSSC **45**(3), 629–639 (2010)

Design and Implementation of a Domain Specific Rule Engine

Mengdong Chen[✉], Xinjian Zhou, Dong Wu, and Xianghui Xie

State Key Laboratory of Mathematical Engineering and Advanced Computing,
Henghua Science and Technology Park, Wuxi 214125, Jiangsu, China
chen.mengdong@meac-skl.cn

Abstract. Security strings are often needed in identity authentication mechanism. Security strings recovery is a reverse process, which does much calculations on a large amount of possible strings to find the right one, so that we can recover lost or forgotten strings and regain access to valuable information. In this reverse process, we need first process basic strings based on transformation rules, so as to generate new ones quickly. Rule processing is complex, which has high requirements for computing power, processing time, especially system power consumption. In response to the above requirements, this work puts forward the idea of accelerating the processing of rules using hardware for the first time, and a domain specific rule engine is designed and implemented on the existing FPGA platform. The experimental results show that the performance of the rule engine on a single Xilinx Zynq 7z030 FPGA is better than that of CPU, its performance power ratio is 3 times higher than that of GPU, and 50 times higher than that of CPU. The speed and energy efficiency of the rule processing is improved effectively.

Keywords: String · Rule · Engine · Domain specific

1 Introduction

With the development of computer technology and the expansion of Internet scale, identity authentication mechanism has gradually become an important way for people to protect their information [1]. The authentication process requires an identity information consists of a username and a security string. The HASH algorithm is usually used to calculate the digests of secure strings and the digests are stored together with user credentials. When the user authenticates his identity, the authentication system receives the security string inputed by the user and uses the HASH algorithm to convert the string into a digest and compares it with the digest value stored in the system to complete the authentication process. The forgetting of security strings can cause inconvenience and loss [2]. The analysis technology of authentication protocol is just to solve this problem.

In the analysis of authentication protocol, a large number of to-be-tested strings need to be quickly generated in a short period of time for the subsequent HASH algorithm to calculate the digest value. And the digest value is then compared with the stored digest, so that the correct string can be found. In the process of generating of possible strings, using dictionary and transformation rules is a very accurate and effective way [3–5]. Based on transformation rules and existing dictionaries consisted of basic strings, it is possible to generate a large number of strings with a higher probability, which in turn can increase the speed of analysis and improve accuracy.

As there are many kinds of transformation rules, and the calculation is complex, rule processing is a task with great demand for computation power and processing time. To the best of our knowledge, the public implementation methods are all based on CPU and GPU now [6, 7], which have many shortcomings in processing speed and system power consumption. Aiming at the rule processing in analysis of authentication protocol, this article presents a hardware-implemented, energy-efficient, reconfigurable rule processing architecture, and implements a domain specific rule processing engine. The research in this article is based on Xilinx Zynq FPGA. The experimental results show that the engine performs well in terms of processing performance and system power consumption.

2 Rule and Its Implementation Platform

2.1 Rules in the Analysis of Identity Authentication Protocal

When setting a secure string, people often set up a new string based on a simple transformation, such as adding a prefix, adding a suffix, etc., this transformation is called a transformation rule [6, 7]. This rule-based approach provides an idea for the analysis of identity authentication protocols. By collecting known security strings, a dictionary can be formed. The analysis can be attempted in the dictionary. Compared to the full-character search space, the amount of calculation here can be significantly reduced and a higher probability of hits can be ensured. At the same time, by applying rules to the dictionary, new strings can be generated, which expands the coverage of the dictionary, and improves the hit rate. The exquisitely set dictionaries and rules can significantly increase the hit rate of the analysis when satisfying the limitations of search scale, time limit, and the like.

In the analysis of authentication protocol, there are many string transformation rules accumulated. Multiple tools have their own supported rules and provide a dictionary plus rule analysis mode.

John the Ripper [6] is an open source and free analysis software, its main purpose is to analyze the weak Unix passwords. It now supports more than 100 kinds of algorithms, and provides support for many different types of system architectures, including Unix/Linux, Windows/DOS and OpenVMS. It supports dictionary analysis mode, and supports more than 40 kinds of string transformation rules and their handling. The rules are processed on CPU.

Hashcat [7] is a widely used multiplatform free analysis kit, which supports various platforms with OpenCL runtime, including CPU, GPU (supporting NVIDIA GPU and AMD GPU), DSP, FPGA, etc. It supports multiple operating systems, including Linux, Windows, MacOS, etc. It supports distributed processing, nearly 200 algorithms, and multiple analysis modes. It supports the processing of dictionaries and rules, and its rules are processed mainly on CPU and GPU.

Based on the rules used by Hashcat, this article studies 41 common basic transformation rules and implements their acceleration engine. Table 1 lists several typical transformation rules. Each rule takes a visible character as its mnemonic, some rules need parameters, and the number of parameters varies from 0 to 3. Table 1 illustrates the transformation results of the rule by taking the string *p@ssW0rd* as an example.

Table 1. Rules and their meanings

Mnemonic	Description	Example	Transform result
u	Uppercase all letters	u	P@SSW0RD
r	Reverse the entire word	r	dr0Wss@p
pN	Append duplicated word N times	p2	p@ssW0rdp@ssW0rdp@ssW0rd
{	Rotates the word left	{	@ssW0rdp
DN	Deletes character at position N	D3	p@sW0rd
iNX	Inserts character X at position N	i4!	p@ss!W0rd
sXY	Replace all instances of X with Y	ss$	p@$$W0rd
*XY	Swaps character at position X with character at position Y	*34	p@sWs0rd
+N	Increment character @ N by 1 ascii value	+2	p@tsW0rd

In actual use, several individual rules can be combined together to carry out one transform, such as *uD3ss$3*, which is combined of 3 individual rules. A new string is generated after all 3 rules are processed

2.2   Rule Processing Platform with High Efficiency

The analysis process of identity authentication protocol needs to search and calculate the string space made up of visible characters to find the correct string. When the length of the string increases, the space of search and the amount of computation all increase exponentially [8, 9]. Moreover, the analysis and calculation include a large number of computationally intensive modules. The computational power of a single computing node cannot meet the requirements. Even in the dictionary and rules mode which is a certain targeted analysis pattern, the number of rules and basic strings is also very large. Take a dictionary file with 50 million entries and a rule file with 100 thousand entries as an example, only the processing of rules will need to generate 5×10^{13} to-be-tested new strings, which contains huge amount of computation. Even we use MD5, the simplest HASH algorithm an example, it still takes more than ten days to finish the analysis process on a single common CPU. It can be seen that the computing power of a single computing node is still far from the analysis task of identity authentication protocol. The usual practice is to build large-scale computing clusters, divide the search space into different computing tasks, and each node conducts search and calculation in its own task space to speed up the entire analysis process [10].

When constructing large-scale analysis clusters, performance and power consumption are two main concerns. Rule processing and authentication protocol analysis are both computationally complex tasks. Common CPUs have encountered bottlenecks in performance improvement, and their computational capabilities have fallen far short of the requirements. The advent of GPU acceleration units has made them clearly superior in performance. And the theoretical computational performance in dealing with high integration, computationally intensive issues, etc. has substantially exceeded that of general-purpose processors [11, 12]. However, the GPU also has problems as an acceleration device. Especially when building a large-scale computing system, its construction cost, frequency wall, power-consumption wall, and storage wall have made the GPU's high cost and high power consumption intolerable [13].

The dedicated ASIC has a high degree of integration and high processing performance. However, the development is complex and the cost is high. Once the function is implemented, it cannot be changed, and it is not suitable for the acceleration of rule processing.

FPGA has the characteristics of low power consumption and high parallelism. It can not only accelerate the computing speed, but also keep power consumption within acceptable range [13–15]. Its wide application and reconfigurable characteristics provide a basis for its application in accelerating rule processing. Its low power consumption, high parallelism and strong expansibility make it suitable for accelerating the processing of rules and the analyzing of identity authentication protocol. Focusing on processing performance and energy efficiency. This article studies the rule processing techniques, designs and implements a rule engine with FPGA.

3 Design of the Rule Engine

The rule engine accelerates the parsing of the rules in a fully hardware-implemented manner. When processing, the software only needs to configure the size and location of the rule and dictionary files. The rule engine can automatically obtain rules and dictionaries from the off-chip, parse them, and generate new strings. The newly generated strings can be written back to the off-chip memory space through a high-speed bus for use by other applications. It can also integrate HASH authentication algorithms on-chip to directly verify the correctness of the string and complete the analysis of the entire identity authentication protocol.

3.1 Structure of the Hardware Platform

The rule engine of this article is based on an identity authentication protocol analysis system. This analysis system is a large-scale reconfigurable computing cluster. Its computing power comes from a large number of low-power reconfigurable Xilinx Zynq XC7Z030 chips. The chip is a hybrid core processor that includes a general-purpose embedded computing core (a dual-core ARM CortexTM-A9 processor running at 1 GHz) and an FPGA-based reconfigurable compute core [16]. The two heterogeneous computing resources are tightly coupled through a high-speed interconnection bus, which can support the parallel collaborative execution of general-purpose computing tasks and accelerated computing tasks. The hybrid processing platform integrates 1 GB of low-power DDR memory, 32 GB of flash memory, Gigabit Ethernet interfaces, and high-speed ring network interfaces and so on. The structure diagram of the computing platform based on Zynq XC7Z030 is shown in Fig. 1. The platform is visible in Fig. 2.

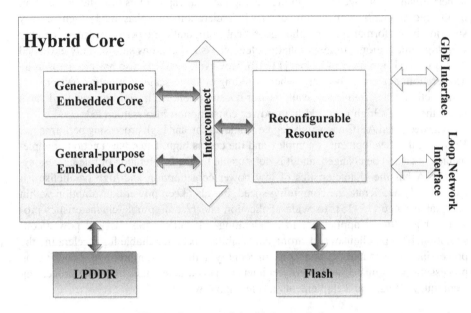

Fig. 1. Structure of the hardware platform

The rule engine is implemented on the reconfigurable FPGA of a single Zynq XC7Z030, and the engine can be integrated in each FPGA in the large-scale system. Rule files and dictionary files are divided into smaller parts according to computing tasks, and stored in off-chip low-power DDR memories.

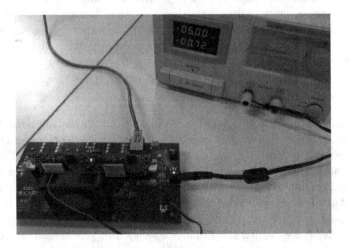

Fig. 2. Physical picture of the hardware platform

3.2   Design of the Data Format

Rule-based identity authentication protocol analysis requires that a large number of transformation rules be organized into rule files and common strings be organized into dictionary files for storage and usage. In the hardware implementation of the rule engine, expansion requirements, storage space limitations, and the readability of the rules should be considered. Each rule is coded with a specific length of 8 bits. We directly encode the rules with ASCII code of their mnemonic. The 8-bit code can theoretically support up to 256 rules, leaving room for new extensions for future rules. The rules are coded and stored by ASCII code, which ensures the readability of rule files and reduces the workload of translation and conversion between hardware and software.

When performing string transformation in reality, several individual rules are often combined together to perform one transform. In designing the hardware storage space, considering the rule combination and its parameters, 40 bytes of storage space is allocated for each transformation. Generally, the length of the string in each dictionary file is the same. In the hardware logic, 32 bytes of storage space is allocated for each dictionary entry, that is, the length of the string is a maximum of 32. The rule file and dictionary file format, as well as its storage form in hardware, are shown in Fig. 3.

Rule file   Rule in storage   320bit

Rule file	6c	44	30	69	35	65	00	00	···	···	00
IDOi5e	6c	44	30	69	35	65	00	00	···	···	00
IDOi5s	6c	44	30	69	35	73	00	00	···	···	00
rsa@	72	73	61	40	00	00	00	···	···	···	00
......						············					

Dictionary file   Dictionary in storage   256bit

Dictionary file	68	65	6c	6c	6f	31	32	33	00	···	00
Hello123	68	65	6c	6c	6f	31	32	33	00	···	00
Password	70	61	73	73	77	6f	72	64	00	···	00
12345678	31	32	33	34	35	36	37	38	00	···	00
......						············					

Fig. 3. The storage format of rule file and dictionary file

3.3   Design of the Engine Core

Rule processing is the process of decoding the rules, and then transforming the strings to get new ones. Because different transformation rules will change the length of the string, even if the input string has the same length, the output string will still be of different lengths, which will cause difficulties for subsequent usage. The solution is to categorize the dictionary files, and each time the processed dictionary file has the same string length. When processing, all the dictionary entries in the dictionary file are first looped for one rule, and thus, these new generated strings are of a same length, which facilitates the use for subsequent HASH pipelines. Then we use another rule, reacquire dictionary file and loop through it. This process continues, change another rule, reacquire dictionary and loop through the dictionary until all rules in the rule file are processed.

For the case where rules are combined together to apply a transformation to a string, the processing of the latter rules depends on the processing result of the preceding ones, the rules can only be executed in order. During the design process, this article optimized the execution time of each rule, and processed each rule within one clock cycle, including the analysis of the rule and the transformation of string. In this way, one rule is processed every clock cycle. Figure 4 depicts the detailed processing of 3 transformations, each time the transformation is a combination of 3 rules and the number of dictionary entries is k. Because each transformation is made up of 3 basic rules, 1 new string can be generated in every 3 clock cycles.

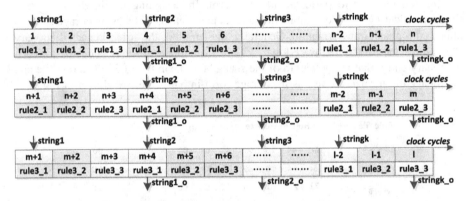

Fig. 4. The procedure of rule processing. The horizontal axis is the time axis and represents the clock period. *string1, string2, string3, ... stringk* are k entries of 1 dictionary. *rule1_1, rule1_2, rule1_3* are 3 basic rules, which together constitute 1 transformation. *rule2_1, rule2_2, rule2_3, rule3_1, rule3_2, rule3_3* are similar to this. *string1_o, string2_o, ..., stringk_o* are k outputs of the transformations. The clock cycles *1* to *n* complete the first transformation of the k dictionary entries, and *n + 1* to *m, m + 1* to *l* complete the second and third transformations, respectively.

The brief structure of the engine core is demonstrated in Fig. 5. Each of the 41 basic rules is designed as a single rule processing element (RPE). The periphery is a preprocessing circuit, a rule decoding circuit, and a memory management circuit. The preprocessing circuit is responsible for dividing the continuously stored rule and dictionary files into entries. The rule decoding circuit decodes the basic rules of each transformation one by one, and then selects the corresponding rule acceleration unit to perform operations. Each RPE completes the transformation according to the input string and the string length, and calculates the length of the newly generated string. The storage management circuit is responsible for using the high-speed bus to obtain rule and dictionary files from off-chip, form on-chip caches at various levels, and output the generated new strings off-chip as needed. All of this work is done automatically by hardware.

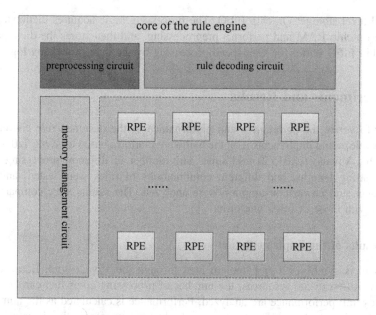

Fig. 5. Brief structure of the engine core

The processing logic of 41 basic rules constitutes a processing core. According to the limitation of hardware resources, one or more processing cores can be placed at the same time within the rule engine, and each core takes its own rule and dictionary to transform.

3.4   The Storage Architecture

The rules engine automatically accesses rules and dictionaries. To meet the speed requirements of the high-speed engine for rules and dictionaries, a total of three levels of storage structures are set.

The first level of storage: off-chip DDR. The rule and dictionary files are stored in DDR. The CPU in Zynq configures the start address and size information of the rule and dictionary files in DDR to the FPGA logic, and the hardware automatically obtains the rules and dictionary. At the same time, if the new strings generated by the rule engine need to be passed off-chip for use by other applications, they are also automatically transferred to the DDR memory by the rule engine.

Second level storage: On-chip RAM. The rule engine in FPGA pre-fetches the rules and dictionary into the FPGA through the AXI (Advanced eXtensible Interface) bus and caches them in the on-chip RAM. The four high-performance AXI_HP interfaces of the AXI bus can achieve a total bandwidth of 4.8 GB/s when operating at 150 MHz, which can guarantee the speed demand of the rule engine. As processing logic continues to consume data in RAM, the rule engine continuously acquires data from off-chip and guarantees the demand.

Third-level storage: On-chip FIFO. The processing logic acquires dictionary data from the on-chip RAM and performs preprocessing, and then stores the dictionary in the on-chip FIFO buffer for high-speed processing by the core processing logic.

4   Experiments and Results

In order to verify the correctness and performance of the designed rule engine, this article develops and implements it on the hardware platform based on Zynq 7z030 chip, through the Vivado (v2015.2) tool suite. The number of different processing cores, different string lengths, and different combinations of rules were tested, and their performance and power consumption were analyzed. The results were compared and analyzed with those of other platforms.

4.1   Results of the Implementation

The design is synthesized and implemented through the Vivado tool. Based on the constraints of hardware resources, the number of processing cores that can be placed and the overall performance are analyzed. Performance is calculated as the number of new strings that can be generated per second when the transformation is combined of 1 rule.

The results show that the maximum implementation frequency is 150 MHz and the maximum number of cores that can be put on chip is 2, so the maximum processing performance is to process 300M basic rules and generate 300M new strings per second. In the case of placing a single processing core on chip, the resource occupancy is 42%, and there are still enough resources to place the HASH algorithm pipeline, which can be used for on-chip verification. If two engine cores are placed on the chip, the resource consumption is about 80%, at this time, the HASH algorithm pipeline cannot be placed on the chip, and the rule engine can be used to transfer the generated new strings to the off-chip for other applications.

4.2   Comparison with Other Platforms

As far as we know, this is the first work that realizes the work of rule processing using hardware.

The comparisons of performance and power consumption are mainly performed with the software implementations on the CPUs and GPUs. The same rule and dictionary files are run on CPU and GPU, respectively. And the results are compared with this work. The two aspects of comparison are performance and power consumption.

Software implementation uses the latest hashcat 4.1.0, which is the industry's fastest analysis tool and supports both CPU and GPU platforms [5]. The result of software has a great relationship with its running platform, for example, in NVIDA GPUs, its desktop products and products specifically designed for high-performance computing have a huge gap in computing power. This work selects two mainstream product platforms for experimentation. The adopted CPU is: Intel(R) Core(TM) i7-6700 CPU @ 3.40 GHz with 32G memory. The adopted GPU is: NVIDIA GeForce GTX 970, with 1664 processing cores, running at 1.18 GHz. The performance comparison results are shown in Fig. 6.

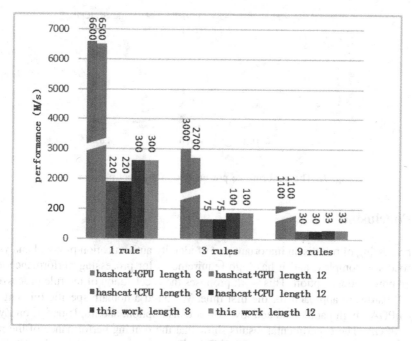

Fig. 6. The comparison of performance between different platforms. For the rule combination, we tested the combination of 1 rule, 3 rules and 9 rules on each platform. For the length of the strings in the dictionary, we tested the situation of 8 bytes and 12 bytes on each platform. Performance is calculated as the number of new strings generated per second.

Through analysis, it can be found that for different string lengths, the processing performance of the three platforms is not affected. The processing performance is greatly affected by the combination of rules. The more rules are combined, the more complex the processing is. Our rule engine can achieve the performance of 300M per second when the transformation is combined of 1 rule. The performance of this work is better than that of the CPU implementation, and is worse than that of the GPU implementation. However, when using the rule engine of this article to build a large-scale, low-power computing cluster, its computing power will increase significantly. But this is not the work of this article.

In actual operation, the running power consumption of the rule engine and the GPU platform is observed in real time. The power consumption of the CPU is calculated as 65 W and the performance power ratio is calculated (the number of rules that can be processed per second per watt). The results are shown in Fig. 7. The operating power of the rule engine is only 2 W, and its performance power ratio is 3 times higher than that of the GPU, and it is 50 times higher than that of CPU. We can see that the processing speed of the rule engine is fast enough, and its power consumption is not large, which is very suitable for building large-scale processing systems.

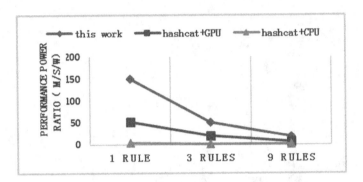

Fig. 7. The performance power ratio of different platforms

5 Conclusion

The processing of rules is an important part of identity authentication protocol analysis. Its process is complex, and it has high requirements for processing performance and system power consumption. This work proposes the acceleration of the rule processing with all hardware approach for the first time. We build a domain-specific rule engine using FPGA's high parallelism and low power consumption, and implement it on Zynq 7z030 FPGA. The experimental results show that the running performance of the rule engine is better than that of Intel i7-6700 CPU. The performance power ratio is 3 times higher than that of NVIDIA GeForce GTX 970 GPU, and about 50 times higher than that of CPU platform.

It effectively improves the speed and energy efficiency of rule processing. The rule engine designed in this paper has high processing performance, low system cost and low operating power consumption. It is particularly suitable for constructing large-scale, distributed, and reconfigurable rule processing systems, thereby providing a basis for the design and implementation of the entire identity authentication protocol analysis system.

Acknowledgements. This research was supported by National Natural Science Foundation of China (No. 91430214; 61732018). I am also grateful to my tutor and colleagues who had helped me in this project.

References

1. Kammerstetter, M., Muellner, M., Burian, D., Kudera, C., Kastner, W.: Efficient high-speed WPA2 brute force attacks using scalable low-cost FPGA clustering. In: Gierlichs, B., Poschmann, A.Y. (eds.) CHES 2016. LNCS, vol. 9813, pp. 559–577. Springer, Heidelberg (2016). https://doi.org/10.1007/978-3-662-53140-2_27
2. Houshmand, S., Aggarwal, S., Flood, R.: Next gen PCFG password cracking. IEEE Trans. Inf. Forensics Secur., 1776–1791, August 2015. https://doi.org/10.1109/tifs.2015.2428671
3. Wang, D., Zhang, Z., Wang, P., Yan, J., Huang, X.: Targeted online password guessing: an underestimated threat. In: Proceedings of the 2016 ACM SIGSAC conference on computer and communications security, pp. 1242–1254. ACM, October 2016
4. Huh, J.H., Oh, S., Kim, H., Beznosov, K., Mohan, A., Rajagopalan, S.R.: Surpass: system initiated user-replaceable passwords. In: Proceedings of the 22nd ACM SIGSAC Conference on Computer and Communications Security, pp. 170–181. ACM, October 2015
5. Melicher, W., et al.: Fast, lean, and accurate: modeling password guessability using neural networks. In: USENIX Security Symposium, pp. 175–191, August 2016
6. John the Ripper password cracker. http://www.openwall.com/john/doc/
7. Hashcat advanced password recovery. https://hashcat.net/hashcat/
8. Ji, S., Yang, S., Hu, X., Han, W., Li, Z., Beyah, R.: Zero-sum password cracking game: a large-scale empirical study on the crackability, correlation, and security of passwords. IEEE Trans. Dependable Secure Comput. **14**(5), 550–564 (2017)
9. Brumen, B., Makari, T.: Resilience of students' passwords against attacks. In: 2017 40th International Convention on Information and Communication Technology, Electronics and Microelectronics, pp. 1275–1279. IEEE, May 2017
10. Chang, D., Jati, A., Mishra, S., Sanadhya, S.K.: Cryptanalytic time–memory trade-off for password hashing schemes. Int. J. Inf. Secur., 1–18 (2016)
11. Qiu, W., Gong, Z., Guo, Y., Liu, B., Tang, X., Yuan, Y.: GPU-based high performance password recovery technique for hash functions. J. Inf. Sci. Eng. **32**(1), 97–112 (2016)
12. Akleylek, S., Tok, Z.Y.: Efficient arithmetic for lattice-based cryptography on GPU using the CUDA platform. In: 2014 22nd Signal Processing and Communications Applications Conference (SIU), pp. 854–857, April 2014 (2014)
13. Li, X., Cao, C., Li, P., Shen, S., Chen, Y., Li, L.: Energy-efficient hardware implementation of LUKS PBKDF2 with AES on FPGA. In: 2016 IEEE Trustcom/BigDataSE/ISPA, pp. 402–409 (2016). https://doi.org/10.1109/trustcom.2016.0090
14. Wang, C., Mao, J., Leng, T., Zhuang, Z.Y., Wang, X.M.: Efficient acceleration for total focusing method based on advanced parallel computing in FPGA. Int. J. Acoust. Vib. **22**, 536 (2017)
15. Abbas, A., Voss, R., Wienbrandt, L., Schimmler, M.: An efficient implementation of PBKDF2 with RIPEMD-160 on multiple FPGAs. In: 20th IEEE International Conference on Parallel and Distributed Systems (ICPADS), pp. 454–461 (2014). https://doi.org/10.1109/padsw.2014.7097841
16. Zynq-7000 All Programmable SoC. https://www.xilinx.com/support/documentation/product-briefs/zynq-7000-product-brief.pdf

High-Speed Circuit Power Integrity Design Based on Impedance Characteristic Analysis

Guangming Zhang[✉]

Jiangsu Automation Research Institute, Lianyungang 222061, China
focuszgm@163.com

Abstract. Power integrity (referred to as PI) issues have become increasingly important in today's high-speed circuit designs, at the same time, the complexity of power integrity analysis has increased. Based on the two-port network model, paper establishes the small signal model of the power system and the transmission matrix model of the PCB power supply ground plane system, innovatively combines power supply design and PCB design to realize the impedance control of the power distribution system and improve the power integrity of the circuit. Taking the design of a certain type of network card as an example, based on the impedance model, through simulation, the target impedance is controlled in different frequency bands. The method is verified by measuring the dynamic characteristics and noise of the chip power supply.

Keywords: Power integrity · Small signal model · Transmission matrix
Impedance control

1 Introduction

With the development of ultra-large-scale integrated circuit technology, the operating voltage of the chip is getting lower and lower, and the working speed is getting faster and faster, the power consumption is getting larger and larger, the density of the single-board is also getting higher and higher, the operation of each transistor inside the chip is usually synchronized by the core clock or on-chip peripheral clock, but due to the internal delay difference, the state transition of each transistor can not be strictly synchronized [1], when some transistors have completed the state transition, other transistors may still be in the conversion process in. A high-level gate inside the chip will transmit power noise to the input of other gates, if the gate receiving power noise is in an unstable state of level shifting at this time, the power supply noise may be amplified and the output of the gate circuit generates a rectangular pulse disturbance, which in turn causes a logic error in the circuit. Noise at the external power supply pins of the chip propagates through the internal gate circuitry and may also trigger internal register generation. In addition to affecting the operating state of the chip itself, power supply noise also affects other parts, for example, power supply noise affects the jitter characteristics of the crystal, PLL, and DLL, and the conversion accuracy of the AD conversion circuit.

Now, the clock frequency of the microprocessor's core and peripherals has exceeded 800 MHz, and the internal transistor's level conversion time has dropped

W. Xu et al. (Eds.): NCCET 2018, CCIS 994, pp. 120–130, 2019.
https://doi.org/10.1007/978-981-13-5919-4_12

below 800 ps, therefore, higher requirements are placed on the stability of the power supply system in the entire operating frequency band. The level of PI design directly affects the performance of the system, such as overall reliability, signal-to-noise ratio and bit error rate, EMI/EMC and other important indicators. Excessive board-level power channel impedance and synchronous switching noise SSN excessively contribute to severe power integrity issues, which can have fatal effects on device and system operation stability.

2 Research Status

PI design is to ensure that the quality of board-level power supply meets the requirements of the device and product through reasonable planar capacitance, discrete capacitance, and planar segmentation applications, ensuring signal quality and stable operation of devices and products. Figure 1 shows the characteristic diagram of a typical power distribution system for a high-speed circuit system. In the figure, we divide the entire power supply band into parts. In the low frequency range, the power supply noise mainly depends on the power conversion chip VRM to filter; in the frequency range of a few MHz to several hundred MHz, the power supply noise is mainly filtered by the board-level discrete capacitors and the PCB's power ground plane pair; in the high frequency part, the power supply noise is mainly filtered by the decoupling capacitor system and the high-frequency capacitors inside the chip [2, 3]. When the transient current of the load is changed, because the internal transistor level of the load chip is extremely fast, the load chip must be supplied with enough current in a very short time, but the voltage regulator source cannot respond to the change of the load current quickly. There are usually many capacitors placed around the load chip to meet the load transient current requirements.

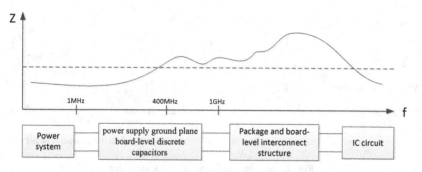

Fig. 1. Power distribution system features

It is relatively intuitive to understand the principle of power supply decoupling from the perspective of energy storage, but it does not help the circuit design. Understanding capacitive decoupling from the perspective of impedance can allow us to design the circuit in a rule-based manner. From the chip point of view, the power supply system, PCB power ground plane and capacitive decoupling system can be called a composite power supply system, when the PI design is carried out, it is necessary to ensure that the voltage of the power supply system remains stable regardless of how the load current of the chip changes. It is required that the impedance of the power supply system in the characteristic frequency band be sufficiently low. Because of the limitation of volume, efficiency and switching frequency, the power system bandwidth is usually lower than 20 MHz, the loop design needs to ensure the dynamic characteristics within the working bandwidth. Output filter capacitors, inductors and other power devices are mainly selected on the output load current and ripple requirements, so the impedance analysis of the power system is mainly concentrated in the working bandwidth, based on the small signal modeling of the power system; Through the reasonable setting of PCB copper foil size, grid distribution shape, board-level discrete capacitors, pcb power ground plane and board-level discrete capacitors can well suppress the mid-range 20 M–1000 M noise; At high frequencies, due to the black box characteristics of the chip, the high-frequency capacitance distribution inside the chip package cannot be known. Therefore, the ground plane and in-package capacitance of the PCB power supply are generally used to suppress high-frequency noise.

The power system, PCB power ground plane, and decoupling capacitor system can all be equivalent to a two-port transmission matrix network. The network has four main parameters: input impedance, output impedance, reverse current gain, and audio attenuation rate. The input and output impedances are reflected its coupling relationship with other cascade systems, so based on the impedance characteristics to analyze the coupling characteristics of the cascade system can reflect some of the system's essential problems, Fig. 2 shows the parameters of the dual-port network model, the input can be expressed as the Norton equivalent circuit and the output can be expressed as the Thevenin equivalent circuit.

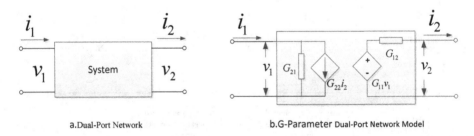

a.Dual-Port Network   b.G-Parameter Dual-Port Network Model

Fig. 2. System dual-port network structure

Among them, G_{11} is the voltage audio attenuation rate, G_{12} is the output impedance, G_{21} is the input admittance, and G_{22} is the reverse current gain. The parameter transfer function can be obtained by measuring the frequency response of the port to describe the dynamic characteristics of the DC/DC converter. Equation (1) describes the relationship between the input and output variables of the converter.

$$\begin{bmatrix} v_2 \\ i_1 \end{bmatrix} = \begin{bmatrix} G_{11} & G_{12} \\ G_{21} & G_{22} \end{bmatrix} \begin{bmatrix} v_1 \\ i_2 \end{bmatrix} \tag{1}$$

3 Method and Model

When the power system operates near a certain steady-state operating point, the relationship between the small-signal disturbance quantities of the circuit state variables exhibits a linear characteristic [4]. Through perturbation and linearization, small-signal AC equations can be obtained. The small signal AC model of the basic DC power system can be unified into a standard form called a unified circuit model. As shown in Fig. 3. The dotted line box is a DC/DC conversion system, and the rear stage is schematic express a board-level discrete capacitor, PCB power supply ground plane system or decoupling capacitor system.

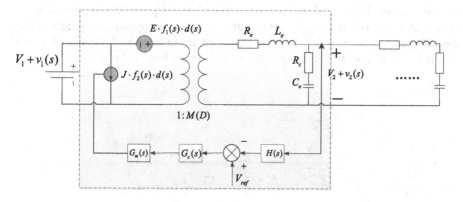

Fig. 3. Unified circuit model of power system

Assume that the input reference voltage perturbation $v_{ref}(s) = 0$, in the case of $v_1(s) = 0$, as shown in Fig. 4, a simplified small signal model system block diagram [5] is established for the output current to the output voltage, deduces the transfer function of the output impedance from the definition of the output impedance, which results in:

$$G_{12CL} = \frac{G_{12OL}}{1+T} \tag{2}$$

Among them, G_{12OL} is closed loop output impedance, G_{12OL} is open loop output impedance, T is loop gain.

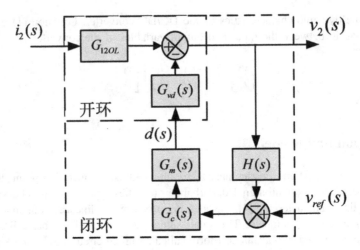

Fig. 4. Simplified small signal model system block diagram for output current to output voltage in $v_1(s) = 0$

The actual size of the planar PCB power supply ground plane is very important for its performance. Figure 5 shows a pair of power/ground plane RLCG equivalent circuits with M * N cell grid equivalent circuits [6], where the equivalent circuit model of the cell grid uses the π model. To ensure the accuracy of the model, the size of the cell grid is less than 1/10 of the shortest wavelength in the band to be analyzed.

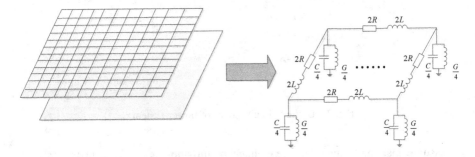

Fig. 5. RLCG equivalent circuit for power/ground plane

The package and PCB power ground plane can be represented by the cascade of the equivalent circuit of the cell grid. Therefore, the two-port transmission matrix method can be used to perform efficient analysis and simulation of arbitrary shapes and complex power/ground planes, as shown in Fig. 5, the power/ground plane is divided into $(M-1) * (N-1)$ cell grids, the transmission matrix has $M * N$ inputs and $M * N$ outputs, and the transmission matrix can be simplified as:

$$T_p = \begin{bmatrix} A_p & B_p \\ C_p & D_p \end{bmatrix} = \begin{bmatrix} I & 0 \\ C_p & I \end{bmatrix} \tag{3}$$

Among them, I represents unit matrix, 0 identifies 0 matrix, C_P is a $(M * N) *$ $(M * N)$ matrix. The decoupling capacitor and transmission matrix of the through hole can be obtained by the same method [7]. After obtaining the transmission matrix of each part of the multilayer power/ground plane, it can be expressed as a total transmission matrix representing multilayer power/ground plane. Figure 6 shows the input and output of the entire model. According to Fig. 6, the total transmission matrix can be calculated. The impedance matrix can be obtained by the relationship between the transmission matrix and the impedance matrix.

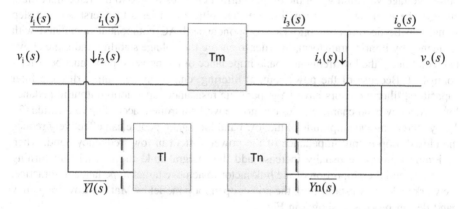

Fig. 6. Block diagram of a multi-layer power/ground plane system

According to the transmission matrix of each part, the required impedance matrix can be expressed as:

$$Z = \begin{bmatrix} Z_A & Z_B \\ Z_C & Z_D \end{bmatrix} = \begin{bmatrix} R_n \times C_{inv} \times D_l & A_n \times C_{inv} \times D_l \\ A_n \times C_{inv} \times D_l & A_n \times C_{inv} \times R_l \end{bmatrix} \tag{4}$$

Among,

$$C_{inv} = \left([C_l \quad D_l] \times \begin{bmatrix} A_m & B_m \\ C_m & D_m \end{bmatrix} \times \begin{bmatrix} A_n \\ C_n \end{bmatrix} \right)^{-1}, R_n = A_m \times A_n + B_m \times C_n, R_l$$
$$= C_l \times B_m + D_l \times D_m$$

4 Simulation and Test

Take a certain type of 10G fiber network adapter module as an example to illustrate the high-speed system power supply integrity design based on impedance analysis [8]. The module core chip uses a T5 network card chip, 5VDC single power input, and the power required by the device is obtained through DC-DC conversion. The chip manual requires the power supply accuracy is within ±4% under any operating conditions, including DC voltage drop and AC disturbances. Based on the DC-DC power supply and the PCB's operating characteristics, in the process of controlling the impedance on full-band, the DC voltage drop, the voltage output overshoot when the load step changes, and the resonance of the possible output line near the operating frequency, may all cause the voltage output to overflow [9]. The above conditions need special consideration.

In the low frequency range, the DC voltage drop is reflected by the load regulation rate, which is usually expressed as a percentage of the output voltage divided by the output voltage variation when the output current changes from 0 to the rated maximum current; the load step change will cause the voltage transients to overshoot, the step signal can be decomposed into DC component and AC component attenuated with frequency by Fourier transform, in order to ensure the voltage stability under the above two conditions, the low frequency band impedance of the power supply must be strictly controlled. Because of the power output filtering. characteristic, output discrete filter capacitors, filter inductors have large parasitic resistance, open-loop output impedance low frequency band characteristics can not be well controlled, according to formula (3–1), by increasing the amplitude of the low band loop gain, people can effectively reduce the closed loop output impedance of the power system in low frequency band. when designing power, we usually increase add the integral link, the inertial link turning frequency and the proportion of the link factor to achieve target impedance, in practice, the work is done by establishing the power open loop model by Matlab. Low frequency band design process is shown in Fig. 7.

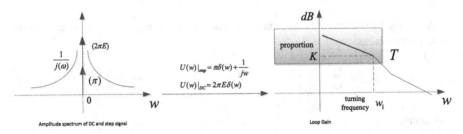

Fig. 7. Low-band impedance control diagram for power system

In the mid-range, to avoid band noise in the power supply coupling into the power supply loop, an inertia section in the middle band is required to reduce the mid-range noise gain, and the loop gain amplitude rapidly decreases [10]. Therefore, in order to control the closed-loop output impedance of the middle band, the output filter transfer function must be controlled to reduce the open-loop output impedance, thereby the closed-loop output impedance is controled. Based on Figs. 3 and 4, combined with the loop gain, a closed-loop model of the power supply is built in Matlab. The mid-band design flow is shown in Fig. 8.

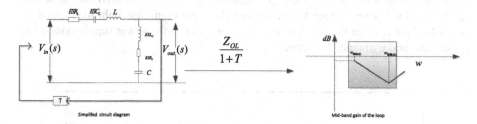

Fig. 8. Mid-range band impedance control diagram in power system

Set up the power system model in Saber simulation software for time domain simulation. Use the constant current source analog power supply at the power load end to simulate the output varies from 20% light load to 80% heavy load to 20% light load. Compare the impedance of output before and after, the voltage overshoot is significantly reduced. The result is as shown in Fig. 9.

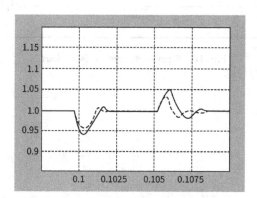

Fig. 9. Comparision of voltage dynamic characteristics in two conditions

In the mid-high band, the characteristics of the power supply and discrete components are inductive. In order to control the output impedance, impedance control in the mid-high frequency band is usually achieved by establishing a reasonable power supply system structure [11]. Since the power supply ground plane forms a resonant cavity in the PCB structure, if the resonant frequency point appears near the operating frequency, it may easily cause abnormal operation of the chip. Based on Fig. 6, passive simulation of the PCB design model is performed through Ansoft SIwave, S-parameters and resonance mode analysis are performed, the resonance occurrence region and frequency are viewed, and the mid-high frequency band is improved by lowering the capacitance (0.1 to 0.01 uF) or making a thin dielectric layer PCB impedance [12], Fig. 10 shows a comparison of PCB parameters before and after the improvement of S-parameters. The resonance is significantly be suppressed.

The PI test is performed on the actual module after the impedance control [13, 14], ripple and noise waveform in mid-high frequency band (20–1000 MHz) are as shown in Fig. 11, load point voltage waveform switching between 20% light load and 80% heavy load is shown in Fig. 12. The waveform proves that the power supply system has good static and dynamic characteristics.

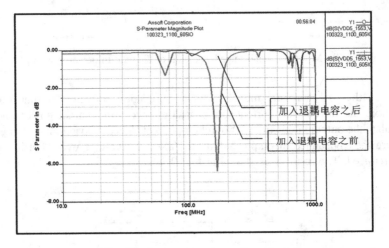

Fig. 10. S-parameter comparison chart

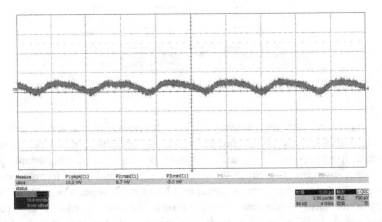

Fig. 11. Measured waveform by oscilloscope (ripple and noise in 20–1000 MHz)

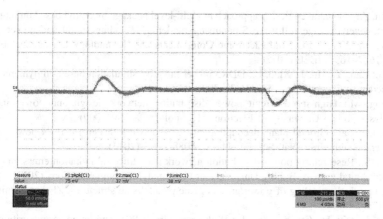

Fig. 12. Measured waveform by oscilloscope (switching between 20% light load and 80% heavy load)

5 Summary

The paper innovatively combines power supply design and PCB design, Conduct impedance analysis and control from the whole process of design. Paper takes the high-speed circuit power integrity design as the background, and studies the method of improving power integrity from the perspective of impedance. Based on the concept of port network, the power system small signal model and PCB power ground plane system impedance model are established, from the low frequency band, the middle frequency range, and the medium high band, the impedance control method was proposed in the aboved three aspects of the frequency band. Using a certain type of network card as a design example, the correctness of the impedance control method is verified by measuring the dynamic characteristics of the power supply and the noise distribution. Based on the research of the paper, in the future [15], a more efficient and dynamic model of the power distribution system needs to be established for precise impedance control in order to improve the power supply efficiency and reduce the development cost.

References

1. Hu, H.: Research on power supply noise suppression in high speed digital system. Xidian University of Electronic Technology (2017)
2. Shuqiang, Y., Chunyan, K., Chaoyang, L.: Research on power integrity of high speed wireless data transmission system. Wirel. Commun. Technol. **34**(4), 55–58 (2012)
3. Su, H.: Optimization design of high-speed circuit power network based on hybrid simulation. Space Return Remote. Sens. **18**(5), 50–56 (2017)
4. Chen, H.: Research on the influence of PDN noise on high speed parallel link. Xidian University of Electronic Technology (2017)

5. Chen, Z.: A general co-design approach to multi-level package modeling based on individual single-level package full-wave S-parameter modeling including signal and power/ground ports. In: 2012 IEEE 62nd Electronic Components and Technology Conference (ECTC), pp. 1687–1694. IEEE (2012)
6. Li, J., Cao, Y., Hu, J., Xiao, L.: DDR3 power integrity simulation based on dynamic target impedance. Comput. Eng. Sci. **36**(3), 399–403 (2014)
7. Zhang, M.: High-speed circuit power distribution network design and power integrity analysis, Xidian University of Electronic Technology, Xi'an (2009)
8. Liu, L., et al.: Ground plane decoupling capacitor network design for PDN power supply. J. Cent. South Univ. Nat. Sci. Ed. **44**(10), 4088–4093 (2013)
9. Wen, S.: Research on power distribution network and structural radiation emission of high speed digital system. Beijing University of Posts and Telecommunications (2017)
10. Jin, H.: PDN modeling of power/ground plane parallel slab structures. Zhejiang University (2017)
11. Peng, D., Xu, H., Gu, Y., Wan, L.: High-speed circuit PCB and its power integrity design. Autom. Instrum. **37**(3), 5–8 (2016)
12. Ren, B.: Simplified design flow of hardware circuit based on PDN principle. Mod. Electron. Technol. **38**(2), 132–136 (2015)
13. Lei, H.: Design optimization of power distribution network based on target impedance matching. Ordnance Autom. **35**(11), 60–67 (2016)
14. Lu, Y.: High-speed circuit PCB signal integrity and power integrity simulation analysis. Xidian University of Electronic Technology (2015)
15. Gu, X., Gu, D.: Power integrity analysis and application. Electron. Packag. **17**(2), 21–24 (2017)

Applying Convolutional Neural Network for Military Object Detection on Embedded Platform

Guozhao Zeng[1], Rui Song[1], Xiao Hu[1(✉)], Yueyue Chen[1],
and Xiaotian Zhou[2]

[1] College of Computer, National University of Defense Technology,
Changsha 410073, Hunan, China
zgzhl993@hotmail.com, xiaohu@nudt.edu.cn
[2] The Target Support Brigade of STCJOCC,
Guangzhou 510080, Guangdong, China

Abstract. Object detection has always been an important part in the field of image processing. The traditional object detection algorithm has complex structure and operations. With the continuous development of deep learning technology, Convolutional Neural Network (CNN) has become an advanced object detection method. Because of its high accuracy, stability, and speed of operation, this method is widely used in many fields. In this work, we use CNN to achieve the detection of military objects. It uses the idea of regression to build a model, which is fast and accurate and can achieve detection in real-time. Unlike image classification, image detection requires more parameters and calculations, and therefore it is difficult to be placed on a small embedded platform. We analyzed some of state-of-the-art object detection network, replace the traditional fully connected layer with global average pool layer, generate region proposals using the anchor boxes, and apply it to military object detection. Finally, we deployed it successfully on TMS320C6678, which is a low-cost, low-power embedded platform. A well-performing and easy-to-deploy military object detection system is realized, which helps to improve the accuracy and efficiency of military operations.

Keywords: Object detection · CNN · YOLO · DSP · Military object

1 Introduction

Convolutional Neural Network (CNN) based models are the current state-of-the-art for the task of object detection. The accuracy of CNN is based on the massive training of large datasets. To satisfy such a large number of operations, GPUs are usually used to accelerate, which dissipate a huge amount of power. On the other hand, embedded processing and DSPs are excellent low-cost, low-power solutions. As an embedded microprocessor, DSPs are not only powerful for image processing, operation and control capabilities, but also with high performance price ratio, performance power ratio, and performance area ratio. And it has the advantages of software development for scalability and scalability, high quality, high reliability, and has a powerful development tools and developers. It's widely used in military, aerospace, medical and other key areas.

In order to run the object detection network on an embedded platform, we must use a model that has a simple structure and few parameters, but we can not lose its accuracy. In this paper, we analyze and compare the existing excellent detection network, and propose a detection network that is friendly to embedded platforms. We use fine-tuning method to reduce the dependence of network training on datasets. At the same time, the Global Average Pooling (GAP) is used to replace the traditional Fully Connected (FC) layer, which also greatly reduces the number of parameters.

We randomly select images of fighters, tanks and so on, which are open on Google as target datasets. On the one hand, these objects are very valuable. On the other hand, random target datasets are selected and different from the source dataset (ImageNet) which is used to finetune. This can prove the stability and reliability of our model.

2 Related Work

2.1 Traditional Object Detection

Traditional object detection algorithms use artificially designed filters and classifiers. In this way, people's experience and knowledge are used to select features with high discrimination as the representation of candidate regions in the image through information such as texture, color, and statistics of the image. The classifier is then trained to classify these regions. Some good traditional object detection algorithm model is shown in [1–4].

2.2 CNN-Based Object Detection

The methods of using CNN to achieve object detection are mainly divided into two directions. On the one hand, using the Region Proposal Network (RPN) to generate bounding boxes and using CNN to classify, these methods mainly include [5–10]. On the other hand, there have been some methods to convert object detection to regression problems, which do not require region proposal network but regression directly on the input image completes the determination of position and category. Such methods are represented by [11, 12].

Both methods have advantages and disadvantages. The method based on the region proposal has better stability and better performance, but it has a larger amount of computation and takes more time. Regression-based algorithms, such as YOLO, as the name suggests, "You Only Look Once", compared to the R-CNN series of algorithms "see two eyes" or "more eyes," YOLO only needs to "look at one", the speed has increased hundreds of times. But the method that based on the regression is not as effective as the former method in detecting small objects and multiple objects.

In this work, we have measured two methods. We combine with the application of the field, borrow from YOLO's regression ideas, aim at the embedded platform and design a light-weight object detection network.

2.3   Embedded CNN Object Detection

High-performance, high-accuracy deep learning networks mostly have deep structure and need to be combined with GPUs for acceleration. However, as CNN usage demands increase day by day, CNN is deployed on platforms such as ASICs, FPGAs, and DSPs. [13, 14] shows successful cases of deploying CNN object detection on FPGAs and DSPs, which gives us hope. We use the TMDSEVM6678LE (hereinafter referred to as EVM) test board for deployment.

2.4   Application of Object Detection on Military Objects

Object detection is critical to the automation of military operations. There are many ways to apply different detection methods in the military field. Due to the requirements of military scenarios, the performance of traditional object detection algorithms is insufficient. CNN's good performance has provided researchers with new ideas. [15] uses the Fast R-CNN structure to propose a military object detection algorithm that incorporates multi-channel CNN. In [16] Automatic Edge Detection (AEDS) was proposed in the three fields of scale spatial analysis, edge detection and neural network. AEDS delivers very quick edge detection of objects within medium-contrast images, through the automatic selection of a single optimum scale for applying the scale space edge detection to an entire image. Our work is based on CNN and combines on the ideas of YOLO to achieve faster and more accurate military object detection.

3   Method

3.1   Network Architecture

Object detection is the extension and development of image classification. After the advent of CNN, the performance of image classification is constantly being refreshed. The annual ImageNet Large Scale Visual Recognition Competition (ILSVRC) is the most authoritative competition in the field of image classification. The accuracy of all networks tested on the large dataset ImageNet is measure. Table 1 shows parameters and float-point operations (FLOPs) of the ILSRVC championship in recent years.

Table 1. Parameters of the ILSRVC Championship in recent years.

	Error (top-5)	Parameters	Fully-Connected Parameters	FLOPs
AlexNet	15.30%	62M	58M	2.27B
ZF-Net	11.20%	386M	375M	5.52B
VGG-19	7.30%	143M	123M	31.54B
GoogLeNet	6.70%	7M	1M	12.59B
ResNet-152	3.57%	57M	0	29.37B

The network architecture of YOLO is inspired by GoogLeNet model for image classification. YOLO divides the input image into 7×7 grids. Each grid only predicts two boxes and can only have one class. The speed is greatly improved, but it loses certain precision. And it struggles with small objects that appear in groups, such as flocks of birds.

Faster R-CNN implements ZF-Net, VGG, and ResNet. Faster R-CNN uses RPN and ROI Pooling to generate regions of interest (RIO) and map them on feature maps. Finally, finetune those ROI. As can be seen from Table 1, although the fully connected layer can obtain global information, the number of parameters is too large, which accounts for more than 80% of the parameters, and too many parameters will lead to too many calculations. This is not friendly to embedded systems.

The application target of our research is military objects. Compared to ImageNet's 1000-class, our military object dataset only has 6-class, which does not require the extraction and classification of too complex features. At the same time, we aim to deploy on the DSP embedded platform. There is a bottleneck for the number of parameters and calculations. Therefore, a light-weight classification network is used in our work. The network structure is shown in Fig. 1. There are 15 layers in total, 7 convolutional layers which use 3 × 3 kernel. We remove the fully connected layers from YOLO, we use a 1 × 1 convolution and a Global Average Pool instead which greatly reduces the number of parameters. After CNN, we use anchor boxes to predict bounding boxes. In addition, we set the input size as 416 × 416 so that the network can adapt to large size images. And the output size of our network is 13 × 13. Compare to YOLO's 7 × 7 output, our network can detect more objects of different scales. The final detection system is shown as Fig. 2.

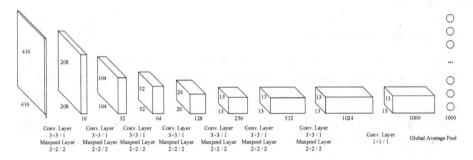

Fig. 1. The classification network in our work uses a fully convolutional network to replace FC with GAP.

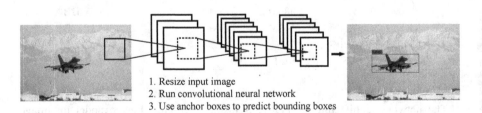

1. Resize input image
2. Run convolutional neural network
3. Use anchor boxes to predict bounding boxes

Fig. 2. The military object detection system.

3.2   Training Methods

For the method of generating bounding boxes, we refer to the anchor boxes used by Faster R-CNN to optimize the YOLO detection method and improve the precision. We don't use the 9 types of anchor boxes in Faster R-CNN. Instead, K-means clustering is used to generate anchor boxes sizes that are more suitable for our dataset. The size of the anchor boxes are relative to the output image, and we regress directly on the final feature map. We know that the down-sampling rate of the network is 32, so only the size of anchor boxes generated by the K-means needs to be scaled ($\times 32$).

We use the transfer learning method to solve the problem of training non-convergence that may be caused due to insufficient datasets. Firstly, we pretrain our classification network on the ImageNet 1000-class competition dataset, and the resulting model was used as the initial parameter for finetuning the entire detection network. In this way, can the network converge faster.

Unlike Faster R-CNN, which deploys a 4-step alternating training strategy to train RPN and detector network, our network is end-to-end training. So, we only need to pay attention to the input and output. Similar to YOLO, we use the same multi-class loss function as YOLO (Eq. 1).

$$
\begin{aligned}
loss = {} & \lambda_{coord} \sum_{i=0}^{S^2} \sum_{j=0}^{K} l_{ij}^{obj} (x_i - \hat{x}_i)^2 + (y_i - \hat{y}_i)^2 \\
& + \lambda_{coord} \sum_{i=0}^{S^2} \sum_{j=0}^{K} l_{ij}^{obj} (\sqrt{w_i} - \sqrt{\hat{w}_i})^2 + (\sqrt{h_i} - \sqrt{\hat{h}_i})^2 \\
& + \sum_{i=0}^{S^2} \sum_{j=0}^{K} l_{ij}^{obj} (C_i - \hat{C}_i)^2 \\
& + \lambda_{noobj} \sum_{i=0}^{S^2} \sum_{j=0}^{K} l_{ij}^{obj} (C_i - \hat{C}_i)^2 \\
& + \sum_{i=0}^{S^2} l_{ij}^{obj} \sum_{c \in classes} (p_i(c) - \hat{p}_i(c))^2
\end{aligned}
\tag{1}
$$

Where l_{ij}^{obj} denotes that the object appears in cell i and the j-th bounding box in cell i is responsible for the detection of the object. The loss function classifies and locates errors differently depending on whether there is an object in the grid cell. x_i, y_i, w_i, h_i corresponds to the ground truth bounding box center coordinates, width and height for objects in grid cell (if it exits) and $\hat{x}_i, \hat{y}_i, \hat{w}_i, \hat{h}_i$ represent the corresponding predictions. C_i and $\hat{C}_i$ denote confidence score of non-object at grid cell i for ground truth and prediction. $p_i(c)$ and $\hat{p}_i(c)$ stand for conditional probability for object class c at cell index i for ground truth and prediction respectively. We use similar settings for YOLO's object detection loss minimization and use values of $\lambda_{coord} = 5$ and $\lambda_{noobj} = 1$.

We output class conditional probabilities, the K bounding boxes and their associated confidence scores for each grid. As in YOLO, we consider a responsible bounding box for a grid cell to be the one among the K boxes for which the predicted area and the ground truth area shares the maximum Intersection Over Union. During training, we simultaneously optimize classification and localization error (Eq. 1). For each grid cell, we minimize the localization error for the responsible bounding box with respect to the ground truth only when an object appears in that cell.

4 Experiments

4.1 Dataset

The pre-training of the classification network was performed using the ILSVRC 2012 dataset. The ImageNet dataset contains 1000 classes and more than 12 million images. It is the most standard dataset for test the performance of image classification models in the current deep learning domain.

In this work, 6 types of valuable open military object images such as tanks and fighters on Google were collected as the original data of our military dataset. According to the standard format of PASCAL VOC, each image was named with 6 numbers and use Labeling to annotate object class and location to form a XML file. The dataset includes 6 classes of tank, fighter, airplane, vehicle, artillery, and helicopters, each with 300 original images. Then, the image is subjected to noise, transformation, and other processing, and the dataset is doubled. 60% of them are training sets and 40% are test sets. Relative to the public dataset, our dataset is small, but through transfer learning we have achieved good results on our model.

4.2 Hardware and Software Environment

In our work, the Nvidia GTX 1080Ti GPU was used for training and testing, and the TMDSEVM6678LE was used for deployment. The GTX 1080Ti has 3,584 CUDA cores, each with a base frequency of 1,480 MHz and a maximum frequency of 1,582 MHz, with 11 GB of memory and 11,000 MHz of memory frequency. The PC uses the Intel Core i7-4900 CPU @ 3.60 GHz × 8 and Ubuntu 16.04.

TMDSEVM6678LE is a high-performance, high-efficiency independent development platform that allows users to evaluate and develop applications for TI TMS320C6678 DSP. As shown in Fig. 3, EVM includes a multi-core DSP TMS320C6678, 512M DDR3, 64M NAND Flash, 1MB local boot I2C EEPROM and other peripherals.

4.3 Experimental Results

We used ImageNet to train the classification network. The batch-size was set to 128. After 450,000 iterations, the classification network model was obtained. The top-5 error of the model tested on ImageNet is only 7%. Based on this, we modify the network configuration, the final feature output channel is controlled to 55 which equal to *numbers of output* × (*classes* + λ_{coord} +1)), and the anchor boxes are used for detection operation. Use our military object dataset to finetune on the detection network. Figure 4 shows some examples of our experimental results.

(a)   (b)

Fig. 3. The collected military object dataset. (a) is the original data image collected on Google; (b) is the image after adding salt and pepper noise.

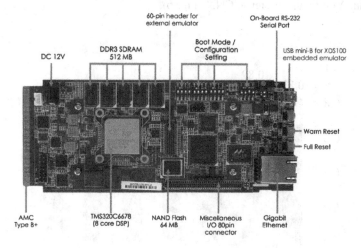

Fig. 4. Texas instruments TMDSEVM6678LE (Evaluation Module) kit.

As shown in Fig. 5, the model of this work can reach 0.75 mAP, and the frames can reach 275 FPS with acceleration of GTX1080Ti and cuDNN. It's so fast and can achieve real-time detection. We randomly select a video to test our model and the result shows that the performance is good.

Since our model lacks a fully connected layer, compared with YOLO and Faster R-CNN, the model parameters and floating-point operations in our work are greatly reduced. The weight file is less than one-tenth, and a small number of parameters are more conducive to our deployment in embedded platform. In order to measure the precision of our model, we also finetune for YOLO and Faster R-CNN with our

Fig. 5. After finetuning, we tested every class with the resulting model.

military object datasets. The results show that a small number of parameters does not lead to a reduction in mean Average Precision (mAP). Instead, the precision of our model is higher than the previous two models. Table 2 shows the comparison of this model with YOLO and Faster R-CNN (Fig. 6).

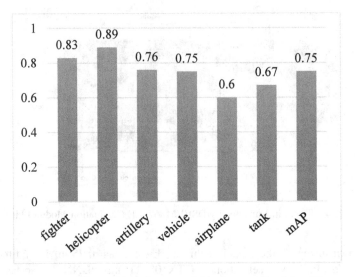

Fig. 6. 6 classes of our military object dataset and it's Average Precision. The mean Average Precision for our model is 0.75.

Table 2. Use our military object dataset to finetune on YOLO Faster R-CNN and our model. Model size FLOPs and mAP are showed that our model is smaller but keeping the precision.

	mAP	Model size	FLOPs
YOLO	0.62	753 MB	34.90 Bn
Faster R-CNN(VGG)	0.73	483 MB	32.65 Bn
This Work	0.75	63 MB	6.97 Bn

4.4 Deployment

We use EVM for network deployment. CCS provides us a platform for compiling codes and downing to EVM. We analyze the time taken by each module to further optimize the acceleration. In Table 3, we use a single core to test our model and list the time for main module on EVM.

Table 3. Time for main module on EVM Single core. Load/Store includes follow steps: load input image, symbol library, weights, save output image. Because the weight file in this test is loaded from the PC, Load/Store wastes most of the time.

	Time consuming (%)
Total	100
Load/Store	80
Convolution	12
Pooling	3
Detection	2

We can find that apart from the data I/O time, the largest proportion of the time in the calculation process is the convolution operation, which is also the main operation of the convolutional neural network. So, if we can optimize the convolution operation, the speed will increase a lot. In Table 3, we use gemm function on Caffe for convolution which is the matrix tiling convolution method. However, TI provides developers with library functions such as MCSDK, CSL, and DSPLIB, optimized for DSP architecture. The DSP_sp_mat_mul function in DSPLIB can be also used for convolution. In Table 4, we compare direct convolution, gemm method and DSP_sp_mat_mul method

Table 4. The result of testing the direct convolution, gemm and DSP_sp_mat_mul. In the test, input map size is set to $3 \times 416 \times 416$, kernel size is set to 3×3 and the stride and pad are both set to 1.

	Time (s)
direct convolution	3.37
gemm	1.75
DSP_sp_mat_mul	0.54

and find the DSP_sp_mat_mul is the fastest method for convolution. So, we use DSP_sp_mat_mul to replace the gemm function.

We use the stbimage image processing library function to perform image prepro- cessing and read/write operations. Master-slave mode is used to perform reasonable parallel scheduling of calculations. Finally, we test the performance of our military object detection network on PC and EVM evaluation board. The result is shown in Table 5. With same frequency, the speed of EVM can be similar to PC.

Table 5. We deploy our network on EVM and optimize it in parallel. After optimizing, the time running on EVM is close to it on i7-4790 CPU.

	mAP	Time
i7-4790 CPU 8 Cores @ 3.6 GHz	0.75	1.36 s
TMS320C6678 Single Core @ 1 GHz	0.75	24.12 s
TMS320C6678 8 Cores @ 1 GHz	0.75	4.85 s

5 Conclusion

Military object detection is an important part of military operations. In this work, we analyze the current CNN classification network and object detection network. Using the ideas of YOLO and Faster R-CNN which are state-of-art, we use a full convolu- tional network and anchor to construct a military object detection network. In the six targets of this paper's dataset, the mAP reaches 0.75. Compared with YOLO and Faster R-CNN, the weight file in this paper is less than one-tenth. The floating-point operation is only 6.97 BFLOPs. Finally, the detection network of this paper was successfully deployed on the EVM platform.

References

1. Viola, P., Jones, M.: Fast and robust classification using asymmetric adaboost and a detector cascade. Adv. Neural. Inf. Process. Syst. **14**, 1311–1318 (2001)
2. Sedaghat, A., Mokhtarzade, M., Ebadi, H.: Uniform robust scale-invariant feature matching for optical remote sensing images. IEEE Trans. Geosci. Remote Sens. **49**(11), 4516–4527 (2011)
3. Zhu, Q., Yeh, M.: Fast human detection using a cascade of histograms of oriented gradients. In: IEEE Conference on Computer Vision and Pattern Recognition (CVPR), New York, pp. 886–893 (2006)
4. Felzenszwalb, P., Huttenlocher, D.: Pictorial structures for object recognition. Int. J. Comput. Vis. **61**(1), 55–59 (2005)

5. Girshick, R., Donahue, J., et al.: Rich feature hierarchies for accurate object detection and semantic segmentation. In: IEEE Conference on Computer Vision and Pattern, pp. 580–587 (2014)
6. He, K., Zhang, X., Ren, S., et al.: Spatial pyramid pooling in deep convolutional networks for visual recognition. IEEE Trans. Pattern Anal. Mach. Intell. **37**(9), 1904–1916 (2014)
7. Girshick, R.: Fast R-CNN. In: IEEE International Conference on Computer Vision, pp. 1440–1448. IEEE Computer Society (2015)
8. Ren, S., He, K., Girshick, R., et al.: Faster R-CNN: towards real-time object detection with region proposal networks. In: International Conference on Neural Information Processing Systems, pp. 91–99. MIT Press (2015)
9. Dai, J., Li, Y., He, K., et al.: R-FCN: object detection via region-based fully convolutional networks (2016)
10. He, K., Gkioxari, G., Dollár, P., et al.: Mask R-CNN. In: IEEE International Conference on Computer Vision, pp. 2980–2988. IEEE (2017)
11. Redmon, J., Divvala, S., Girshick, R., et al.: You only look once: unified, real-time object detection. In: Computer Vision and Pattern Recognition, pp. 779–788. IEEE (2016)
12. Liu, W., et al.: SSD: single shot multibox detector. In: Leibe, B., Matas, J., Sebe, N., Welling, M. (eds.) ECCV 2016. LNCS, vol. 9905, pp. 21–37. Springer, Cham (2016). https://doi.org/10.1007/978-3-319-46448-0_2
13. Nakano, T., Morie, T., Iwata, A.: A face/object recognition system using FPGA implementation of coarse region segmentation. In: SICE 2003 Conference, vol. 2, pp. 1552–1557. IEEE (2004)
14. Tripathi, S., Dane, G., Kang, B., et al.: LCDet: low-complexity fully-convolutional neural networks for object detection in embedded systems. In: Computer Vision and Pattern Recognition Workshops, pp. 411–420. IEEE (2017)
15. Liu, S., Liu, Z.: Multi-channel CNN-based object detection for enhanced situation awareness (2017)
16. Khashman, A.: Automatic detection of military targets utilizing neural networks and scale space analysis. In: Proceedings of the NATO RTO-IST Symposium RTO-MP-049, pp. 25.1–25.6 (2001)

An Optimization Scheme for Demosaicing Algorithm on GPU Using OpenCL

Tongli Wang, Wei Guo, and Jizeng Wei[✉]

School of Computer Science and Technology, Tianjin University, Tianjin, China
{tongliwang,weiguo,jizengwei}@tju.edu.com

Abstract. With the popularity of GPU which has the high performance computing feature, more and more algorithms have been successfully transplanted to the GPU platform and achieved high efficiency. But existing videos or images processing methods, such as demosaicing algorithm, have not fully exploited the parallel computing capacity of heterogeneous processing platform and the video frame rates can't meet real-time requirements. In order to take full advantage of the computing power of GPU under the heterogeneous processing platform, an optimization scheme is proposed in this paper. We use the demosiacing algorithm as a case and modify the algorithm. By exploiting the GPU's memory hierarchy, the optimization scheme improves the parallelism of the algorithm while reducing the memory access latency, and greatly reduces the execution time. Then we achieve the zero-copy at the same time. The experimental results show that optimization version has a significant performance improvement, the optimized OpenCL version is up to 6x comparing with the basic OpenCL version about kernel execution.

Keywords: Parallel processing · Image demosaicing
Heterogeneous platform · OpenCL

1 Introduction

Digital cameras are increasingly widespread, and camera modules are now embedded in a variety of handheld devices including mobile phones and tablet PCs. Due to the cost of imaging, most digital camera imaging chips only have one CMOS or CCD sensor chip, each sensor surface is covered with a color filter array [1,2] (Color Filter Array, CFA), such as Fig. 1. The conventional color filter array limits the arrival of only one base light per pixel location, capture only one color component at each spatial location. The remaining components must be reconstructed by interpolation from the captured samples. So that the other two colors of the color image will be interpolated with the sampling result of the adjacent pixels of the sampling matrix in the case of single block inductive chip samples [3]. This color plane interpolation algorithm is called image to mosaic. In the early stage of the computer technology, graphics processing and computing are relatively simple, we can use the CPU to achieve graphics processing.

© Springer Nature Singapore Pte Ltd. 2019
W. Xu et al. (Eds.): NCCET 2018, CCIS 994, pp. 142–152, 2019.
https://doi.org/10.1007/978-981-13-5919-4_14

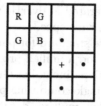

Fig. 1. Bayer CFA

But with the development of computer technology, especially the requirements on the quality of graphics processing and computing speed continue to improve, this needs to find new ways to meet the increasing requirements.

Nowadays, parallel computers are not expensive and exquisite because almost all PCs have multicore hardware. Basically, there are two main multi-core approaches: integrating some of the core into a single microprocessor (multi-core CPU), or integrating a large number of cores to the current graphics processing unit (GPU) as an example [4]. The GPU was originally designed specifically for graphics applications and image rendering required during the rasterization process. Over time the computational resources of modern graphics processing units became suitable for certain general parallel computations because of the inherent parallel processing capabilities of the architecture [5]. By starting multiple execution threads, we can take advantage of all of these multicore hardware.

So, heterogeneous computing of CPU and GPU become the mainstream platform of high performance computing, which has great advantages in computing energy efficiency compared with multi-core processors and has been well verified by the parallelization of multiple algorithms.

In this paper, we propose an optimization scheme for demosaicing algorithm. The objective of this implementation is to demosaic image as fast as possible, so that the video editing workflow will be accelerated. To achieve this, we first introduce the parallel processing of the algorithm as the base method. Then we propose two implementation methods, one is reducing input and output transfer between global and shared memory when data transmission between GPU and CPU, another is reducing the number of work items and queuing time by changing the distribution of working groups. Finally, we come to the conclusion.

2   Related Work

[6] proposed an improved linear interpolation for demosaicking of Bayer-patterned color filter array (CFA) images. An efficient edge-based technique for color filter array demosaicking is presented in [2]. The authors in [1] introduce an efficient demosaicking method based on an advanced nonlocal mean filter using adaptive weight with consideration of both neighborhood similarity and patch distance.

Meanwhile, several works have been dedicated to implement demosaicing using GPU. An efficient implementation of Bayer demosaic filtering on GPUs was published in [7]. McGuire accelerated MalvarHe-Cutlere [8] image demosaicing algorithm using OpenGL in real-time speed.

OpenCL is the first open, free standard for parallel programming for general purpose heterogeneous systems and a unified programming environment, which is used to program multiple devices, including GPU and CPU, as well as other computing devices as part of a single computing platform. OpenCL uses parallel execution SIMD (single instruction, multiple data) engines found in General Purpose Graphics Processing Units (GPGPU) and Compute Cores(CC) to enhance data computational density by performing massively parallel data processing on multiple data items, across multiple compute engines. Each compute unit has its own ALUs, including pipelined floating-point (FP) units, integer (INT) units that can perform computations as well as transcendental operations.

Due to the good cross platform and parallelism of OpenCL, in recent years, OpenCL has also been widely used in image processing and algorithm acceleration. For example, [5] proposes a parallel implementation and optimization method for the real-time dehazing of the high definition videos based on a single image haze removal algorithm.

In this paper, we further modified and optimized the demosaicing algorithm. The presented OpenCL implementation in paper is 6 times faster than the GPU implementation in [7] using the same filter. And we use the 4th Generation Intel® Core^{TM} Processor family which includes complex SoCs integrating multiple CPU Cores, Intel® Processor Graphics, and potentially other fixed functions all on a single shared silicon die. And the GPU and CPU share the Last Level Cache (LLC).

3   Parallel Implementation and Optimization of Demosiacing Algorithm Based on OpenCL

In an OpenCL execution model, the host program is responsible for managing and scheduling OpenCL-supported computing devices. When the host side submits the kernel to computing devices, serial code defines the organization structure of the work item through the global index space (NDRange) and the operation mode of the kernel on the computing device through the mapping method on the computing device, as shown in Fig. 2.

Figure 3 shows that the OpenCL memory architecture is divided into four parts: global memory, constant memory, local memory, and private memory, as shown in the figure. The sizes and corresponding access speeds of these memory types are different. Data can flow along the channel of host memory, global memory, local memory, private memory. When optimizing the OpenCL kernel program, it's an important part to fully tap the potential of the GPU's storage hierarchy based on the characteristics of the algorithm.

3.1   Algorithm Modification

The Intel Graphics device is equipped with several Execution Units (EUs). EUs are Simultaneous Multi-Threading (SMT) compute processors that drive

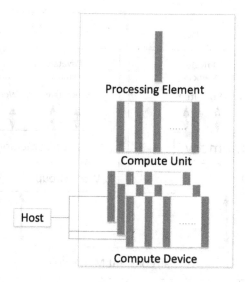

Fig. 2. OpenCL platform model

multiple issuing of the Single Instruction Multiple Data Arithmetic Logic Units (SIMD). Compiler generates SIMD code to map several work-items to be executed simultaneously within a given hardware thread. The SIMD-width for kernel is a heuristic driven compiler choice. Therefore, the basic algorithm version suffers a significant performance improvement.

[6] presented an OpenGL implementation of the Malvar-HeCutler filter. [7] also provide a GPU Filters which includes the filter coefficients. And the GPU Filters can achieve SIMD such as MADD and ADD on 4-vectors at the same speed as on scalars. For example, when calculating the float4 value PATTERN, we use the following formula:

$$
\begin{aligned}
PATTERN+\ =&(kA.xyz * (float3)(value.x, value.x, value.x)).xyzx+ \\
&(kE.xyw * (float3)(value.z, value.z, value.z)).xyxz
\end{aligned}
\tag{1}
$$

There are many similar formulas in the kernel to adapt to the characteristics of SIMD. This will make the most advantage of SIMD and reduce the amount of calculation steps and running time.

For a given SIMD-width, if all kernel instances within a thread are executing the same instruction [12], then the SIMD lanes can be maximally utilized. Moreover, the GPU instruction execution is SIMD, the GPU Vector ALU hardware is more flexible and can efficiently use the floating-point hardware [13]. In this paper, we modified the algorithm code, a lot of uchar8 and float8 data types are used to further speed up the program running time, including addition, multiplication, dot times and other operations. So we can make full use of the SIMD-width. For example:

$$
uchar8\ lineA = (uchar8)(vload8(0, psrc + mad24(j - 2, 1920, i * 4 - 2)))
\tag{2}
$$

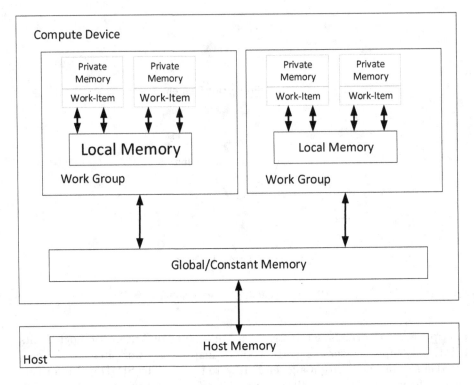

Fig. 3. OpenCL memory architecture

$$
\begin{aligned}
out =&(uchar16)(lineC.s2, convert_u char2(PATTERN\_One.xy), 255,\\
&PATTERN\_Two.z, lineC.s3, PATTERN_Two.w, 255,\\
&lineC.s4, convert_u char2(PATTERN\_Three.xy), 255,\\
&PATTERN\_Four.z, lineC.s5, PATTERN\_Four.w, 255);
\end{aligned}
\tag{3}
$$

Due to the SIMD-width is fully occupied when operations execute, an obvious performance improvement when executed on GPU environment [12]. In addition, by doing so, we can handle four pixels at a time. Algorithm 1 shows the steps of the modified version.

3.2 Data Transmission Optimization

When mapping OpenCL on CPUs, the host and device share the same memory space [4]. Since OpenCL requires explicit data transfers but does not impose restrictions on memory access patterns, it is up to the compiler and to the device driver to select whether or not to actually replicate the data or just read it from already allocated space, and Fig. 4 is the traditional mode of data transmission. To overcome this irregularity, we applied the so called zero copy technique.

To achieve zero copy, the Intel Processor Graphics has a congenital advantage. Intel® Processor Graphics architecture shares DRAM physical memory

Algorithm 1. Optimization demosiacing algorithm

Input: input A 8-bit gray 1920 × 1080 image
Output: output A 32-bit color 1920 × 1080 image
1: Using vload8 instruction to obtain the pixels and assigned to lineA˜ lineE
2: Calculate the filter coefficients
3: Calculate the pattern 4-vector of filter terms
4: Using the pattern to restore the four color pixels A,B,C,D
5: **return** out = (uchar16)(A,B,C,D)

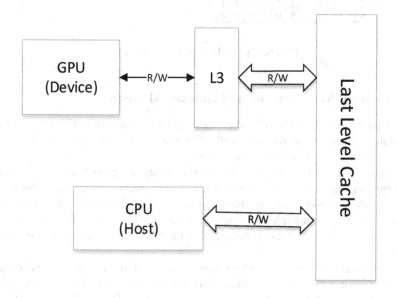

Fig. 4. The original data transfer method

with the CPU like Fig. 5. Thus, the advantage is that shared physical memory enables zero-copy buffer transfers between CPUs and Gen7.5 compute architecture. Moreover, the architecture further augments the performance of this sharing with shared caches. This reduces the overhead of the data transfer.

All data into and out of the samplers and data ports flows through the L3 data cache in units of 64-byte wide cachelines. This includes read and write actions on general purpose buffers. L3 cache bandwidth efficiency is highest for read/write accesses that are cacheline aligned and adjacent within cacheline. Compute kernel instructions that miss the subslice instruction caches also flow through the L3 cache. A kernel should access at least 32-bits of data at a time, from addresses that are aligned to 32-bit boundaries.

In order to improve performance, we use the vload8 and vstore8 to read data from shared memory. On one hand, this will reduce the data transfer time. On the other hand, this also allows four pixels are restored at one time in kernel like Fig. 6.

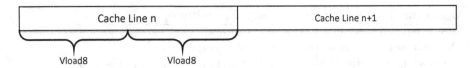

Fig. 5. The optimized data transfer mode

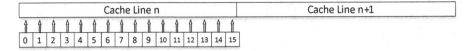

Fig. 6. Vload data to cache at once

3.3 Memory Management and Indexes Memory

There are global memory and local memory in INTEL® PROCESSOR GRAPH-ICS. How to manage the memory will influence the data progress. In this paper, we use a 1920 × 1080 image as an example.

In general, we will allot the size of the image as global memory. Because our kernel will use vload8 to read data, this will waste the memory. So we can shrank a quarter in size and shorten the time about a half. Further, we can set the local memory a multiple of 32, which is the SIMD-width. This is because the work-item will share the local memory, and a SIMD-width size can be suitable the data width.

To optimize performance when accessing __global memory, a kernel must minimize the number of cache lines that are accessed [11]. If a kernel indexes memory, where index is a function of a work-item global id(s), the following factors have big impact on performance:

i The work-group dimensions
ii The function of the work-item global id(s)

The work-group dimensions can affect memory bandwidth. We call a "row" work-group: <16, 1, 1>. With the "row" work-group, get_global_id(1) is constant for all work-items in the work-group, myIndex increases monotonically across the entire work-group, which means that the read from, and myArray comes from a single L3 cache line (16 x sizeof(int) = 64 bytes) like Fig. 7. This will make full use of the bandwidth to read data from cache line.

Also, the function of the work-item global ids can affect memory bandwidth [11]. In our kernel, we use the following way to get work-item ids.

$$
\begin{aligned}
&int\ i = get\_global\_id(0);\\
&int\ j = get\_global\_id(1);\\
&int\ src\_idx = mad24(j, 1920, i * 4);\\
&int\ x = psrc[src\_idx];
\end{aligned}
\tag{4}
$$

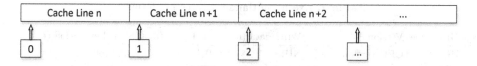

Fig. 7. The read is cache-aligned, and the entire read comes from one cache line. This case should achieve full memory bandwidth

The read is cache-aligned, and the entire read comes from one cache line. This case should achieve full memory bandwidth. This will get full the memory performance. The read from psrc comes from same L3 cache line for 16 work-items. This means a single L3 cache line (16 x sizeof(int) = 64 bytes) will full used.

4   Experimental Results and Performance

We implement the demosiacing algorithm by three ways. First, we use a straight-forward CPU implementation with the filter in [8] using C++ programming. Second, we first implement the basic OpenCL version using the GPU filter in [7]. And the final implementation is the optimized OpenCL version. And the time are divided into three parts: write data to device, read Data from device and kernel execution.

The tests reported in this study were performed on a multiprocessor PC with an Intel(R) HD Graphics 4600 and an Intel core i7-4590 3.30 GHz CPU. Each CPU of the pc has 4 physical cores. As each physical core hosts two virtual cores. The C++ development environment is Microsoft Visual Studio 2017. The OpenCL development environment is an intel sdk with OpenCL version 1.2.

In our paper, we use the 8-bit gray images of three size including 640 × 480, 1024 × 768 and 1920 × 1080. To evaluate the performance on GPU, all versions were run 50 times. Table 1 shows the execution times.

Table 1. Execution times for three image sizes

Image size	Version	Write data (ms)	Read data (ms)	Kernel execution (ms)
640 × 480	CPU version	NULL	NULL	52.8441
1024 × 768		NULL	NULL	81.4833
1920 × 1080		NULL	NULL	131.3766
640 × 480	Basic OpenCL	0.6958	0.8429	0.7288
1024 × 768		0.8958	1.3232	1.0784
1920 × 1080		1.2533	2.0968	1.9415
640 × 480	Optimized OpenCL	0.0154	0.0123	0.2876
1024 × 768		0.0165	0.0133	0.4249
1920 × 1080		0.0167	0.0143	0.7473

Table 2. Execution times for three platforms

GPU type	Version	Write data (ms)	Read data (ms)	Kernel execution (ms)
HD4600	CPU version	NULL	NULL	131.3766
HD530		NULL	NULL	108.4523
HD630		NULL	NULL	90.5148
HD4600	Basic OpenCL	1.2533	2.0968	1.9415
HD530		1.0542	1.3376	1.1365
HD630		0.9856	1.1232	0.9147
HD4600	Optimized OpenCL	0.0167	0.0143	0.7473
HD530		0.0163	0.0145	0.5173
HD630		0.0158	0.0139	0.3473

From Table 1, we can see that the Optimized version has a very significant speedup relatively to the basic OpenCL version, including data transfer and kernel execution no matter which size. The speed of the optimized OpenCL version is improved approximately 200% compared with the CPU version.

In the optimized OpenCL version, the data copy spend little time in memory access and time can be ignored. This result highlight the importance of that GPU and CPU share Last Level Cache (LLC). Due to this reason, data transfer between devices can easily achieve the really zero-copy.

Moreover, the data-width has the fastest kernel execution time. It has improved roughly 60% faster than the basic OpenCL version. This is reason that we make full use of the SIMD optimization. The entire SIMD-width size is fully filled with the data at once, and this reduces the problem of repeated reading of data and cache miss. No matter basic OpenCL version or optimization version, we already use the SIMD instructions, but we can see that the speedup can be greatly improved by make full use of the SIMD-width size.

To further verify the generality of the optimization scheme, we continue to test two multiprocessor PCs. One has an Intel(R) HD Graphics 530 and an Intel core i7-6700 3.40 GHz CPU and another has an Intel(R) HD Graphics 630 and an Intel core i7-7700 3.6 GHz CPU. Other environments are consistent with previous tests. To evaluate the performance on GPUs, we use the 8-bit gray image of 1920 × 1080, and all versions were run 50 times. Table 2 shows the execution times.

As can be seen from the table, the optimization scheme greatly improves the execution speed of the algorithm comparing with the CPU version and basic OpenCL version. Because of zero-copy, the read and write actions take almost no time in the optimized OpenCL version no matter which platform. Due to the improvement in GPU performance, the PC with an Intel(R) HD Graphics 530 is about 40% faster in the basic OpenCL version and about 40% faster in the optimized OpenCL than the PC with HD4600 about kernel execution. The PC with an Intel(R) HD Graphics 630 has the less execution time in all OpenCL versions. In the optimized version, the kernel execution speed is improved by

53% than the PC with HD4600 and 32% than the PC with HD530. This also shows that our scheme is possessed of stronger applicability and generality.

5   Conclusion

The paper presents an optimized scheme about a parallel implementation of demosaicing algorithm using OpenCL. We detailed describe each step about how the original algorithm is implemented, parallelized and optimized. In addition, we introduce how the algorithm executes on the GPU. Specifically, our optimized scheme makes full advantage the modern parallel computing architecture, which increases the parallelism of the process and reduces the computational complexity and the execution time. We implement a basic OpenCL version and further optimized this version. The results show that optimization version has a significant performance improvement about kernel execution, the optimized OpenCL version is up to 6x and the data transmission time is almost zero. And experimental results shows the good applicability of the optimized scheme.

It confirms that the algorithm should be adapted to OpenCL codes accordingly to the hardware execution environments. Indeed, by optimizing the OpenCL code, a 6 speedup yielded by the Optimized OpenCL version comparing with the basic OpenCL version. For some algorithms, it can be well optimized. OpenCL can play a greater role in heterogeneous computing.

Acknowledgements. The work is supported by the Science and Technology Key Project of Tianjin under Grant No. 17YFZCGX01180 and Tianjin Key Laboratory of Advanced Networking (TANK).

References

1. Wang, J., Wu, J., Wu, Z., Jeon, G.: Filter-based bayer pattern CFA demosaicking. Circ. Syst. Sig. Process. **36**(7), 2917–2940 (2017)
2. Chen, R., Jia, H., Wen, X., Xie, X.: Bayer demosaicking using optimised mean curvature over RGB channels. Electr. Lett. **53**(17), 1190–1192 (2017)
3. Lien, C.Y., Yang, F.J., Chen, P.Y.: An efficient edge-based technique for colour filter array demosaicking. IEEE Sens. J. **PP**(99), 1 (2017)
4. Andrade, D.C.D., Trabasso, L.G.: An opencl framework for high performance extraction of image features. J. Parallel Distrib. Comput. **109**, 75–88 (2017)
5. Tan, H., He, X., Wang, Z., Liu, G.: Parallel implementation and optimization of high definition video real-time dehazing. Multimedia Tools Appl. **76**, 1–22 (2016)
6. Wang, D., Yu, G., Zhou, X., Wang, C.: Image demosaicking for Bayer-patterned CFA images using improved linear interpolation. In: Seventh International Conference on Information Science and Technology, pp. 464–469 (2017)
7. McGuire, M.: Efficient, high-quality bayer demosaic filtering on GPUs. J. Graph. GPU Game Tools **13**(4), 1–16 (2008)
8. Malvar, H.S., He, L.W., Cutler, R.: High-quality linear interpolation for demosaicing of Bayer-patterned color images. In: IEEE International Conference on Acoustics, Speech, and Signal Processing, vol. 3, pp. iii–485-8 (2004)

9. Al-Hashimi, B.M.: Energy-efficient run-time mapping and thread partitioning of concurrent openCL applications on CPU-GPU MPSoCs. ACM Trans. Embed. Comput. Syst. **16**(5s), 147 (2017)
10. Dashti, M., Fedorova, A.: Analyzing memory management methods on integrated CPU-GPU systems. ACM SIGPLAN Notices **52**(9), 59–69 (2017)
11. Jang, B., Schaa, D., Mistry, P., Kaeli, D.: Exploiting memory access patterns to improve memory performance in data-parallel architectures. IEEE Trans. Parallel Distrib. Syst. **22**(1), 105–118 (2011)
12. Holewinski, J., Sadayappan, P.: High-performance code generation for stencil computations on GPU architectures. In: ACM International Conference on Supercomputing, pp. 311–320 (2012)
13. Pereira, P.M.M., Domingues, P., Rodrigues, N.M.M., Falcao, G., Faria, S.M.M.D.: Optimizing GPU Code for CPU Execution Using OpenCL and Vectorization: A Case Study on Image Coding. Springer (2016)

The Various Graphs in Graph Computing

Rujun Sun[✉][ID] and Lufei Zhang[ID]

State Key Laboratory of Mathematical Engineering and Advanced Computing,
Wuxi, China
{sun.rujun,zhang.lufei}@meac-skl.cn

Abstract. The world is full of relationships, and graph is the most evident representation for them. With the increasing of data scale, graphs become larger and have encountered a new world of analyzing. What can we learn from a graph? How many kinds of graphs are there? How different is graph from one area to that from another? All these questions need answers, but previous research on graph computing mainly focused on computing frameworks and systems, paying little attention to graph itself.

In this paper, we studied graphs of different kinds, different scales and different mining methods, trying to give a sketcher and classification of graph categories. Besides, we studied characters and analyzed algorithms in each category. We researched public graph datasets to show current graph scale and its trend for future infrastructure.

Keywords: Graph category · Extremely large scale graph
Graph characters

1 Introduction

Relational data plays an important role in big data analysis. Graph is an intuitive and expressive method for relational data representation.

Moreover, graphs have diversity in scale, structure, density, connectivity etc. Different graphs apply to variety kinds of algorithms and applications.

Most graph computing articles focus on computing, while few talk about graph itself. When it comes to graph computing system's evaluation, PageRank, BFS and WCC are most popular benchmark algorithms. Besides, Graph 500 [3] suggests BFS for graph computing ability evaluation. However, are these algorithms enough for diverse graph applications? Will different types of graphs apply to such algorithms?

In this research, we focus on graph itself, to find out its characters and diversity in different domains. Section 2 will introduce some cataloging methods and a brief category of graphs. Section 2.3 will study on scale of graphs and the infrastructure. In Sect. 4 we will talk about algorithms and characters of a graph. Future work will be in Sect. 5, and conclusion will be drawn in Sect. 6.

W. Xu et al. (Eds.): NCCET 2018, CCIS 994, pp. 153–164, 2019.
https://doi.org/10.1007/978-981-13-5919-4_15

2   Graph Structures

2.1   Graph Basic Structures

As is well known to us, graphs can be regarded as a collection of vertices and edges between them.

Each vertex may have different number of neighbors, which will be shown as degree distribution in the whole graph.

Apart from single relationships, graphs can be complex. Vertices may have various properties and different kind of relationships. The complexity can be categorized and described as dimensions.

Degree Distribution. Power law, or logarithmic degree distribution, has been a common sense in graph computing, especially in web graphs. But the base of power varies. We have seen domain networks with average degree of 8 and web graph with 20 or higher [37].

Moreover, not all realistic graphs obey power law. Road graph, biomedical graph and genome network have their own characters. Sometimes we are not able to obtain the whole graph and some partial graphs may show weak power law or even too small to observe power law.

Self-similarity. Initial research on web graph shows self similarity [21]. Other complex networks indicate the same feature [50]. It happens in most social/information networks and web graphs. Self similarity can help with analysis of extremely large graphs, sampling a subgraph for a brief outline or regarding groups of nodes as item of a sketched graph.

2.2   Graph Dimensions

Graphs are typically multi-model, multi-relational and dynamic. In this subsection, we divided graphs into numbers of dimensions. Dimension(**D**) here means a kind of property in the graph, which is wild-ranging.

1D: Examples contain web graph, a web page hyperlinking to other pages, social network, a person being a friend of another one, as well as road graph, one city connecting to another city by a specific distance. 1-D graph has one kind of items, which include relationship between them.

2D: Examples contain online reviews, a user commenting on a product, flue spread graph, a patient at a location. Sometimes a 2-D graph is also regarded as a bipartite graph.

3D: Examples contain temporal or spacial bipartite graphs, for example, a patient stops at a location with a time-record, a person trusts a website at a time. Another example is person-vehicle-location graph, a person drives a car at a location.

4+D etc: For multi relational graphs, each party of a relation is one dimension.

With number of dimensions increasing, graph can include everything in the world as we want. The dimensions and ranges of a graph only depend on what we care about. Once an aspect of character is defined, it can be a dimension.

Although Dimensions are innumerable, temporal-dimension and special-dimension are the most important.

Temporal Graph. A static graph is probably the snapshot of a temporal graph. Temporal-dimension is object's property of time, creation time, modification time or something else. The available largest research temporal graph is Wikipedia temporal pages [47]. It includes Wikipedia's web page information about not only link between pages, but also page creation time.

With temporal graphs, researchers can analyze graph evolution and predict future vertex/edge creations. Insertion and deletion performance of graph databases can be experimented.

Spacial Graph. Some graphs may have spacial information. Road network is 1-D graph of only spacial information. Information networks, such as Twitter's Tweets graph, have location information of each tweet. Some tweets coming from the same person may have relations, some created from the same location may also have relations.

Except for direct relation, spacial information offers a second view of relations, edge. It can help with some listed item sets, drawing relationships between items and making the set able to do graph computing. Undeniably, spacial information is just an addition to other direct relationships sometimes.

2.3   Graph Scales

With increasing number of netizens, ubiquitous sensors and devices, larger storing capability and higher computing power, graphs are bigger and related to more area.

The scale of a graph may indicate its mining capability and denote the computing resources it needs.

Commercial servers analyzed Weibo graph with 44.27 billion edges [28] and .uk domain web graph with 47.61 billion edges [11]. Graph in Neo4j for IBM Power with 56 TB memory can be larger, which would hold over 1,000 billion edges if vertex is properly and succinctly represented. Known largest FPGA cluster analyze twitter graph with 1.4 billion edges [19].

We analyzed over 1000 graphs from some public data collections (Table 1), which include over 10,000 datasets. (Some item-based datasets for machine learning was omitted.)

Figure 1 shows number of graphs whose edge number are less than 1 million, between 1 million and 1 billion, between 1 billion and 10 billions, between 10 billions and 100 billions and more than 100 billions in Table 1.

Table 1. List of public datasets

DataSets	Scale
SNAP datasets [37]	Small, large
UF Sparse Matrix Collection [20]	Small
Kaggle datasets [33]	Small, large
Pajek datasets [8]	Small
Yahoo web graphs [2]	Large, extreme
LWA datasets [9,10,12]	Small, large, extreme
Datahub of The Linking Open Data cloud diagram [5]	Small, large, extreme

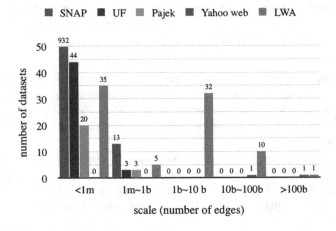

Fig. 1. Scale distribution of selected graph datasets

Small Graphs. Most graphs can be stored and analyzed in a single machine. Personal computer can easily work out an 1 million edge graph. Regular server with 1TB memory can hold over 1 billion edges.

From Fig. 1, there are over 80% graphs within 1 million edges, and over 90% graphs have less than 1 billion edges. Graphs in UF matrix collection and SNAP datasets are almost PC analyzable, which may be caused by needs of variety and easy-glance in such collections. Besides, some graph categories are naturally small in size. For example, road graph, as there are nearly 3 million roads in CA, U.S. [37], 58 millions in U.S. and 45 million in Europe [54]), and we can infer a graph of less than 10 billion edges of the whole world according to limited land-size. Human protein-coding genes can be as few as 19,000 [24].

However, great percentage of small graphs may be caused by limited data collecting abilities and bounded storage power previously. We believe it will be alleviated in the near future.

Large Graphs. Size of some realistic graphs can be inferred as we have done in previous subsection, such as specific social networks, biomedical networks and web graphs.

When we gather more information, graphs become larger. A single PC can not hold such big graphs and thus comes cluster with distributed graph computing frameworks. A regular cluster with tens to hundreds computing nodes can analyze as many as 100 billion edges. Most research work (Table 2) announced 64 to 512 node clusters to prove scalability of graph computing frameworks, with largest graph of nearly hundreds billion edges/items.

Table 2. Scale experiment of distributed graph frameworks

Framework	Cluster size	Largest graph size	Graph type
PBGL [39]	112	256m vertices, 1b edges	Random graph
Pregel [40]	300	50b nodes	Binary trees and lognormal random graphs
GraphLab [25]	64	5.5b edges	(uk) web graph
GraphX [26]	128	3.7b edges	(uk) web graph
Trinity [49]	128	13b edges	Synthetic
Giraph [16]	300	256b edges	(Facebook) social network

m: million, b: billion

As we can see, most big realistic graphs are social networks and web graphs. Generated graph data obeys power law, and is suggested by Graph 500 [3] to have average degree factor of 4.

Extremely Large Graphs. When it comes to extremely large graphs, say 1 trillion edges, clusters need more computing nodes and complicated network solutions, which may still lead to inefficiency. However, cluster is not the only solution. HPC can also deal with graphs, starting from BFS traversal in graph 500 benchmark.

Published largest graph analysis was done by IBM BlueGene/Q, traversing synthetic graph of 2^{41} nodes, with 8.8 trillion edges [3].

We list some large graphs in Table 3. Graphs with trillions of edges are common, let alone that with tens and hundreds billion edges.

However, analysis of extremely large graph is still restricted to basic traversal or structure calculation. Categories of graphs are most web graphs or synthetic power law graphs. Besides, indexing of these graphs is more frequent than analyzing, which has a different (fast and real-time v.s. accurate and informative) computing request. Those variety needs both time-efficient and cost-efficient facilities.

Table 3. Selected large graphs

Graph	Nodes	Edges	Category	Algorithms
Twitter2010	41.7m	1.47b	Social network	Basic structure
Weibo	349.7m	44.27b	Social network	Basic structure (PageRank, SSSP), important nodes
UK-2014	747.8m	47.61b	Web graph	PageRank, WSD
Clueweb	978.4m	42.57b	Web graph	PageRank, WSD
Yahoo web [2]	1.4b	6.6b	Web graph	Basic structure
Facebook12 [7]	721m	137b	Social network	Basic structure
Twitter2012	175m	20b	Social & information network	Basic structure [43]
Facebook	2b	400b	Social network	Label propagation, pagerank, friends of friends score [17]
Google web	1t	-	Web graph	Basic index [6]
Kronecker Gen.	1.1t	4.4t	Gen. graph	BFS on K, Sunway TaihuLight, BlueGene/Q [3]
Kronecker Gen.	2.2t	8.8t	Gen. graph	BFS on BlueGene/Q [3]

m: million. b: billion. t: trillion.

Basic structure: degree distributions, connected components, shortest path lengths, clustering coefficients, and degree assortativity.

Despite of such large graphs and the ability to generate larger ones, extremely large graphs are still around trillion scales, owning to human population and landscape. Graphs of molecule can be larger but may have a different computation model than graph computing (vertex centric, matrix calculation or bulk synchronous parallel iteration).

3   Graph Resources and Characters

Some graph dataset collections have already classified graphs roughly. SNAP [37] has categories such as social networks, communication networks, transportation networks, citations, web graph, product co-purchasing graph, as well as wiki graph, twitter graph and some organization-based graphs. However, such categories may have overlaps and hide features of similar ones.

Graphs of different resource categories have dissimilar structures and may apply to distinct analytical algorithms. Such division is more acceptable in data mining area. In the following subsections, we divide graphs to social networks, web graphs, information networks, road graphs, biology or other domain specific graphs and synthetic graphs. Characters of each category will be listed.

Resource 1: Social Networks

Social Network is a popular kind of graph in data mining. It describes relations between people or group of people in some society, such as a web community, or even bigger, the whole society.

Some famous social networks include Facebook's friends network, Twitter's or Weibo's follower network, academic co-author network, etc.

Basic social network properties come with the structure of a graph. Centrality and prestige help to point out "important nodes" in a graph, which is akin to PageRank algorithm in web graph area. Degree, closeness, betweenness, and information can all weight centrality relations. Besides, clusterability values the ability to gather similar graph nodes. Clustering coefficient, cliques discovering and subgroup comparison come along with this. Roles and positions analysis gives a realistic application in structure analyzing. It also needs a closer look at the local circumstances of our interested nodes. Further more, statistical analyzing is a wild spread method in social network analysis. Examples are simplification of multirelational networks and triad census [29].

Resource 2: Web Graph

Web graph represents for web-page linkage graph. Page-set may be limited in a local network, limited to a domain or expand to the whole web. SNAP has some public web graphs including Stanford's network domain and that of Google. Others contain Yahoo! web graph [2], Clueweb12 [1] dataset and some crawling frameworks such as [12].

Web graph analysis was first developed by search engines [44], and later entered an explosive growth phase. Ranking is the most important application in web graph analysis. Link based [30], visit based [35] and path recommendation based [22] ranking are all variations of initial PageRank. Web graph analysis includes structure analysis, for instance degree distribution, connected component counting, and BFS reachability rates [13]. Another example is evolution analysis, focusing on structure development, which involves temporal graph analysis. As web pages increase, current research changes to web graph compression [11], semantic mining [41], and simulation.

As web graph is naturally large in scale, it becomes a convinced experimental dataset for evaluating large graph computing infrastructure. Google announced that the world websites have reached 1 trillion in 2008 [6] and the number is still growing.

Resource 3: Information Networks

Information network stands for information flow. Some well-known information networks are Twitter's tweets graph by forward, citation graphs(paper cites papers), Wechat's article forward graph, etc.

There are two directions of research, how to design the flow path of information and what can we learn when observing information flow. In such networks, we can design advertisement's broadcast pattern and observe how news spreads [36] or how an idea develops. As information is semantic aware, topic modeling is another application [52].

Information networks often have several dimensions. Pure social network can be its base. [43] analyzed Twitter graph's two-hop neighborhoods and concluded its effectiveness for information dissemination and reception. Other applications include in-network caching, clustering [53] and decoupling of senders and receivers.

Resource 4: Communication Networks

Communication network is also based on social network or some other objects, but is different from information network that it focuses on ordinary communications rather than a piece of information flow.

Previous research has studied group evolving [46] based on change of communication. Some other studies focus on "network" in computing system, design of connections and capacity of cluster's network, such as [18,34,42].

Recent research of communication network in graph computing includes pattern discovery [48], abnormal detection [14] and behavior analysis [31].

Resource 5: Road Graph

Literally, road graph is a description of road network. There is road-net CA, PA and TX in SNAP datasets. Public road network information can be reached at government's website. Similar graphs are realistic or virtual maps.

Algorithms and applications of road network are often related to traversal problems. Single source shortest path, graph coloring and flow/traffic analysis are representations.

Since road graph is based on physical space, the distribution of degree does not obey "power law". Graph algorithms such as coloring may be extremely slow on it than that on power law graphs of the same scale. Diameter of the graph is also large, indicating longer traversal time.

Such graph and algorithms indicate a more weighable standard for graph iterating models and result in a great diversity of the latter, synchronous [40], asynchronous [25] and hybrid-(a)synchronous.

Resource 6: Biology, Physics, etc.

Biological network is a domain specific application in graph computing. Such domains vary from physics to chemistry. Objects in biology (protein, gene and metabolism etc.) have relationships and need both bottom-up inspection and systematic analysis. Engineers have studied graph structures of such biological networks and implied ranking method and clustering analysis [45], helping with similar biological entities identification and co-expressed gene recognition from different organisms. Subgraph finding contributes to functional discovery [32].

Biomedical [38], physics and chemistry networks are similar [51].

Resource 7: Synthetic Graph

Beside realistic graphs, synthetic graph is an addition to relational data analytics. We can generate graphs with parameters that we learned from realistic ones, such as degree distribution, scale and connectivity. Generating methods include

Kronecker product [27], Erdos Renyi method [23], LUBM dataset generator [4] and R-MAT generators [15].

With graph generators, we can obtain large graphs without collecting data exhaustedly, and focus on the development of analysis facilities.

4   Graph Algorithms

Graph algorithms help to study a graph. In this subsection, we will list some graph algorithms to show a brief application of different graphs.

Of a graph: When observing a graph, basic structures of it are calculated, for example, nodes and edges of a graph, degree distribution, (weakly or strongly) connected components number, (single source or multi source) shortest path, clustering coefficients, regular PageRank etc. These structures can not only give a sketch of the graph but also help to decide future computation on it.

On a graph: When we are computing on a graph, it becomes facilities or the "roads" for information flow. Graph coloring, label propagation, network flow design and pestilence simulation are all examples. Algorithms on a graph are more close to realistic applications and other domains.

In a graph: When we are analyzing in a graph, semantics or detail of nodes appear. We could find some subgraphs of a graph, which have some characters, or inspect a small group according to graph clustering result. Algorithms in a graph are more related to the graph itself, which can help with network analysis or relationship mining. Semantic information will be needed after these algorithms for further digging.

5   Future Works

Graphs in graph computing vary from domain to domain. Techniques in one area have been imported to others, but still need deep integration.

Characters of web graph and social networks have been researched, but some specific domain graphs are just a new start to the public. As algorithms are multitudinous, the adaptiveness in different categories needs additional research.

Extremely large graphs are more regular in recent analyzing works. But the they are limited to synthetic graphs. We should aware that realistic graphs are not strictly the same as synthetic ones. Large public datasets will be urgently needed for framework and system evaluations.

What's more, graph computing is still important in relationship analyzing. Facilities for extremely large graphs, including frameworks and hardware systems, are limited in scale and need further development.

6   Conclusion

In this paper, we focused on graphs in graph computing, analyzing different categories and characters of each kind, showing algorithms and applications. We have proved that graphs vary in different domains and resources. Besides, we have studied scale of graphs and computing infrastructure for each scale. From such study, we have drawn a trend for future research on integration of algorithms, collection of larger datasets and innovation of infrastructures.

References

1. The clueweb12 dataset (2012). http://lemurproject.org/clueweb12/
2. Yahoo! altavista web page hyperlink connectivity graph (2012). http://webscope.sandbox.yahoo.com/
3. Graph 500, May 2017. www.graph500.org
4. Lehigh university benchmark (lubm) (2017). http://swat.cse.lehigh.edu/projects/lubm/
5. The linking open data cloud diagram: Datahub (2017). https://datahub.io/dataset
6. Alpert, J., Hajaj, N.: We knew the web was big (2008). http://googleblog.blogspot.com/2008/07/we-knew-web-was-big.html
7. Backstrom, L., Boldi, P., Rosa, M., Ugander, J., Vigna, S.: Four degrees of separation. In: Proceedings of the 4th Annual ACM Web Science Conference, pp. 33–42. ACM (2012)
8. Batagelj, V., Mrvar, A.: Pajek datasets (2006)
9. Boldi, P.: The laboratory for web algorithmics (lwa) datasets, May 2017. http://law.di.unimi.it/datasets.php
10. Boldi, P., Rosa, M., Santini, M., Vigna, S.: Layered label propagation: a multi resolution coordinate-free ordering for compressing social networks. In: Srinivasan, S., Ramamritham, K., Kumar, A., Ravindra, M.P., Bertino, E., Kumar, R. (eds.) Proceedings of the 20th International Conference on World Wide Web, pp. 587–596. ACM Press (2011)
11. Boldi, P., Vigna, S.: The webgraph framework i: compression techniques. In: Proceedings of the 13th International Conference on World Wide Web, pp. 595–602. ACM (2004)
12. Boldi, P., Vigna, S.: The WebGraph framework I: compression techniques. In: Proceedings of the Thirteenth International World Wide Web Conference (WWW 2004), pp. 595–601. ACM Press, Manhattan (2004)
13. Broder, A., et al.: Graph structure in the web. Comput. Netw. **33**(1), 309–320 (2000)
14. Cesa-Bianchi, N., Gentile, C., Mansour, Y., Minora, A.: Delay and cooperation in nonstochastic bandits. In: Conference on Learning Theory, pp. 605–622 (2016)
15. Chakrabarti, D., Zhan, Y., Faloutsos, C.: R-mat: a recursive model for graph mining. In: Proceedings of the 2004 SIAM International Conference on Data Mining, pp. 442–446. SIAM (2004)
16. Ching, A.: Giraph: production-grade graph processing infrastructure for trillion edge graphs. ATPESC ser. ATPESC **14** (2014)
17. Ching, A., Edunov, S., Kabiljo, M., Logothetis, D., Muthukrishnan, S.: One trillion edges: graph processing at facebook-scale. Proc. VLDB Endowment **8**(12), 1804–1815 (2015)

18. Coppola, M., Locatelli, R., Maruccia, G., Pieralisi, L., Scandurra, A.: Spidergon: a novel on-chip communication network. In: 2004 International Symposium on System-on-Chip, Proceedings, p. 15. IEEE (2004)
19. Dai, G., Huang, T., Chi, Y., Xu, N., Wang, Y., Yang, H.: Foregraph: Exploring large-scale graph processing on multi-FPGA architecture. Proc. Multi-FPGA Archit. Vertex **1**(4), 5 (2017)
20. Davis, T.A., Hu, Y.: The university of Florida sparse matrix collection. ACM Trans. Math. Softw. **38**(1), 1:1–1:25 (2011). http://www.cise.ufl.edu/research/sparse/matrices
21. Dill, S., Kumar, R., McCurley, K.S., Rajagopalan, S., Sivakumar, D., Tomkins, A.: Self-similarity in the web. ACM Trans. Internet Technol. (TOIT) **2**(3), 205–223 (2002)
22. Eirinaki, M., Vazirgiannis, M., Kapogiannis, D.: Web path recommendations based on page ranking and markov models. In: Proceedings of the 7th Annual ACM International Workshop on Web Information and Data Management, pp. 2–9. ACM (2005)
23. Erdős, P., Rényi, A.: Asymmetric graphs. Acta Math. Hung. **14**(3–4), 295–315 (1963)
24. Ezkurdia, I., et al.: Multiple evidence strands suggest that there may be as few as 19 000 human protein-coding genes. Hum. Mol. Genet. **23**(22), 5866–5878 (2014)
25. Gonzalez, J.E., Low, Y., Gu, H., Bickson, D., Guestrin, C.: PowerGraph: distributed graph-parallel computation on natural graphs. In: OSDI, vol. 12, p. 2 (2012)
26. Gonzalez, J.E., Xin, R.S., Dave, A., Crankshaw, D., Franklin, M.J., Stoica, I.: Graphx: graph processing in a distributed dataflow framework. In: OSDI, vol. 14, pp. 599–613 (2014)
27. Graham, A.: Kronecker Products and Matrix Calculus: With Applications, p. 130. Wiley, New York (1982)
28. Han, W., Zhu, X., Zhu, Z., Chen, W., Zheng, W., Lu, J.: Weibo and a Tale of two worlds. In: Proceedings of the 2015 IEEE/ACM International Conference on Advances in Social Networks Analysis and Mining 2015, pp. 121–128. ACM (2015)
29. Hanneman, R.A., Riddle, M.: Introduction to social network methods (2005)
30. Henzinger, M.R.: Hyperlink analysis for the web. IEEE Internet Comput. **5**(1), 45–50 (2001)
31. Hildorsson, F., Kvernvik, T.: Method and arrangement for supporting analysis of social networks in a communication network. US Patent 9,305,110, 5 Apr 2016
32. Hu, H., Yan, X., Huang, Y., Han, J., Zhou, X.J.: Mining coherent dense subgraphs across massive biological networks for functional discovery. Bioinformatics **21**(suppl 1), i213–i221 (2005)
33. Kaggle Inc.: Kaggle datasets, May 2017. https://www.kaggle.com/datasets
34. Kistler, M., Perrone, M., Petrini, F.: Cell multiprocessor communication network: built for speed. IEEE Micro **26**(3), 10–23 (2006)
35. Kumar, G., Duhan, N., Sharma, A.: Page ranking based on number of visits of links of web page. In: 2011 2nd International Conference on Computer and Communication Technology (ICCCT), pp. 11–14. IEEE (2011)
36. Lerman, K., Ghosh, R.: Information contagion: an empirical study of the spread of news on digg and twitter social networks. ICWSM **10**, 90–97 (2010)
37. Leskovec, J., Krevl, A.: SNAP datasets: stanford large network dataset collection, Jun 2014. http://snap.stanford.edu/data

38. Li, C., Liakata, M., Rebholz-Schuhmann, D.: Biological network extraction from scientific literature: state of the art and challenges. Briefings Bioinform. **15**(5), 856(2014). https://doi.org/10.1093/bib/bbt006

39. Lumsdaine, A., Gregor, D., Hendrickson, B., Berry, J.: Challenges in parallel graph processing. Parallel Process. Lett. **17**(01), 5–20 (2007)

40. Malewicz, G., et al.: Pregel: a system for large-scale graph processing. In: Proceedings of the 2010 ACM SIGMOD International Conference on Management of data, pp. 135–146. ACM (2010)

41. McBride, B.: Jena: a semantic web toolkit. IEEE Internet Comput. **6**(6), 55–59 (2002)

42. Merolla, P.A., et al.: A million spiking-neuron integrated circuit with a scalable communication network and interface. Science **345**(6197), 668–673 (2014)

43. Myers, S.A., Sharma, A., Gupta, P., Lin, J.: Information network or social network?: the structure of the twitter follow graph. In: Proceedings of the 23rd International Conference on World Wide Web, pp. 493–498. ACM (2014)

44. Page, L., Brin, S., Motwani, R., Winograd, T.: The pagerank citation ranking: Bringing order to the web. Tech. rep, Stanford InfoLab (1999)

45. Pavlopoulos, G.A., et al.: Using graph theory to analyze biological networks. BioData Min. **4**(1), 10 (2011)

46. Rogers, E.M., Kincaid, D.L.: Communication networks: toward a new paradigm for research (1981)

47. Sallinen, S., Iwabuchi, K., Poudel, S., Gokhale, M., Ripeanu, M., Pearce, R.: Graph colouring as a challenge problem for dynamic graph processing on distributed systems. In: Proceedings of the International Conference for High Performance Computing, Networking, Storage and Analysis, p. 30. IEEE Press (2016)

48. Schneider, B., Acevedo, C., Buchmüller, J., Fischer, F., Keim, D.A.: Visual analytics for inspecting the evolution of a graph over time: pattern discovery in a communication network. In: 2015 IEEE Conference on Visual Analytics Science and Technology (VAST), pp. 169–170. IEEE (2015)

49. Shao, B., Wang, H., Li, Y.: Trinity: a distributed graph engine on a memory cloud. In: Proceedings of the 2013 ACM SIGMOD International Conference on Management of Data, pp. 505–516. ACM (2013)

50. Song, C., Havlin, S., Makse, H.A.: Self-similarity of complex networks. Nature **433**(7024), 392–395 (2005)

51. Strogatz, S.H.: Nonlinear Dynamics and Chaos: With Applications to Physics, Biology, Chemistry, and Engineering. Westview press, Boulder (2014)

52. Sun, Y., Han, J., Gao, J., Yu, Y.: itopicmodel: information network-integrated topic modeling. In: Ninth IEEE International Conference on Data Mining ICDM 2009, pp. 493–502. IEEE (2009)

53. Sun, Y., Han, J., Zhao, P., Yin, Z., Cheng, H., Wu, T.: Rankclus: integrating clustering with ranking for heterogeneous information network analysis. In: Proceedings of the 12th International Conference on Extending Database Technology: Advances in Database Technology, pp. 565–576. ACM (2009)

54. Yan, D., Cheng, J., Lu, Y., Ng, W.: Blogel: a block-centric framework for distributed computation on real-world graphs. Proc. VLDB Endowment **7**(14), 1981–1992 (2014)

The Implementation and Evaluation of High-Speed Link Monitoring Tool for Supercomputer

Jiaqing Xu[(✉)], Jie He, Xiaotao Hu, Jijun Cao, Lei Zhang,
and Chongfeng Wang

School of Computer, National University of Defense Technology,
Changsha, China
xujiaqing@nudt.edu.cn

Abstract. With the increase of system scale and link speed, the link failure has become the most important type of interconnect fault in supercomputers, which has brought great challenges to the maintenance of high-performance inter-connect networks. In order to meet the needs of operation and maintenance personnel to monitor the status and performance of all high-speed links of supercomputer in real-time, this paper designs a high-speed link monitoring tool based on in-band network, which has good scalability and robustness for real-time monitoring of high-speed link status and performance information. The tool has been practically utilized in the operation and maintenance of domestic supercomputers to speed up the process of locating and troubleshooting link failures, effectively reducing the downtime of supercomputers.

Keywords: Supercomputer · Interconnection networks · High-speed link
Monitoring tool

1 Introduction

Supercomputer refers to a type of computer that has extremely fast computing speed, great storage capacity, and extremely high communication bandwidth. It is mainly used in the fields of big sciences, large projects, and industrial upgrading, and plays an important role in national security, economic, and social development. It is an important symbol of national scientific and technological development level and comprehensive national strength. To meet the demand for higher computing power in scientific research and production activities, the performance of supercomputers increases 1000 times every ten years. At present, the maximum computing speed of these computers is close to 200 Petaflop/s [1] and is expected to reach Exaflop/s [2] around the year of 2020.

High performance interconnection networks [3, 4] is an important global infras-tructure for supercomputers. It is the key to achieve high-speed collaborative parallel computing for all types of nodes in the system, directly affecting the performance and scalability of the system. The high-performance interconnection network is mainly composed of high performance adapters, high-radix switches, and high-speed links.

W. Xu et al. (Eds.): NCCET 2018, CCIS 994, pp. 165–178, 2019.
https://doi.org/10.1007/978-981-13-5919-4_16

Although the probability of failure of a single interconnect component is very low, as both the system scale and the link rate are increasing, the overall failure rate of high-performance interconnect networks will continue to rise [5], giving great challenge to the reliability of supercomputers.

Systems A, B and C are three operating domestic supercomputers. Their online operating hours, interconnected network scale, and link rates are shown in Table 1. Among them, System A has the longest service life and has been online for more than 7 years. System B has the largest scale of interconnected networks. It has used more than 2,000 switches, more than 46,000 optical fibers, and more than 18,000 adapters. The deployment time of System C is the latest, but its link rate is the highest, reaching 25 Gb/s.

Table 1. The scale and link speed of three supercomputers

	System A	System B	System C
System online time	>7 years	>4 years	>2 years
Link speed	QDR (10 Gb/s)	FDR (14 Gb/s)	EDR (25 Gb/s)
Number of switches	220+	2000+	340+
Number of links	3100+	46000+	4600+
Number of NICs	3000+	18000+	11300+

According to different properties, interconnection faults can be classified into software faults and hardware faults, where hardware faults can be divided into switch, link, and adapter faults. Because the two ends of the link are connected to different switches, the failure of the link usually indicates that the port of the switch is in faulty. In real systems, link failures can be discovered by monitoring the port state of the switch.

Due to different deployment time of each system, the time span of operation and maintenance data statistics are also different. The first investigated HPC system, System A, in operation from December 2015 to May 2018. The system B was in operation from January 2017 to May 2018. The third investigated HPC system, System C, was online from January 2017 to June 2018. The proportions of various types of interconnection failures in the three systems are shown in Table 2. Hardware failures account for more than 90% of total interconnection failures in all three systems. Among them, the proportion of adapter failures is relatively small, mainly focusing on switch and link failures. In system A, the switch failures reached 81.05%, and the link failures were only 10.53%. The reason is that the link rate of system A is QDR, and as the service time of the system increases, the aging of electronic components leads to increased switch failures. System B and System C, on the other hand, use FDR and EDR fibers, and their link failure ratios reach 76.61% and 61.94%, respectively.

The first investigated foreign HPC system, Deimos, in operation from March 2007 to April 2012 at TU-Dresden, is a 728-node cluster with 108 IB switches and 1,653 links. Their hardware failure ratios reach 87%. The second foreign HPC system, TSUBAME2.0, online from April 1997 to August 2005, uses a dual-rail QDR IB network with 501 switches and 7,005 links to connect the 1,408 compute nodes. The dominated hardware failure is link failure, which reached 93% [5].

It is not difficult to find that with the increase of the system scale and the link rate, the link failure has become the most important type of failure in the interconnection network, bringing great challenges to the maintenance of the interconnection network.

Table 2. Percentage of different kinds of interconnection failures

	System A	System B	System C	Deimos	TSUBAME2.0
Percentages of network-related failures					
Software	6.86%	0.53%	3.6%	13%	1%
Hardware	93.14%	99.47%	96.4%	87%	99%
Percentages for hardware only					
NIC/NIS	8.42%	0.46%	6.72%	59%	1%
Switch	81.05%	22.93%	31.34%	14%	6%
Link	10.53%	76.61%	61.94%	27%	93%

At present, the fault localization and recovery of the interconnection network have become an important part of daily operation and maintenance of the supercomputers. When interconnection faults occur, how to assist the system operation and maintenance personnel to quickly locate and eliminate interconnection faults, so as to reduce the scope of the interconnection faults as much as possible, is an important issue that needs to be solved in the process of operation and maintenance of interconnection networks. In order to meet the needs of operation and maintenance personnel to monitor the status and performance of all high-speed links in the system in real-time, this paper designs a high-speed link monitoring tool based on in-band access [6] to monitor link connectivity, stability, bandwidth, etc. Information, with good real-time, scalability and robustness, has now been practically used in the operation and maintenance of domestic supercomputers to speed up the process of locating and troubleshooting link failures, which can effectively reduce the downtime of supercomputers.

The contributions of this paper can be summarized as follows:

The probe, aka Network Management Agent, based on hardware implementation reduces the latency of acquiring the status information of high-speed link, and improves the real-time performance of monitoring tools.

The process of information collection and processing is optimized from dimensions of time and space, which effectively reduces the time overhead of information collection and processing, and increases the scalability of monitoring tools.

A dynamic in-band path construction method is proposed, which can effectively solve the problem of unreachable switch caused by link failure, and improve the robustness of monitoring tools.

The structure of this paper is as follows. Section 1 introduces the background. Section 2 presents the related work. Section 3 details the structure and implementation of the high-speed link monitoring tool, and Sect. 4 provides the performance evaluation of the high-speed link monitoring tool, as well as robustness analysis. Finally, Sect. 5 concludes this paper.

2   Related Work

At present, there are two major categories in supercomputers: general networks represented by Ethernet and high-performance networks represented by InfiniBand [7].

Ethernet uses the SNMP network management protocol [8] to implement network management. This protocol checks the port status by periodically sending BFD packets between network ports. In normal circumstances, the operation and maintenance personnel need to log in to the network device to view the status information of the port. This method is directly monitored and has low efficiency, which cannot meet the requirements for real-time monitoring of system-wide links of large-scale systems. Pingmesh [9] adopted the idea of indirect detection and implemented link fault detection by sending an end-to-end probe. However, this method requires maintaining one probe between each pair of servers in the network. As the network scales growing, the number of probes that need to be maintained will increase exponentially, which results in a prolonged period of time for each probe and at the same time excessive bandwidth load, yielding it difficult to implement real-time detection. Both [10, 11] have improved the Pingmesh method based on topology-aware thinking. By simplifying the detection path, the number of end-to-end probes is effectively reduced. Microsoft's NetBouncer [12] also belongs to indirect monitoring. It sends a large number of IP-in-IP probe messages firstly, and then infers the location of the failed link based on the success or failure of probe packets. Compared with direct monitoring, indirect detection methods still have the possibility of false positives.

Mellanox's InfiniBand and Intel's OPA [13] are the main representatives of high-performance networks. Both have added a layer of subnet management [14], and the subnet manager perceives the status of the entire interconnect network through the subnet management agent. The Unified Fabric Manager (UFM) [15] developed by Mellanox and the Fabric Suite Fabric Manager (FM) [16] developed by Intel can efficiently monitor and manage the entire high-performance network. However, UFM and FM are proprietary software developed by vendors for their own high-performance networks and are not open source. This paper draws on the design concept of UFM and uses a combination of hardware and software to design and implement a high-speed link monitoring tool for domestic high-performance networks, which can monitor the status of the entire system's link in real time and fill the gaps in the country.

3   High-Speed Link Monitoring Tool Design

The aim of this paper is to design a tool that can monitor all high-speed links in the system in real-time. This tool will be deployed in home-grown supercomputers to achieve the effect of real-time acquisition of all link status and performance information in the system.

3.1   Overall Structure of the High Speed Link Monitoring Tool

The overall structure of the high speed link monitoring tool is shown in Fig. 1. It consists of link status register, link performance register, Network Management Agent

(NMA) [6], in-band network, in-band path construction module, link information collection and processing module, and link information display module. The link state register, link performance register, network management agent and in-band path are implemented by hardware. The in-band path construction module, link information collection and processing module and link information display module are implemented by software.

Link Status Register: The function of the link status register is to record the basic status information of the current link, including linkup, handup, retry, lane, and credit.

Link Performance Registers: The Link Performance Registers feature records link performance information, namely real-time transceiver traffic and bandwidth.

Network Management Agent: Each Switch contains a hardware-based network management agent module. Its role is to receive management request messages, read and write the corresponding link state or performance registers based on the contents of the messages, and then construct a management response report.

In-band network: The in-band channel is responsible for the transmission of in-band management packets. It forwards the management request packet of the management server to the destination NMA or forwards the management response packet constructed by the NMA to the management server.

In-band path construction module: The path construction module is implemented by software, and its function is to build an in-band path to each switch of the access system.

Link information collection and processing module: The function of the link information collection and processing module is to collect link status and link performance information through an in-band path and process the information. After processing is completed, it is passed to the link information display module for display.

Link information display module: The function of the link information display module is to receive the data of the link information collection and processing module, and then visually display it.

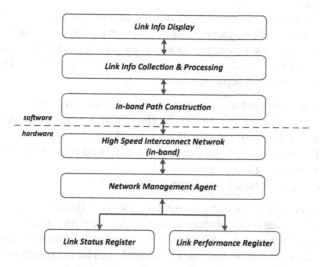

Fig. 1. The architecture of high-speed link monitoring tool

3.2   The Operating Mechanism of the High-Speed Link Monitoring Tool

The operating mechanism of the high-speed link monitoring tool is shown in Fig. 2. It mainly includes three steps: in-band path construction, information collection and processing, and information display.

Step 1: The path construction module will construct an in-band access path according to the position of each Switch in the system.

Step 2: The link collection module sequentially obtains the port state information of all the switches in the system through the in-band path.

Step 3: The link information display module completes the display of the port status information.

Step 2 and Step 3 successively display the real-time status of the system. If the link information cannot be acquired in a certain cycle, Step 1 is triggered to rebuild the in-band path. The detailed operation of each step will be detailed later.

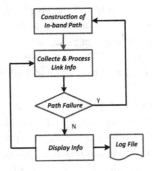

Fig. 2. The operating mechanism of the high-speed link monitoring tool

Path Construction

In-band path construction is the basis of in-band access. The path construction algorithm adopts a breadth-first search strategy. The first switch is searched from the adapter of the management server, and an access path to this switch is constructed, and then all the ports of this switch are accessed. Depending on the status of the port, the following cases are handled separately:

(1) If the port is connected to an adapter, no processing is required.
(2) If the port is connected to a switch and the switch does not construct an in-band path, an in-band path of the switch is built and added to the seed queue.
(3) If the port is connected to the switch and the in-band path of the switch already exists, no processing is required.
(4) No processing is required if the port is disconnected.

Figure 3 shows an in-band path schematic diagram of a 10 switches tree network. In this figure, svr0 is taken as the starting point, and the thick line is the built-in in-band path. The switch with the number X is represented by switchX. The specific construction process is: first find that svr0 is connected to switch0, then build the path to switch0, and then scan ports 1–7 of switch0. Ports 1–3 connected to the adapter are not processed.

Ports 4–7 are connected to switch4 and switch5. Since switch4 and switch5 have not constructed the in-band path, the in-band path to switch4 and switch5 are built, and two switches are added to the seed queue at the same time. After scanning all the ports of switch0 is completed, there are switch4 and switch5 in the seed queue. Then switch4 and switch5 perform port scanning in turn. When scanning switch4, new seeds switch8 and switch9 are generated, then these new seeds will be scanned in sequence. After the scanning of switch8 and switch9 is completed, the new seeds switch6 and switch7 are generated, and then switch6 and switch7 will be scanned in sequence. After that, new seeds switch2 and switch3 are generated. Finally, when the scanning of switch2 and switch3 is completed, no new seeds will be generated and the seed queue will be empty. At this point, the construction of in-band path to each switch is completed.

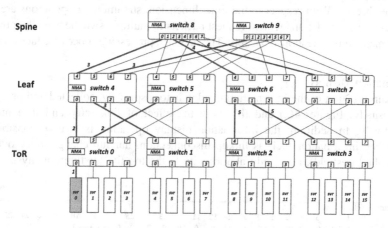

Fig. 3. The schematic diagram of in-band path

The port number Y of the switch with the number X is represented by switchX.pY. Each hop of in-band path is represented by the remote port of link from the starting point (svr0). Table 3 shows the in-band path of each switch that is constructed. In this example tree network, the maximum number of hops for the in-band path is 5.

Table 3. The in-band path of each switch

Switch name	Hops	In-band path
switch0	1	$svr0 \rightarrow switch0.p0$
switch1	3	$svr0 \rightarrow switch0.p0 \rightarrow switch4.p0 \rightarrow switch1.p4$
switch2	5	$svr0 \rightarrow switch0.p0 \rightarrow switch4.p0 \rightarrow switch8.p0 \rightarrow switch6.p4 \rightarrow switch2.p4$
switch3	5	$svr0 \rightarrow switch0.p0 \rightarrow switch4.p0 \rightarrow switch8.p0 \rightarrow switch6.p4 \rightarrow switch3.p4$
switch4	2	$svr0 \rightarrow switch0.p0 \rightarrow switch4.p0$
switch5	2	$svr0 \rightarrow switch0.p0 \rightarrow switch5.p0$
switch6	4	$svr0 \rightarrow switch0.p0 \rightarrow switch4.p0 \rightarrow switch8.p0 \rightarrow switch6.p4$
switch7	4	$svr0 \rightarrow switch0.p0 \rightarrow switch4.p0 \rightarrow switch8.p0 \rightarrow switch7.p4$
switch8	3	$svr0 \rightarrow switch0.p0 \rightarrow switch4.p0 \rightarrow switch8.p0$
switch9	3	$svr0 \rightarrow switch0.p0 \rightarrow switch4.p0 \rightarrow switch9.p0$

Link Information Collection Processing

The link information collection processing is divided into two subtasks: information collection and information processing. The information collection is responsible for collecting the status and performance information of all the links in the network through in-band access. The information processing is responsible for disconnection of link, the change of handup, the oversize of retry, the credit abnormality and other key information extraction. The time required for information collection and processing is an important factor affecting the real-time and scalability of the monitoring tools. In order to speed up the process of information collection and processing and shorten the information collection and processing time, the information collection and processing module is optimized from two dimensions: space and time. Regarding to spatial dimension, when tasks are too large, tasks are grouped and processed in parallel by multiple threads. With respect to the time dimension, streamlining operations are used to concurrently send management request packets to multiple switches and then receive switch management response packets. The message processing process reduces waiting time.

Information Display

The main function of the information display is to display the collected and processed data visually. Figures 4(a) and (b) show the effect of link retry and lane number respectively. In addition, the information display operation is also responsible for saving key information such as linkup disconnection, handup change, retry oversize (above the threshold), and credit abnormality to the log file for future analysis.

The retry of ToR Switch

	0	1	2	3	4	5	6	7	8	9	10	11	12	13	14	15	16	17	18	19	20	21	22	23
Switch0	-	0	0	0	0	0	0	0	0	0	0	0	0	0	0	0	0	0	0	0	0	0	0	0
Swtich1	-	0	0	0	0	0	0	0	0	0	0	0	451	0	0	0	0	0	0	0	0	0	0	0
Switch2	0	0	0	0	0	0	0	0	0	0	0	-	0	0	0	0	0	0	0	0	0	0	0	0
Swtich3	0	0	0	0	0	0	0	0	0	0	0	-	0	0	0	0	0	0	0	0	0	0	0	0

(a)

The lane of ToR Switch

	0	1	2	3	4	5	6	7	8	9	10	11	12	13	14	15	16	17	18	19	20	21	22	23
Switch0	-	8-8	8-8	8-8	8-8	8-8	8-8	8-8	8-8	8-8	8-8	8-8	8-8	8-8	8-8	8-8	8-8	8-8	8-8	8-8	8-8	8-8	8-8	8-8
Swtich1	-	8-8	8-8	8-8	8-8	8-8	8-8	8-8	8-8	8-8	8-8	8-8	7-8	8-8	8-8	8-8	8-8	8-8	8-8	8-8	8-8	8-8	8-8	8-8
Switch2	8-8	8-8	8-8	8-8	8-8	8-8	8-8	8-8	8-8	8-8	8-8	-	8-8	8-8	8-8	8-8	8-8	8-8	8-8	8-8	8-8	8-8	8-8	8-8
Swtich3	8-8	8-8	8-8	8-8	8-8	8-8	8-8	8-8	8-8	8-8	8-8	-	8-8	8-8	8-8	8-8	8-8	8-8	8-8	8-8	8-8	8-8	8-8	8-8

(b)

Fig. 4. The monitoring result of switches' retry and lane

3.3   Basic Functions of the High-Speed Link Monitoring Tool

The basic functions of the high-speed link monitoring tool are shown in Table 4, which include two parts: the status monitoring and performance monitoring. The state monitoring is responsible for real-time monitoring of the basic state of high-speed links in the interconnection system, including linkup, handup, retry, lane, and credit. The performance monitoring is responsible for real-time detection of the performance of high-speed links in the interconnected system, including traffic and bandwidth.

Linkup: This status indicator reflects the connectivity of the link. When the link is down, the link status register will be linked up.

Handup: This status indicator reflects the link stability, which will cause the value of the handup register to change.

Retry: This status indicator reflects the link quality. The smaller the retry, the better the link quality.

Lane: This status indicator reflects the link's communication capabilities. Decreasing the number of port lanes will cause the current link's communication capabilities to decrease.

Credit: This status indicator reflects the size of the buffer at the receiving end of the link.

Traffic: This performance indicator reflects the number of packets sent and received by the link over a period of time.

Bandwidth: This performance indicator reflects the utilization of the link.

According to the long-term accumulation of operation and maintenance experience, when operation and maintenance personnel can obtain the above-listed link information in real time, they can fully grasp the current operating conditions of the interconnection network, and quickly discover and locate various link failures, even the gray failures [17].

Table 4. The basic functions of the high-speed link monitoring tool

Function		The description of function
Status monitoring	Linkup	Get the linkup register of each link, report the disconnect link
	Handup	Get the handup register of each link, report the change of handup
	Retry	Get the retry register of each link, report the oversize of retry
	Lane	Get the lane register of each link, report the decreasing of port lanes number
	Credit	Get the credit register of each link, report the credit abnormality
Performance monitoring	Traffic	Monitor the real-time traffic of all links
	Bandwidth	Monitor the real-time bandwidth of all links

4 Performance Evaluation and Analysis

4.1 Real-Time Property

The in-band path construction and information collection processing time are two key factors that affect the real-time property of the monitoring tools. System D, System E, and System F are three online domestic supercomputers. Link monitoring tools are deployed on three systems. Table 5 shows the average in-band path construction time and information collection processing time, which can meet the need for real-time monitoring of all high-speed links in each system. Table 5 also shows the single switch information collection and processing time of System D, E and F, and compares it with Tianhe-2. It can be seen that the single-switch information collection and processing time of System D, E and F are about 0.5 ms, which is obviously better than the 1.01 ms of Tianhe-2 [6].

Table 5. The results of real-time property test

System name	Number of switches	In-band path construction time (ms)	System-wide information collection and processing time (ms)	Single switch information collection and processing time (ms)
System D	86	3.862	1.818	0.4963
System E	86	4.439	1.837	0.5051
System F	96	5.183	2.219	0.4981
Tianhe-2	5856		2000	1.01

4.2 Scalability

This section discusses the scalability of the proposed tool from two aspects: topology change and system scale.

Topology Change

During usage, the monitoring tool is deployed on the management server and uses the server as the root node to build an in-band access path, as shown in Fig. 3. Different topologies will affect the hops of the in-band path from the management server to the switch.

Figure 5(a) shows the relationship between the number of hops and the time taken to collect and process single switch information on system D. When the number of hop steps increases by 5, the corresponding information collection processing time will increase by 74.2 µs (515.3 µs–441.1 µs), an increase of 16.8%. From the trend of the curve, it can be predicted that when the difference in the number of hop steps increases to 10, the increase in access time will not exceed 40%. According to the actual construction of the supercomputer, the difference in the number of hops caused by the topology will not exceed 10. It can be seen that the topology change has little impact on the performance of the monitoring tool and can be deployed on domestic supercomputers with different topologies.

System Scale

As the scale of the system increases, the processing time for system-wide information collection will inevitably increase. In order to reduce information collection processing time, this tool optimizes the information collection process. On system B, the time required for the collection and processing of different numbers of switch links was tested. Table 6 shows the comparison of the time required for collection and processing of different numbers of switches before and after optimization. When the number of switches increases to 1024, the optimized information is obtained. Approximately 34 times the speedup ratio can be obtained before the collection processing time is optimized.

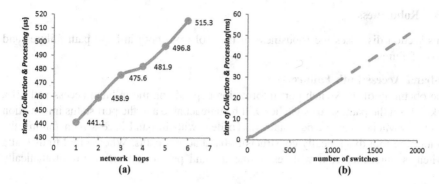

Fig. 5. The test of collection and processing time with system scale

Table 6. The required time for collection and processing before and after optimization

Number of switches	Required time before optimization (ms)	Required time after optimization (ms)	Speedup
1	1.33	1.24	1.077
2	2.27	1.12	2.022
4	4.09	1.06	3.858
8	7.72	1.12	6.876
16	15.12	1.12	13.443
32	28.37	1.57	18.071
64	58.14	1.64	35.327
128	116.84	3.39	34.411
256	229.73	6.50	35.339
512	458.37	13.21	34.693
1024	917.44	26.98	33.999

Figure 5(b) shows the curve of the change of the information collection processing time with the number of switches after optimization. From the figure, we can see that when the number of switches is less than 64, the time-consuming curve changes smoothly and the acceleration ratio increases linearly. When the number of switches is greater than 64, the time-consuming curve rises linearly, and the acceleration ratio remains basically unchanged. China is expected to complete the deployment of the exascale supercomputer around 2020. If 36-port switches and a 4-level fat-tree topology are adopted, the number of switches in the system will reach more than 40,000. According to the trend of the time-consuming curve, the time for completing the system-wide link information collection and processing with this monitoring tool is about 1.08 s, which can meet the needs of the operation and maintenance personnel to monitor the link status in real time.

4.3 Robustness

This section discusses the robustness of the tool from both in-band path failures and server failures.

In-band Access Path Failure

The obtaining of the switch port information depends on the in-band access path. If a link fails on the path, some switches will be unreachable and the port status information of these switches cannot be obtained. To deal with in-band access path failure, the monitoring tool dynamically constructs in-band access paths. When a tool finds that a switch is unreachable, it will restart the in-band path construction to automatically

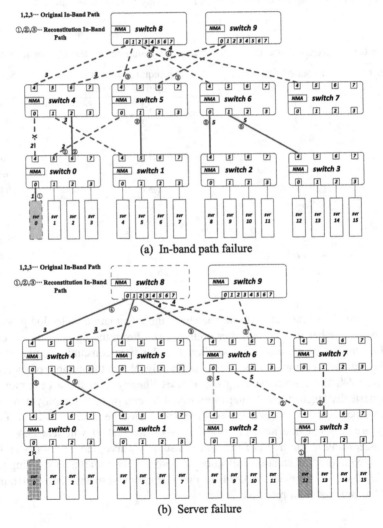

(a) In-band path failure

(b) Server failure

Fig. 6. The schematic diagram of in-band path reconstitution after failure

avoid failure links. The specific process is shown in Fig. 6(a). When the port switch4.port0 fails, the original in-band path from svr0 to switch4 svr0→switch0. p0→switch4.p0 is unreachable. After the tool detects that switch4 is unreachable, it will rebuild the in-band path from svr0 to switch4, which is svr0→switch0. p0→switch4.p2, and at the same time svr0 to switch1 ∼ switch3 and switch6 ∼ switch9 in-band paths have also been rebuilt. It can be seen that for a specific switch, only one reachable port is needed to build its in-band access path, ensuring that the status of all the ports on the switch can be obtained in real time.

Server Failure

The server failures are divided into server itself failure and server link failure. The consequences of the two failures are that the server cannot monitor the link informa-tion. In actual operation, the monitoring tool is deployed on at least two servers. One is the main server and the other is the standby server. When the main server fails, the standby server will take over the monitoring of system link information. In order to avoid the simultaneous failure of the main server and the standby server caused by the switch failure, the main server and the standby server may be connected to different switches in the system. As shown in Fig. 6(b), svr0 is the main server, and svr12 is the standby server, which is connected to switch0 and switch3. When the main server svr0 fails, the system can also be monitored by the standby server svr12. The link infor-mation in the system effectively tolerates server failures.

5   Conclusion

This paper draws on the design idea of Unified Fabric Manager and uses a combination of hardware and software to design and implement a high-speed link monitoring tool for domestic high-performance networks. According to the actual performance eval-uation and analysis, the tool has good real-time performance, robustness and scala-bility, which can meet current and even future exascale supercomputer system-wide link monitoring requirements, and can speed up the process of locating and trou-bleshooting link failures as well as shorten the supercomputer's downtime.

Acknowledgements. This work is mainly supported by the National Key Research and Development Program of China (2016YFB0200203), the National Natural Science Foundation of China (61572509).

References

1. https://www.top500.org/. Last Accessed 30 May 2018
2. The Opportunities and Challenges of Exascale Computing. Summary Report of the Advanced Scientific Computing Advisory Committee (ASCAC) Subcommittee, Office of Science, DOE (2010)
3. Duato, J., Yalamanchili, S., Ni, L.: Interconnection Networks: An Engineering Approach. Morgan Kaufmann Publishers, California (2003)

4. Dally, W.J., Towles, B.: Principles and Practices of Interconnection Networks. Morgan Kaufmann Publishers, California (2004)
5. Domke, J., Hoefler, T., Matsuoka, S.: Fail-in-place network design: interaction between topology, routing algorithm and failures. In: Proceedings of the International Conference for High Performance Computing, Networking, Storage and Analysis (SC 2014), pp. 597–608. IEEE Press, New Orleans (2014)
6. Cao, J.J., Xiao, L.Q., Wang, K.F.: The implementation and evaluation of in-band network management in supercomputing system. Chin. J. Comput. **39**(9), 1717–1732 (2016)
7. Introduction to InfiniBand-White Paper. https://www.mellanox.com/pdf/whitepapers/IB_Intro_WP_190.pdf. Last Accessed 3 June 2018
8. Wang, H.R., Xu, M.W.: Survey on SNMP network management. Mini Micro Syst. **25**(3), 358–366 (2004)
9. Guo, C.X., Yuan, L.H., Xiang, D., et al.: Pingmesh: a large-scale system for data center network latency measurement and analysis. In: Proceeding of ACM SIGCOMM 2015, pp. 139–152. ACM Press, London (2015)
10. Peng, Y., Yang, J., Wu, C., et al.: deTector: a topology-aware monitoring system for data center networks. In: 2017 USENIX Annual Technical Conference (USENIX ATC 2017), USENIX Association, pp. 55–68. USENIX Association, California (2017)
11. Wang, J.X., Qi, H.: Real-time link fault detection as a service for datacenter netwrok. J. Comput. Res. Dev. **55**(4), 704–716 (2018)
12. CloudBrain for Automatic Troubleshooting for the Cloud. https://www.microsoft.com/en-us/research/project/cloudbrain/. Last Accessed 5 June 2018
13. Birrittella, M.S., Debbage, M., et al.: Intel omni-path architecture: enabling scalable, high performance fabrics. In: Proceeding of 23rd IEEE Annual Symposium on High-Performance Interconnects, pp. 1–9. IEEE Press, California (2015)
14. Wen, J.W.: Infiniband subnet management technology. Master thesis, National University of Defense Technology (2009)
15. Unified Fabric Manager for InfiniBand User Manual. http://pleiades.ucsc.edu/doc/mellanox/UFM_5.2_User_Manual_IB_DOC-00600.pdf. Last Accessed 28 May 2018
16. Intel Omni-Path Fabric Suite Fabric Manager – User Guide. https://www.intel.com/content/dma/support/us/en/documents/network-and-i-o/fabric-products/Intel_OP_FabricSuite_Fabric_Manager_UG_H76468_v8_0.pdf. Last Accessed 12 June 2018
17. Huang, P., Guo, C.X., Zhou, L.D, et al.: Gray failure: the Achilles' heel of cloud-scale systems. In: Proceedings of the 16th Workshop on Hot Topics in Operating Systems (HotOS 2017), pp. 150–155. ACM Press, Whistler (2017)

A Survey of Approaches for Promoting Honest Recommendations in Reputation Systems

Junsheng Chang$^{(\boxtimes)}$, Liquan Xiao, and Weixia Xu

School of Computer, National University of Defense Technology,
Changsha, China
cjs7908@163.com

Abstract. The efficiency of the reputation mechanism fully depends on the number of received recommendations and the quality of each of them, but a peer may not be willing to provide honest recommendations actively in order to pursue its own interest. To address this problem, a number of schemes have been proposed. It is therefore necessary to give an overview of the representative schemes. In this paper, we present a comprehensive discussion on approaches for promoting honest recommendations in reputation systems. We first classify the existing schemes into two categories: protecting the privacy of recommenders and providing incentive to recommenders. The latter can then be subdivided into two categories: market-based incentive schemes and policy-based incentive schemes. We then survey some representative schemes in the literature belonging to each category, and summarize their unique characteristics and working principles. Moreover, some open problems in each category are also discussed.

Keywords: Incentive mechanism · Privacy · Reputation system
Reputation

1 Introduction

The rapid growth of Internet and ubiquitous connectivity has spurred the development of various collaborative computing systems such as service-oriented computing (SOC), Peer-to-Peer (P2P) and on line community systems. In these applications, the accessibility of information and services offered by these communities, makes it both possible and legitimate to communicate with strangers and carry out interactions anonymously, as rarely done in "real" life. However, the service consumer usually knows little about the service providers, which often makes the consumer accept the risk of working with some providers without prior interaction or experience. To mitigate the potential risks of the consumers, reputation systems [1–4] are deployed as a popular approach to predict how much the service provider can be trusted. Reputation systems provide communities with means to reduce the potential risk when communicating with people hiding behind

Supported by National Major Scientific Research Program (2016YFB0200203).

virtual identities. These utilize the experience and knowledge accumulated and shared by all participants for assigning reputation values to individuals, and attempt to identify dishonest members and prevent their negative effect.

One major challenge associated with designing reputation mechanisms is to ensure that truthful information is gathered about the actual outcome of the transaction. In the absence of independent verification means, the efficiency of the reputation mechanism fully depends on the number of received reputation information and the quality of each of them. It is however not at all clear that it is in the best choice of a rational peer to provide honest recommendations actively because [5]: (1) feedback reporting is usually costly. Users need to understand the rating scale, must fill in feedback forms and supervise the submission of the report. All these require the time and the conscious effort of the reporters. As feedback reporting does not bring direct benefits (the information is valuable only to subsequent buyers), rational agents are better off not to report at all. (2) providing honest positive recommendations lifts the reputation of other peers, so it may be a disadvantage to report them truthfully, and (3) a peer may be afraid of retaliation for honest negative recommendations.

To address the above problems, many researchers have proposed a lot of approaches for promoting honest recommendations. One solution is provided by Miller, Resnick and Zeckhauser [6]. They compare the quality reports of two agents about the same good with one another and apply strictly proper scoring rules to compute a payment scheme that makes honest reporting a Nash equilibrium. Jurca and Faltings [7] study a largely similar setting but use automated mechanism design to compute a budget-optimal payment scheme. Furthermore, they developed numerous extensions to the base model, such as incorporating collusion resistance [8, 9]. Gudes et al. [10] used another approach of protecting the privacy of recommendation providers to solve the problem of fear of retaliation in reputation systems. They presented three different schemes for the private computation of reputation, and analyzed the advantages and disadvantages in terms of privacy and communication overhead.

A number of strategies have been proposed to prevent the impact of selfish behavior. It is therefore necessary to give an overview of the representative strategies. In this paper, we present a comprehensive discussion on approaches for promoting honest recommendations in reputation systems. Different classes of approaches are described along with their unique characteristics and working principles. A number of schemes proposed are critically reviewed and compared with respect to their effectiveness and efficiency of performance. Some open problems in the area of promoting honest recommendations in reputation systems are also discussed. To the best of our knowledge, we are the first to systematically analyze the schemes for promoting honest recommendations in reputation systems.

The reminder of this paper is structured as follows. In the second section, Section two presents a classification and brief description of existing schemes for motivating honest recommendations in reputation systems. The detailed discussion on two main category approaches along with their unique characteristics and working principles is presented in the following two sections. Conclusions and future works are in the end.

2 Taxonomy of Approaches for Promoting Honest Recommendations

Many reputation systems make an assumption that all peers are willing to provide recommendations, but this assumption always is not true. In a self-organized systems (e.g. file sharing, collaboration, and e-commerce) dominated by rational agents acting to maximize their revenues, it is not clear that sharing truthful information is in the best interest of the reporter. To address this problem, current solutions can be divided into two categories: preserving the privacy of recommenders and providing incentives to recommenders. Taxonomy is shown in Fig. 1.

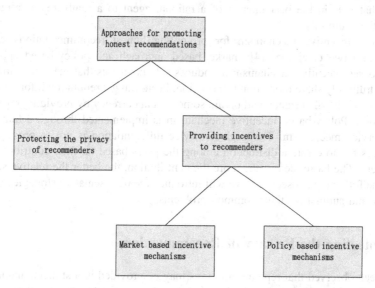

Fig. 1. Taxonomy of approaches for promoting honest recommendations in reputation systems.

It has been observed that users in a reputation system often hesitate in providing negative feedback. Resnick and Zechhauser reported some interesting statistics about eBay's reputation system [2]: Only 0.6% and 1.6% of all the feedbacks provided by buyers and sellers, respectively, were negative, which seem too low to reflect the reality. This might be due to the fact that mutually satisfying transactions are simply the (overwhelming) norm. However, it might also be the case that when feedback providers' identities are publicly known, reputation ratings can be provided in a strategic manner for reasons of reciprocation and retaliation, not properly reflecting the trustworthiness of the rated parties. For example, a user may have an incentive to provide a high rating because he expects the user he rates to reciprocate, and provide a high rating for either the current interaction or possible future ones.

A more general solution to this problem is computing reputation scores in a privacy preserving manner [11–19]. A privacy preserving reputation system operates such that the individual feedback of any entity is not revealed to other entities in the system.

The implication of private feedback is that there are no consequences for the feedback provider and thus he is uninhibited to provide honest feedback.

Moreover, in a large network, there is little incentive for a particular individual to expand resources to maintain the reputation system. Moreover, from a game theoretic perspective not reporting feedback may be advantageous to an agent in a competitive situation. To address these two problems, researchers have been working on developing incentive mechanisms [5–9, 20–26]. Incentive mechanism rewards the peers who give honest recommendations actively and penalizes the peers who are not willing to give recommendations or give dishonest recommendations. So the peers can behave as we expected to provide honest recommendation actively. Thus, the aim of incentive mechanism is how to make a reputation mechanism incentive-compatible, i.e. how to ensure that it is in the best interest of a rational agent to actually report reputation information truthfully.

Current incentive mechanism for promoting honest recommendations can be divided into two categories [4]: market-based approach and policy-based approach. Market-based incentive mechanism introduces side payments that make it rational for peers to truthfully share reputation information. Peers can get reputation information by paying some virtual currency and obtain some virtual currency by providing reputation information. Policy-based incentive mechanism is implemented through a fair differential service mechanism. The goal of service differentiation is not to provide hard guarantees but to create a distinction among the peers based on their contributions to the system. The basic idea is, the more the contribution, the better the relative service.

In the following subsections, we will introduce the representative strategies in each category and summarize their common problems.

3   Protecting the Privacy of Recommenders

It has been observed that reputation ratings may be provided in a strategic manner for reasons of reciprocation and retaliation, and therefore may not properly reflect the trust worthiness of rated parties. It thus appears that supporting privacy of recommendations providers could improve the quality of their ratings [12, 13].

Privacy preserving reputation computation is straightforward in the presence of a trusted central authority, each provider submits his feedback value to the central authority who aggregates all feedback and reveals the reputation score while keeping the individual feedback private. Zhang et al. [11] propose a reputation system which can protect the privacy of users offering feedback with the help of a trusted central server. In their scheme, reputation scores submitted to the central server are encrypted and can only be decrypted by it. In addition, the central server only returns to the querying user an aggregated reputation score instead of collected raw reputation scores. Therefore, it is impossible for any server to know the reputation score a particular client gives for him, and clients can be assured of offering honest reputation scores without incurring retaliation.

However, preserving privacy in decentralized reputation systems is not trivial, since no such universally trusted central authority is present to collect and report reputation ratings.

Pavlov et al. [12] argues that supporting perfect privacy in decentralized reputation systems is impossible, but as an alternative presents three probabilistic schemes that support partial privacy. On the basis of these schemes, they offer three protocols that allow ratings to be privately provided with high probability in decentralized additive reputation systems. The first protocol is not resilient against collusion of users, the other two protocols are probabilistically resistant to collusion of up to n–1 users, and require respectively $O(n^2)$ and $O(n^3)$ messages among n users.

Kinateder and Pearson [13] suggest a privacy-enhanced peer-to-peer reputation system on top of a Trusted Computing Platform (TCP). The platform's functionality along with the use of pseudonymous identities allow the platform to prove that it is a trusted platform, yet to conceal the real identity of the feedback provider. A possible privacy-breach in the IP layer is handled by the use of MIX cascades or anonymous web-posting. This approach is dependent on a specific platform, which is currently arousing controversy in the computing community [14].

Gudes et al. [10] discusses the computation of reputation while preserving members' private information. Three different schemes for the private computation of reputation are presented, and the advantages and disadvantages in terms of privacy and communication overhead are analyzed.

Hasan et al. [15] present three different privacy preserving protocols for computing reputation. They vary in strength in terms of preserving privacy, however, a common thread in all three protocols is that they are fully decentralized and efficient. Their protocols that are resilient against semi-honest adversaries and non-disruptive malicious adversaries have linear and loglinear communication complexity respectively.

Liu et al. [26] presents a hybrid approach for privacy-preserving recommender systems by combining randomized perturbation and differential privacy. Users' private data are protected by randomized perturbation and the privacy of recommendation result is guaranteed by differential privacy.

The approach protecting the privacy of recommenders needs to ensure the anonymity of recommenders during collecting reputation information and computing trust value. The logic of anonymous recommendation to a reputation system is thus analogous to the logic of anonymous voting in a political system. It potentially encourages truthfulness by guaranteeing secrecy and freedom from explicit or implicit influence. Although this freedom might be exploited by dishonest recommendation providers, who tend to provide exaggerated recommendations, it seems highly beneficial for honest ones, protecting the latter from being influenced by strategic manipulation issues. For example, a peer may have an incentive to provide a high rating because he expects the peer he rates to reciprocate, and provide a high rating for either the current interaction or possible future ones.

4 Providing Incentives to Recommenders

Providing rewards is effective way to improve feedback, according to the widely recognized principle in economics which states that people respond to incentives. Game theory plays a major role in the design of these mechanisms. This is the mathematical study of interaction among independent, self-interested agents in multi-agent systems. A mechanism is a set of rules that provide a mapping between the actions of the agents and the outcomes (payment) for these actions. The aim of providing rewards is to make a reputation mechanism incentive-compatible, i.e. how to ensure that it is in the best interest of a rational peer to actually report reputation information truthfully.

Recent years have witnessed a growing interest in incentive mechanism for promoting honest recommendations research. Current incentive mechanism for promoting honest recommendations can be divided into two categories [4]: market-based approaches and policy-based approaches.

4.1 Market Based Incentive Mechanism

Market-based incentive mechanism introduces side payments that make it rational for peers to truthfully share reputation information [5–9, 20]. Peers can get reputation information by paying some virtual currency and obtain some virtual currency by providing reputation information.

Dellarocas [20] proposes "Goodwill Hunting" (GWH) as a feedback mechanism for a trading environment based upon the argument that truthful feedback will benefit the community as a whole. If buyers provide random feedback, sellers with high product qualities will be driven out of the market and buyers will lose profit. This mechanism elicits truthful feedback from buyers by offering rebates of a buyer's periodic membership fee if the mean and variance between the buyer's and seller's perception of quality of their transactions are consistent across the entire buyer community. In this mechanism, buyers will receive less payment if their feedback of seller's product qualities deviates from the community-wide reporting. To provide incentives for buyer participation in this mechanism, buyers will not receive a rebate if they do not provide feedback. Buyers may behave badly before they exit from the market. To solve this problem, part of the membership fee will be refunded only at the end of the period on the basis of the buyer's behavior. However, the GWH mechanism does not deal with buyers' strategic behavior of misreporting and only works when each buyer buys from a given seller only once.

In order to stimulate reputation information sharing and honest recommendation elicitation, Jurca and Faltings [5, 7–9] propose an incentive compatible reputation mechanism to deal with inactivity and lies. A peer buys a recommendation about a service provider from a special broker named R-nodes. After interacting with the provider, the peer can sell its feedback to the same R-node, but gets paid only if its report coincides with the next peer's report about the same service provider. One issue is that if the recommendation from an R-node is negative such that a peer decides to avoid the service provider, the peer will not have any feedback to sell. Or in the existence of opportunistic service providers that, for example, behave and misbehave alternatively, an honest feedback does not ensure payback. This opens up the possibility of an honest entity to have negative revenue and thus is unable to buy any recommendation. Besides, the effectiveness of their work depends largely on the integrity of R-nodes, which is assumed to be trusted a priori.

Miller et al. [6] introduce a mechanism which is similar to that proposed by Jurca and Faltings [5]. In this mechanism, there is a center that maintains peers' ratings. The center rewards or penalizes each peer on the basis of its ratings and ensures that the mechanism at least breaks even in the long run. More specifically, a peer providing truthful ratings will be rewarded and get paid not by broker agents but by the buyer after the next buyer. To balance transfers among peers, a proper scoring rule is used to determine the amount that each peer will be paid for providing truthful feedback. Scoring rules used by the center (i.e. the Logarithmic Scoring Rule) make truthful reporting a Nash equilibrium where every peer is better off providing truthful feedback given that every peer else chooses the same strategy. Furthermore, proper scaling of scoring rules and collection of bonds or entry fees in advance ensure budget balance and incentives of the mechanism. This mechanism assumes that service providers have fixed quality, which limits its usefulness. As with the mechanism proposed by Jurca and Faltings [5], the truthful equilibrium is not the only equilibrium in this mechanism. There may be non-truthful equilibria where every peer is better off providing untruthful feedback given that other peers choose the same strategy. Therefore, this mechanism also can not deal with the situation where strategic peers collude in giving untruthful feedback.

To encourage the exchange of reputation information, Pinocchio [21] rewards participants that advertise their experience to others. At the same time, to protect the reward system from users who may submit inaccurate or random statements to obtain rewards, they use a probabilistic honesty metric to detect dishonest users and deprive them of the rewards. The trust management system will set up a credit balance for each participant, which will be credited with a reward for each statement advertised and debited for each query made by that user. The trust management system can set a maximum limit to the amount of credit given as rewards to a participant per minute. If a participant's credit balance is positive, she can use it to get a discount on queries she will make in the future. There is no way to cash the credit for money. Pinocchio does not intend to protect against conspiracies or bad-mouthing.

To obtain the truthful feedbacks on the non-verifiable information environment, inspired by the mechanism design paradigm in a hidden knowledge setting, Zhao et al. [22, 23] model the feedback reporting process as a reporting game, and design a wage-based incentive mechanism and provide numerical solutions to obtain the minimum wage required to reinforce the truthful strategies. Under their mechanism, querists are not required to estimate/know truthfulness of feedbacks when paying wage. The wage paid to reporters only depends on the feedbacks regardless of truthfulness. By following their scheme, truthful revelation will be a dominant strategy for all reporters. Different from most of the comparison based schemes, their proposed solution does not require peers to verify the information truthfulness. That is, the scheme does not require the peers to compare the feedback submission with other feedbacks. The solution requires only localized wage payment schemes, which greatly reduce the risk of collusion in reporting.

In summary, market based schemes allow for rich and flexible economic mechanism, and offer side payment to peers that truthfully rate results of transaction with service providers. Providing truthful feedback of service providers is a Nash Equilibrium in these mechanisms. However, these mechanisms suffer the notable drawback of seeming highly impractical since they need an infrastructure for accounting and micropayments. Much of the research in this field is less concerned with the feasibility of micropayments but instead considers problems that remain under the assumption that monetary exchanges are possible. Second, these mechanisms assume that all the peers share the same truthful opinion and the majority peers behave truthfully, and therefore have difficulty with the situation where peers collude in giving dishonest recommendations. Furthermore, the mechanisms do not work well if the majority of peers select to provide dishonest recommendations because each of these dishonest peers will also get a reward. This means that honest peers that will not be giving similar recommendations as many other peers, will not be rewarded and will be discouraged from being honest in the future. Third, in addition to the desirable truth-telling equilibria, these incentive mechanisms induce additional equilibria where peers do not report the truth. Equilibrium selection is an important consideration in practical implementations.

4.2 Policy Based Incentive Mechanism

Policy based incentive mechanism induces peers to participate reputation information sharing as expected by establishing the proper policy according to their behavior characteristics, namely, whether providing honest recommendations actively. The principle of establishing the policy is that active and honest recommenders, compared to inactive or dishonest ones, can always benefit more from other peers, such as the higher trust value, more interaction chances, larger amount of honest recommendations.

PeerTrust [4] presents a policy based incentive scheme which adds a reward as a community context for peers submitting feedback. It may alleviate the feedback incentive problem to some extent. This can be accomplished by providing a small increase in reputation whenever a peer provides feedback to others. The community context factor can be defined as a ratio of total number of feedbacks a peer give others during the given time period, over the total number of transactions the peer has. The weight factors can be tuned to control the amount of reputation that can be gained by rating others. However there are still some problems. First, how to allocate the weight for community context in the trust metric, if allocated high weight, peers can gain high trust value by providing the honest recommendations, and have no motivation to provide high quality services. Oppositely, if allocated low weight, the effectiveness of incentive mechanism is in doubt. Second, PeerTrust proposes the feedback credibility valuation algorithm PSM (Personal Similarity Measure), however, it ignores the feedback credibility and gives reward to all peers providing feedback. This may induce the peers to submit a lot of random or dishonest feedback.

T. G. Papaioannou et al. propose a mechanism for providing the incentives for reporting truthful feedback in a peer-to-peer system for exchanging services [24, 25]. Under their approach, both transacting peers (rather than just the client) submit ratings on performance of their mutual transaction. If these are in disagreement, then both transacting peers are punished, since such an occasion is a sign that one of them is lying. The severity of each peer's punishment is determined by his corresponding non-credibility metric, this is maintained by the mechanism and evolves according to the peer's record. When under punishment, a peer is not allowed to transact with others for a period that is exponential in their non-credibility values. For each peer, both non-credibility and punishment state are public information, they are appropriately stored so that they are available to other peers. The punishment of not transacting with other peers causes the punished peer to lose value offered by others. This provides incentives for peers to truthfully report of their business with others. however this approach does not deal with collaborated liars, moreover, the policy for punishing the dishonest peers is in doubt from the viewpoint of improving the system availability, for example, there are some peers who provide the high quality service, at the same time, and submit dishonest recommendations, using the punishment policy these peers will have no chance to provide service because of the dishonest recommendations, so the availability of the whole system is weakened.

Zhang et al. [27] develop a novel trust-based incentive mechanism where buyers first model other buyers using their personalized approach and select the most trustworthy ones as their neighbors from which they can ask advice about sellers. They use the term "neighbor" to refer to a buying agent that is accepted as an advisor of the buyer, and becomes part of that buyer's social network. In addition, however, sellers model the global reputation of buyers based on the social network. Since buyers are modeling the trustworthiness of potential advisors, advisors that always provide truthful ratings of sellers are likely to be neighbors of many other buyers and are considered reputable in the social network. These agents will be able to attract a larger audience to witness their feedback (also known as increasing "broadcast efficiency"). In marketplaces operating with their mechanism, sellers will increase quality and decrease prices of products to satisfy reputable buyers, in order to do business with many other buyers in the market. In consequence, their mechanism is able to create incentives for buyers to provide truthful ratings of sellers.

Liu et al. [28] present in this paper an incentive compatible reputation mechanism to facilitate the trust worthiness evaluation in ubiquitous computing environments. It is based on probability theory and supports reputation evolution and propagation. Our reputation mechanism not only shows robustness against lies, but also stimulates honest and active recommendations. The latter is realized by ensuring that active and honest recommenders, compared to inactive or dishonest ones, can elicit the most honest (helpful) recommendations and thus suffer the least number of wrong trust decisions, as validated by simulation based evaluation.

From the above discussion, we can see that in policy based incentive mechanisms, peers maintain recommendation credibility of other peers and use this information in their decision making processes. Recommendation credibility measures the truthfulness of a peer as a provider of recommendations. Peers in these mechanisms have incentives to provide truthful ratings, in order to increase their credibility or decrease their non-credibility. In doing so, they are able to gain higher profit, such as the higher trust value, more interaction chances, larger amount of honest recommendations. Many policy based incentive mechanisms differ from one another primarily in the computation of recommendation credibility and the mapping of credibility to strategies.

5   Conclusions and Future Work

The success of current trust and reputation systems is on the premise that the honest recommendations are obtained [29, 30]. However, without appropriate mechanisms, in most reputation systems, under-participation and lying strategies usually yield higher payoffs for peers than honest recommendations strategies. Thus, to address this problem, a number of schemes have been proposed to motivate honest recommendations in

Table 1. Comparison of existing approaches for promoting honest recommendations in reputation systems.

	Category	Remuneration type	Reward /Penalty	Enforcement	Decentralization	Collusion-resistance	Non-participation Detection
Pavlov Ref[12]	PP	-	-	√	√	-	×
Hasan Ref[17]	PP	-	-	√	√	-	×
Gudes Ref[10]	PP	-	-	Need TTP	×	-	×
Kinateder Ref[13]	PP	-	-	Depend on TCP	×	-	×
Jurca Ref[5,7-9]	MI	VM	No service	×	×	Partial	√
Miller Ref[6]	MI	VM	No service	×	×	×	√
Zhao Ref[22,23]	MI	VM	No service	×	×	√	√
Dellarocas Ref[20]	MI	VM	No service	×	×	Partial	√
Zhou PeerTrust[4]	PI	DS	Enhance reputation value	√	√	√	Partial
Papaioannou Ref[24,25]	PI	DS	Prohibit transacting with others	×	×	×	√
Zhang Ref[27]	PI	DS	Increase quality and decrease prices of products	√	√	√	Partial
Liu Ref[28]	PI	DS	Get more recommendations	√	√	√	Partial

PP: Protecting Privacy; MI: Market-based Incentive; PI: Policy-based Incentive; VM: Virtual Money; DS: Differentiated Service; TTP: Trusted Third Party; TCP: Trusted Computing Platform;

reputation systems. In this paper we give an overview of existing and proposed schemes. Moreover, we categorize them, and analyze the representative strategies in each category and summarize their common problems. Their principles are explained along with the limitations against the system requirements, which are shown in Table 1.

Since all existing incentive mechanisms aim for maximizing the network's performance without taking into account the privacy protection of peers, it is necessary to introduce an incentive mechanism with the privacy protection to peers. The combination of privacy and incentive mechanisms promoting honest recommendations will make reputation systems more robust than ever. Because meeting the demands of peers' privacy protection definitely raises the complexity of the incentive mechanism, and increases computation and communication overheads, it is a challenge to design an efficient incentive mechanism with privacy protection for reputation systems. The addressing of this challenge will be part of future work.

In addition, we plan to study schemes and protocols achieving privacy in the general case, i.e., in decentralized reputation systems which are not necessarily additive.

References

1. Abdul-Rahman, A., Hailes, S.: Supporting trust in virtual communities. In: Proceedings of the Hawaii International Conference on System Sciences 33, Maui, Hawaii (HICSS), January 2000
2. Resnick, P., Zeckhauser, R.: Trust among Strangers in internet transactions: empirical analysis of Ebay's reputation system. In: Baye, M.R. (ed.) The Economics of the Internet and E-Commerce, Applied Micro Economics, vol. 11. Elsevier Science (2002)
3. Stahl, D.O.: An experimental test of the efficacy of a simple reputation mechanism to solve social dilemmas. J. Econ. Behav. Organ. **94**, 116–124 (2013)
4. Xiong, L., Liu, L.: PeerTrust: supporting reputation-based trust in peer-to-peer communities. IEEE Trans. Data Knowl. Eng. **16**(7), 843–857 (2004). Special Issue on Peer-to-Peer Based Data Management
5. Jurca, R., Faltings, B.: An incentive compatible reputation mechanism. In: Proceedings of the IEEE Conference on Electronic Commerce, Newport Beach, CA, USA, pp. 285–292 (2003)
6. Miller, N., Resnick, P., Zeckhauser, R.: Eliciting informative feedback: the peer-prediction method. Manage. Sci. **51**(9), 1359–1373 (2005)
7. Jurca, R., Faltings, B.: Minimum payments that reward honest reputation feedback. In: Proceedings of the ACM Conference on Electronic Commerce (EC 2006), Ann Arbor, Michigan, 11–15 June 2006, pp. 190–199 (2006)
8. Jurca, R., Faltings, B.: Collusion resistant, incentive compatible feedback payments. In: Proceedings of the ACM Conference on E-Commerce (EC 2007), San Diego, 11–15 June 2007, pp. 200–209 (2007)
9. Jurca, R., Garcin, F., Talwar, A., Faltings, B.: Reporting incentives and biases in online review forums. ACM Trans. Web (TWEB) **4**(2), 1–27 (2010)
10. Gudes, E., Gal-Oz, N., Grubshtein, A.: Methods for computing trust and reputation while preserving privacy. In: Gudes, E., Vaidya, J. (eds.) DBSec 2009. LNCS, vol. 5645, pp. 291–298. Springer, Heidelberg (2009). https://doi.org/10.1007/978-3-642-03007-9_20
11. Zhang, Y.C., Fang, Y.G.: A fine-grained reputation system for reliable service selection in peer-to-peer networks. IEEE Trans. Parallel Distrib. Syst. **18**(8), 1134–1145 (2007)

12. Pavlov, E., Rosenschein, J.S., Topol, Z.: Supporting privacy in decentralized additive reputation systems. In: Jensen, C., Poslad, S., Dimitrakos, T. (eds.) iTrust 2004. LNCS, vol. 2995, pp. 108–119. Springer, Heidelberg (2004). https://doi.org/10.1007/978-3-540-24747-0_9

13. Kinateder, M., Pearson, S.: A privacy-enhanced peer-to-peer reputation system. In: Proceedings of the 4th International Conference on Electronic Commerce and Web Technologies (EC-Web), Prague, Czech Republic, pp. 206–215 (2003)

14. Yonezawa, K.: A novel protocol for communicating reputation in P2P networks. In: Proceedings of 4th International Conference on Trust Management, iTrust 2006, Pisa, Italy, pp. 412–422 (2006)

15. Hasan, O., Brunie, L., Bertino, E.: Preserving privacy of feedback providers in decentralized reputation systems. Comput. Secur. (2012). https://doi.org/10.1016/j.cose.2011.12.003

16. Lajoie-Mazenc, P., Anceaume, E., Guette, G., Sirvent, T., Viet Triem Tong, V.: Privacy-preserving reputation mechanism: a usable solution handling negative ratings. In: Damsgaard Jensen, C., Marsh, S., Dimitrakos, T., Murayama, Y. (eds.) IFIPTM 2015. IAICT, vol. 454, pp. 92–108. Springer, Cham (2015). https://doi.org/10.1007/978-3-319-18491-3_7

17. Hasan, O., Brunie, L., Bertino, E., Shang, N.: A decentralized privacy preserving reputation protocol for the malicious adversarial model. IEEE Trans. Inf. Forensics Secur. 8(6), 949–962 (2013)

18. Schaub, A., Bazin, R., Hasan, O., Brunie, L.: A trustless privacy-preserving reputation system. In: Hoepman, J.H., Katzenbeisser, S. (eds.) ICT Systems Security and Privacy Protection. SEC 2016. IFIP Advances in Information and Communication Technology, vol. 471, pp. 398–411. Springer, Cham (2016). https://doi.org/10.1007/978-3-319-33630-5_27

19. Lin, H., Xu, L., Mu, Y., Wu, W.: A reliable recommendation and privacy-preserving based cross-layer reputation mechanism for mobile cloud computing. Future Gener. Comput. Syst. 52(C), 125–136 (2015)

20. Dellarocas, C.: Goodwill hunting: an economically efficient online feedback mechanism for environments with variable product quality. In: Padget, J., Shehory, O., Parkes, D., Sadeh, N., Walsh, W.E. (eds.) AMEC 2002. LNCS (LNAI), vol. 2531, pp. 238–252. Springer, Heidelberg (2002). https://doi.org/10.1007/3-540-36378-5_15

21. Fernandes, A., Kotsovinos, E., Östring, S., Dragovic, B.: Pinocchio: incentives for honest participation in distributed trust management. In: Jensen, C., Poslad, S., Dimitrakos, T. (eds.) iTrust 2004. LNCS, vol. 2995, pp. 63–77. Springer, Heidelberg (2004). https://doi.org/10.1007/978-3-540-24747-0_6

22. Zhao, H., Yang, X., Li, X.: An incentive mechanism to reinforce truthful reports in reputation systems. J. Netw. Comput. Appl. 35, 951–961 (2012)

23. Zhao, H., Yang, X., Li, X.: WIM: a wage-based incentive mechanism for reinforcing truthful feedbacks in reputation systems. In: Global Telecommunications Conference, pp. 1–5 (2010)

24. Papaioannou, T.G., Stamoulis, G.D.: An incentives' mechanism promoting truthful feedback in peer-to-peer systems. In: Proceedings of the 5th IEEE/ACM International Symposium in Cluster Computing and the Grid, Cardi, UK, vol. 1, pp. 275–283 (2005)

25. Papaioannou, T.G., Stamoulis, G.D.: A mechanism that provides incentives for truthful feedback in peer-to-peer systems. Electron. Commer. Res. 10, 331–362 (2010)

26. Liu, X., et al.: When differential privacy meets randomized perturbation: a hybrid approach for privacy-preserving recommender system. In: Candan, S., Chen, L., Pedersen, T.B., Chang, L., Hua, W. (eds.) DASFAA 2017, Part I. LNCS, vol. 10177, pp. 576–591. Springer, Cham (2017). https://doi.org/10.1007/978-3-319-55753-3_36

27. Zhang, J., Cohen, R., Larson, K.: A trust-based incentive mechanism for e-marketplaces. In: Falcone, R., Barber, S.K., Sabater-Mir, J., Singh, M.P. (eds.) TRUST 2008. LNCS (LNAI), vol. 5396, pp. 135–161. Springer, Heidelberg (2008). https://doi.org/10.1007/978-3-540-92803-4_8

28. Liu, J.H., Issarny, V.: An incentive compatible reputation mechanism for ubiquitous computing environments. In: Proceedings of International Conference on Privacy, Security and Trust, Toronto, Canada, pp. 297–311 (2006)

29. Sicari, S., Rizzardi, A., Grieco, L.A., Coen-Porisini, A.: Security, privacy and trust in Internet of Things: the road ahead. Comput. Netw. **76**(15), 146–164 (2015)

30. Xie, H., Lui, J.C.S., Towsley, D.: Incentive and reputation mechanisms for online crowdsourcing systems. In: IEEE International Symposium on Quality of Service, pp. 207–212 (2016)

Author Index

Printed in the United States
By Bookmasters